UNLOCKING THE HEART OF HEALING

BRIDGET HUGHES

For Karen
woohoo!
I love you

Bridget Hughes

Healing Point Press Maryland
Cover design by Paul Fisher
Front Cover photo by Jean-Luc Devis

"Many books have been written about the mind-body connection, some of which speak to unlocking the power of the connection in the context of healing. But few have been written by an awakener such as Ms. Hughes who has unlocked the door and has made herself at home there. Her view—the product of a unique confluence of personal experience, technical knowledge, awareness, curiosity and humor—provides practical and stimulating discussion as to how to access one's vital energy. Her style invites readers to nurture their capacity for full-being healing by living well in their minds, hearts and with each other. Heart of Healing is a must-read for everyone interested in all that can still go right."

-Bill Kraynak, Technology Manager and Connectivity Ponderer

"Unlocking the Heart of Healing is truly a masterpiece. Bridget Hughes is one of the kindest, most knowledgeable and extraordinary people I have had the pleasure of meeting. As a patient, I have witnessed first hand her sheer genius, unique healing through finding my mind-body connection, and her immense compassion. This book is a refuge for all searching and trying to finally heal. I can wholeheartedly vouch for its' validity as Bridget has been my guiding compass throughout my personal journey to healing my body. It is a wealth of knowledge vastly needed in today's society and medical world. To know her is to love her. Bridget–thank you for your love and friendship, I am profoundly grateful."

-Anne Fava, Owner, Pure Barre Annapolis

"Bridget Hughes writes an amazing illustration about the importance of the mind-body connection. She is a wonderful teacher and storyteller who uses personal examples from her own experiences (and the experiences of so many patients she has helped) to illuminate her salient points. I absolutely recommend this book to anyone who has lived through a life-changing illness and wants to learn about the importance of wellness. Ms. Hughes teaches us that healing is not a one-size-fits all model but rather something anyone can learn and utilize."

-Elissa Bantug, 2x cancer survivor & Program Manager for the Johns Hopkins Breast Cancer Program

"*Unlocking the Heart of Healing*, Bridget Hughes' first book, is the most practical, enlightening, humorous, comforting and just plain useful book I've EVER read. The way she writes, while educational and inspirational, leaves the reader feeling they've found their new best friend, basking in the joy of knowing they are not alone and there are concrete, loving ways to heal and thrive. Her authenticity shines through every word, inviting us all to love ourselves and each other more fiercely. This will stay on my bedside table."

-Mary M. Dowling, LCSW-C

"Bridget Hughes has created another wonderful gift to share with the world. Many times over the years I have heard the statement 'Great Wisdom dwells within **you**, where the only TRUE HEALER resides – the one deep within every cell. The one that calls you back to the very awareness of your own true nature.' With her book *Unlocking The Heart of Healing* Bridget offers numerous reminders of this very fact. Further, in addition to reminding us of this inherent ability we all possess, Bridget offers simple strategies for accessing this on a regular and consistent basis.

However, and even more importantly, Bridget reminds us that the simple act of savoring the memory of a special moment has profound healing qualities which accesses this True Healing deep within every cell.

Thank you Bridget for this simple reminder."

-Stanley L. Fox II, CZB, L.Ac.

"This book changes my life as I read it. In these pages Bridget has gathered together wisdom and blended it with real life stories. I find the mix enjoyable, it's readily digestible and it's very compelling. I'm applying it and it's making a difference. This is an unconventional approach to healing but not new. Simple, but not necessarily easy. This is not a fix-it book, it's not "30 Days to a Better You." It's more like the voice of Bridget inviting us to be in love with life and to enjoy the remarkable side-effects of being in love with life."

-Edward Kentish Lic. Ac.

"Bridget Hughes shows us an entirely different highway to health. Informed by her own amazing healing journey (recovery, reversal or radical reduction of 24 medically diagnosed illnesses and injuries including Multiple Sclerosis), the healing experiences of hundreds of her patients who formerly suffered with major life threatening conditions, and the latest findings about Mind-Body-Spirit and wellness, she shows us how to take control of our own healing.

This book doesn't belong on your bookshelf. It belongs within arms reach for reading, re-reading, and daily application."

-Stephen Carter
CEO, Stress Solutions, LLC

Acknowledgments

All of the stories included in this book are true, though changed and modified where necessary to protect privacy. I am profoundly grateful to each of you who has shared deeply with me, that we may all learn, be uplifted, enlightened, inspired, and emboldened by our shared human experiences. Growth and learning don't just conveniently stop at some developmental milepost along the way in our lifetimes, and the more willing we are to share our stories, our vulnerabilities, our blessings, our struggles, our victories, our hardships, our insight, and our wisdom with each other, the more easily the consciousness of our families and communities may grow and flourish in ways that would otherwise be inaccessible.

Just as young learners who are living amongst highly articulate thinkers and readers rise to "the norm," whichever state of mind, heart, and consciousness we live in becomes a "norm." It matters greatly that each of us educates and transforms ourselves to a new heart/mind/consciousness "normal" so that we all rise up. Our deepest capacity for full-being healing arises not from a top-down approach in which we try to "fix" our body, but rather, is a bottom-up side-effect that comes when we are living well in our minds, living well in our hearts and living well with each other. When that happens, our body cannot help but change. This becomes abundantly clear in the stories that follow. Again, to the subjects of these stories–I thank you.

For their keen insight and extraordinarily time intensive help in improving this book, my deepest gratitude to Katie Herman, Dr. Meredith Hostetter, and Don Benson. Katie, you kept me laughing in the early stages when it was tempting to shelve the project. Meredith, thank you for wisdom, suggestions, and for being one of my most meaningful friends for over 23 years. Don, your keen editing eye and ready humor are a cherished gift. Any flaws remaining are because I couldn't stop tinkering. And to my treasured friend who prefers anonymity, you are my brain trust and heart trust and I can't imagine writing this without you.

Enormous thanks too to my beloved Beth Duckett, Anne Fava, Elissa Bantug, Janice Adams-King APRN, FNP-BC, MSN, CPHN, Edward Kentish M.Ac., L.Ac., Bill Kraynak, Normale Doyle, Christina O'Meara, Mary Dowling LCSW-C, Rosemary Bredeson CMH, Reverend Richard Bredeson, Robin Harling M.Ac., L.Ac., Stan Fox M.Ac., CZB, L.Ac., Stephen Cowan M.D., John Sullivan Ph.D., Brother/Doctor Bernard Seif, Jeanette Linder M.D., Frans Johansson, M.B.A., Bob Duggan M.A., M.Ac., L.Ac., Thea Elijah M.Ac., L.Ac., Dianne Connelly Ph.D., M.Ac., L.Ac., Captain Mary R. Vienna U.S.P.H.S., M.H.A., R.N., Ruby Racine, and Dave Daughters. I am grateful for your help along the way. Life would not be as rich without you.

Thank you to the many friends, patients, colleagues and teachers who have helped in so many large and small ways. I am filled with gratitude daily.

Bonnie Grauer, I cannot thank you enough for inspiring me to take leaps I didn't know I had left to leap, and for your unimaginable help that brings tears to my eyes, surpassing anything in the realm of normal human kindness.

Thank you to my friend Wendy Letow, founder of The Little Things for Cancer. You are an inspiration and a soul sister. Thank you to Cindy Carter and Steve Carter and The Cancer Support Foundation, I love you both and salute what you do. Thank you to Linda Roebuck, Gloria Hesseloff and A Community of Transformation (ACT) Annapolis. Without your early encouragement to teach and speak, I may have never taken flight. A huge thank you to all the staff at the Claudia Mayer/Tina Broccolino Cancer Resource Center and the Howard County General Hospital/Johns Hopkins Medicine Wellness Center for nourishing the spark and encouraging and supporting my HeartMindBody programs. Thank you to the staff at the Riviera Beach library who cheerfully told me it "helped the library" when I consistently checked out 20 to 30 books every week.

Thank you to my parents, you are two of the most interesting, charismatic, creative people I have ever met. You were my original mentors in "anything is possible." I am so blessed to know you and have you as my family. Thank you to all of our family members, especially Yvonne and Steve Hughes for raising such an amazing son.

Thank you to my husband Brandon for sharing the joy of practicing a greater consciousness and an open loving heart through all of the adventures and challenges of our life together. Your philosophical discernment and loving application makes it that much easier for me to not lose my way, or our way together. Thank you to our son Bain for living in a pure state of Open Heart Consciousness without even knowing what that is. You two are the foundation for it all. Your playfulness, joking, belly laughs, and deeply loving hearts make it so much easier to live with courage, hope, and lightheartedness and to refill my heart at a wellspring of love every day. I cherish our time together.

Contents

Key #1   Open Your Heart

Key #2   Practice a Feeling Mantra

Key #3   Change Your Mind

Key #4   Nourish Your Body

Key #5   Take on Healing

Key #6   Love

Disclaimer: Do No Harm

The best prescription is knowledge.
Dr. C. Everett Koop
Former U.S. Surgeon General

I take very deeply to heart the Hippocratic Oath "First do no harm." At no point in this book is it my intention to suggest or imply that you try a health practice that may cause harm, and so it is with great sincerity that I state:

Any information or advice contained in this book is not meant to be a substitute or replacement for medical care. Please consult with your physician on all decisions related to your health and health care. Do not follow any ideas mentioned in this book without first consulting a qualified health care provider.

That said, we must enter a wisdom dialogue with our own body, and earnestly aim to listen and follow its counsel and its unique and individual needs. You likely already know quite a bit about what is good for you and what helps you heal, and how to avoid that which causes harm. When people take responsibility for their health and are paying attention, they almost always know the right thing to do.

As I write this legal disclaimer, Vibram, the manufacturers of the FiveFingers minimalist shoe, has been charged with paying $3.75 million in a class-action settlement. This suit was brought about by buyers who felt they were misinformed by marketing that stated, "FiveFingers footwear is effective in strengthening muscles or reducing injury" a claim said to be made without scientific merit. Angry consumers who filed the suit claimed their feet were injured while running in the FiveFingers shoes. I have no doubt they were. Though I didn't wear FiveFingers, I healed a lingering back injury by converting to running both barefoot and in a minimalist shoe; if I had tried to run as usual in the minimalist shoe I would have had at best bad bone bruises, and at worst, possibly bone fractures, as anyone would after pounding away on pavement without any padding. The point of minimalist footwear is that it forces you to completely recreate your gait to avoid injury to the foot, and it forces you *off* surfaces like sidewalks.

Without Vibram's marketing that inspired my subsequent research, I wouldn't have ever thought to try minimalist shoe running to heal my back. If consumers had "listened to their feet," pain would have likely told them something was wrong before the bones were badly bruised or fractured.

Occasionally, stories in this book include mention of people who used unusual means to get well: coffee enemas (even while it is possible to perforate a rectum, or disrupt colonic colonies of good bacteria), allergen elimination diets (even while it is possible to alter diet to such an extreme as to cause malnutrition), megadoses of vitamin C (even while this may in unusual circumstances cause kidney stones), or even took matters entirely into their own hands when conventional medicine failed by trying unvalidated remedies suggested on blogs (even while this could cause injury, worsening of condition, or death). Similar to how I healed my back in minimalist shoes while millions of others injured themselves, the stories that follow are stories of individuals who found something that helped them, but that *won't necessarily help or even be safe for you*. Even if a treatment makes it through all the right channels, it may not necessarily be safe (think: Vioxx, or Thalidomide for nausea in pregnant women. Do an Internet search for "drugs that have been recalled" for the lengthy list the FDA provides each year.)

I have been advised that my frequent use of the term Inner Molecules of Medicine may raise the ire of the more litigious crowd. Please know that I in no way mean to suggest that a person should use their Inner Medicine in place of their prescription medication. I do mean to suggest that you be sure to not forfeit cultivating your own precious Inner Molecules of Medicine even if you also take prescription medicine in your journey toward health. In many cultures other than ours, the words "medicine" and "Medicine Man" or "Medicine Woman" have far broader meaning and much greater scope than the prescription drugs and doctors prescribing them that we think of today.

Information of any kind is potentially dangerous when we apply it unthinkingly like a one-size-fits-all fix to a problem, and don't weigh it against our own keen observations of our body. Once you can hear the whisper of your own captain navigating the ever-fluctuating seas of your life, you will find your innate ability to steer true, and properly confer with outside counsel the way one consults a navigation chart—for informational purposes.

On Possibility

Anyone who doesn't believe in miracles is not a realist.
David Ben-Gurion

Years ago, my blood type changed. Excitedly, with my birth certificate citing one blood type, and a more recent lab test citing a different blood type in hand, I approached about twenty of my savviest doctor and scientist friends with what I figured was an absolutely fascinating question: How did such a thing happen?

I was shocked at the near-identical responses I received. "Can't happen" the party line went. "Blood types never change." "Our testing has improved over the years, so clearly, the first lab just tested it wrong." Without exception, besides one scientist who thought it was curious but highly unlikely, every authority I consulted dismissed it as impossible, because of course we all know, *blood type can't change*.

I knew that the information available to my intelligent colleagues supported that conclusion, but I believed that it was possible that something else had occurred. Dr. Ignaz Semmelweis, the first physician to correctly suggest that lack of hand washing was contributing to increased hospital infections was ridiculed and committed to an insane asylum where he died from severe beatings for his "unusual" beliefs. Clearly, convention can be clung to rigorously and upheld violently even when data to the contrary suggests something otherwise. As Nobel Prize winning physicist Max Planck once wryly observed, "Science progresses funeral by funeral."

At a holiday party, I fell into conversation with an executive of the American Red Cross. With excitement, I asked him about my blood changing type. To my delighted surprise, he said to me, "Actually, there is a woman working for the Red Cross in Pennsylvania whose work is entirely devoted to understanding people like you. When we get a donation of blood that is documented to have changed types, we send it directly to her for research. She is quite busy. She is looking at things like whether there is an enzyme in the blood that is digesting the antigens off the blood, or whether a bacteria or virus may have caused the change."

So there it was, the "impossible" being enthusiastically and rigorously studied just a few hours drive away from my home. What science recognizes about the human body expands and changes every day. And though I had no pressing interest in reverting to my previous blood type, if doing so would in some way improve my health, I would be knocking on that scientist's door to learn more.

This book is about finding what is possible amidst what is popularly or reflexively considered impossible. It is about unlocking the mysterious and miraculous resources for healing that lie dormant within each of us. It is about understanding the states of heart, mind and body that promote powerful changes within us and make it more likely we may heal, be well. As William James, the famous American philosopher, psychologist, and physician observed, "(M)ost people live, whether physically, intellectually, or morally, in a very restricted circle of their potential being. They make use of a very small portion of their potential consciousness...We all have reservoirs of life to draw upon, of which we do not dream."

Just because something is not commonly experienced or popularly discussed does not mean it is not possible or does not exist. As Sir Bannister eloquently described after breaking the world record for running a four-minute mile, "No longer conscious of my movement, I discovered a new unity with nature. I had found a new source of power and beauty, a source I never dreamed existed." Once he demonstrated a new possibility in the domain of running, others were quick to follow.

In the domain of healing, there is also a source, a source of power and beauty, a source that allows for the seemingly impossible to occur that many of us have never dreamed of. I have seen and personally experienced the "impossible" barrier in healing broken many times. May the stories that follow awaken the possibility of such things for you.

The Big Picture

The doctor of the future will give no medicine, but will interest his patients in the care of the human frame, in diet, and in the cause and prevention of disease.
Thomas A. Edison

Every human being is the author of his own health or disease.
Buddha
c. 563 B.C.E.-c. 483 B.C.E.

There is a state of heart noted by many ancient and modern traditions and cultures to spontaneously heal disease from the body. Whether we profoundly heal illness, or learn what it means to live in a state of holy joy irrespective of circumstances, living in this state of heart changes the way we think, feel, and heal. Such a state of heart is alluded to and illuminated through the teaching stories, scriptures, and oral traditions of many diverse people through time. I have some stories to add, and offer them to unlock a deeper understanding not only of this mysterious state of heart, but to unlock other often unrecognized or neglected heart, mind, and body resources for healing. Some of the stories within this book are my own personal stories, and others are those of the friends, family members, and patients in my life. Each story has something to say about how we can help our bodies *make* medicine, or at the very least learn to stop getting in the way of the body's natural efforts to heal.

Researchers around the world have long demonstrated the power of the mind-body connection in healing. In Chinese, the term "xin" translates to HeartMind, a single entity thought to be intimately interwoven and interdependent. In my experience it is all three: our heart, mind, and body that are seamlessly interwoven and interconnected, one influencing the other in every moment. I have adopted the term HearttMindBody connection in place of mind-body connection in recognition of this dynamic interconnectedness. Understanding the HeartMindBody connection yields many clues for unlocking hidden healing resources.

It is well documented that our bodies make many medicinal substances in every second, and accessing the HeartMindBody connection is a proven means to changing our internal levels of these biochemicals that heal. By unlocking our hidden healing resources, we gain access to what I call *Inner Molecules of Medicine*. As we will see, our body makes many medicinal substances in every second, and meditation is a proven means to changing our internal levels of the biochemicals that heal. My learning of this skill turned what I thought was exclusively a personal medical journey into a journey of consciousness and a journey of the heart. Ultimately I came to think of illness as a call to living in a state of heart that we might not set out to cultivate otherwise. Illness and poor health become pathways into that state of heart the ancients in so many cultures knew about. A healthier body is often the side effect.

So often we are tempted by the challenges of life to unlock *Molecules of Misery*. It takes awareness, skill, and practice to change which molecules we are manufacturing. By way of example, I later tell the story of a time when a neighbor got angry at me for something that I didn't think warranted anger. My calm, reasonable, gentle responses further stoked the flames of her rage. A higher level of consciousness and a vaster heart of love are available to any person in any moment. Instead, unskilled as I was at the time of the confrontation, I walked away. It would be months before I realized exactly how I could have stepped outside of old habits and find that state of heart which has the power to heal, irrespective of her behavior. By not sharing that state of heart, I was violating a universal principle of healing. True healing ripples out and touches everyone involved. When I walked away from my neighbor's attack, it allowed for a situation whereby the whole neighborhood took sides in grand "Lord of the Flies" style. Divided factions that gossip and criticize are sure signs of an ill community.

When we learn and practice the principles that support healing in our own body, we learn something greater of how to heal our families, our relationships, our communities, and the global community, and we realize the true heart of healing. Many healing and spiritual traditions suggest that our personal impulse for enlightenment is a benefit to all beings. I believe our personal work to transform and heal is our most precious gift to ourselves, and the most generous contribution we may *ever* make to humanity. As Lao Tzu said, "If you want to awaken all of humanity, then awaken all of yourself, if you want to eliminate the suffering of the world, then eliminate all that is dark and negative in yourself. Truly, the greatest gift you have to give is that of your own self-transformation."

In every moment we are either creating Inner Molecules of Medicine, or Molecules of Misery. There is no "off" switch for the minute titrations in hormones, neurotransmitters, immune complexes and many other biochemical and electromagnetic events within our body in each moment. As we will see, those titrations fluctuate based on our thoughts, moods and feelings. Ask yourself these questions: Did your thoughts and feelings today nourish your kidneys? Did they bathe your lungs in an elixir of love? Is your heart awash in unrestrained compassion? Were the people around you comforted, nourished, and uplifted by your presence? If not, why not? What part of the human drama enticed you to choose to live in unresourceful thoughts and feelings? The state of heart described by ancient cultures and traditions, once accessed, is said to allow disease to be vaporized from the body. That same state of heart that allows for radical health, ripples out to bring radical health to families and communities, irrespective of the human drama, and irrespective of circumstances, *if we so choose it*. Unlocking the Heart of Healing is a personal journey with global impact. We can afford no less.

If you are going to *take* medicine, make sure you *make* medicine

In my work as an acupuncturist, meditation teacher, and Qigong teacher, I often suggest that my patients and students adopt what I call a Feeling Mantra meditation. A Feeling Mantra uses a feeling tone in the heart as a tool for inner transformation. This meditative practice is based on deepening a state of heart that heals, irrespective of how difficult, disheartening, or painful circumstances may be. "That's easy for you to suggest," the person convinced that their situation is just too difficult and challenging to change may retort. "You're cute, healthy, have a career you love, and aren't stressed." They have no idea that for me to know with such certainty that we can profoundly influence whether or not we heal *came from my experience* of being obese, deeply ill, stressed, anxious, and chronically miserable. In fact, if life had carried on effortlessly, I may have never discerned the distinctions I share here. It took my hitting rock bottom to realize that our circumstances aren't what matters most. It is what we make of our inner state, even in the presence of challenging circumstances, that holds the potential for unlocking untapped resources for healing our heart, mind, and body. A Feeling Mantra meditation is one of the most powerful tools.

Once I started cultivating a particular feeling tone in my heart despite the fact that I felt awful, looked awful, and didn't think my prospects proffered any hope besides things that were awful, my body started to change in ways that could be called unusual or "miraculous." Healing that had stymied the cleverest physicians and thwarted the efficacy of the most potent medications seemed to bubble up from my inner state. I realized then that the HeartMindBody connection is one of the most egregiously ignored resources for healing available to us.

To share my personal stories was an idea that took some getting used to. I had no great eagerness to sacrifice the comfort of my personal privacy by telling the intimate health details of my journey in print, and it would be far safer to stand at a cool distance and only tell stories about others. When my very wise and spiritually uplifted 76-year-old friend realized how much of my health journey I chose to share in this book, she asked me, "Are you sure you want to share of yourself so fully?" She told me she holds her beliefs, her spirituality, and the miracles that have happened in her life close and quiet like an "inner treasure" because otherwise, she explained, people are always agreeing and disagreeing, debating the merits or validity, or explaining why such rich blessings don't or can't work for them. The spirit of such exchanges could diminish or cheapen the "inner treasure" in the same way bulldozing the natural habitat of an endangered species in the name of progress might. For my friend, it is prudent to identify a more life-affirming, conservation-minded type of company with whom to selectively share the gift of her inner treasure. Yet I lay my inner treasure out against her counsel in hopes of increasing the nesting habitat of our most important endangered species: the deeply conscious, full feeling, loving heart that is awake and awash in true bliss and holy joy. I share the incredibly long list of diagnoses I grappled with in hopes that the reader tempted to think, "What she is saying might work if I didn't have such difficult things to deal with," will instead think, "If she can do it, so can I."

I've come to think of diagnoses as labels offered in a spirit of help by the medical community that sometimes are useful and sometimes are not. They are temporary snapshots of our fluid and ever-changing bodily processes. A diagnosed disease may or may not exhibit all the associated or expected symptoms, and as I well found, an expected disease process may or may not be as predictable a thing as we expect. That many of my diagnoses reversed would inspire many doctors to suggest I never really had the diseases I had been diagnosed with. I believe that by acting committedly through lifestyle intervention, particularly through the inner transformational work of changing the feeling tone in my heart, the fact that many diseases remitted for me or for anyone is not surprising at all.

Heal from the inside out

Though it is considered impossible that I reversed or radically minimized any of the following diseases, illnesses, or injuries, my diagnoses remarkably include: a hemi-paresis (a one-sided paralysis that was categorized as cerebral palsy), multiple sclerosis, a grapefruit sized abdominal mass, fibroids, hormonal imbalance with hemorrhagic menstrual bleeding, irritable bowel syndrome, major depression, bipolar disorder, anxiety disorder, schizophrenia, hypoglycemia, hyperinsulinemia, rheumatoid arthritis, chronic year-long antibiotic resistant urinary tract infection, nephrogenic diabetes insipidus, infertility, extreme insomnia, chronic fatigue immune deficiency syndrome, candida, environmental and chemical sensitivity, chronic sinusitis, severely herniated discs of the neck and back, celiac disease, metabolic syndrome that led to 90 pounds of excess weight, and at one point, 5 pieces of 400 degree glass that fused to my eye. It's a long list. Life gave me plenty of opportunities to realize that no amount of medical intervention could do more than wildly swing at my symptoms like a spirited game of Whac-a-mole. To heal, I had to change from the inside out.

Many of the stories that follow capture ways my patients or I changed the ways we think and feel in a profound enough manner to change the capacity of our body to heal. While many people I have treated have resorted to *take* medicine for their ailments and illnesses, few have ever explicitly thought to *make* medicine in their body until introduced to the concepts that follow. The learning of that skill changes lives.

While the dramatic quantity of health crises I experienced is unique, many of the illnesses were illnesses you or anyone else could experience if you lived with a poor lifestyle and a grim inner feeling tone in your heart for long enough. My constitution wasn't as hardy as some, so my body filed a complaint earlier in life than most. That spared me from blaming my problems on "aging" and made me face the facts head-on, after conventional treatments failed, that what I was suffering from was not the normal decline of aging, but was lifestyle-induced illness. When those illnesses lifted or lessened through lifestyle reform, the case was cinched.

Live more lovingly in your body

The most profound component of lifestyle reform I found was the ability to utilize my HeartMindBody connection to make medicine in my body by living in that state of heart the ancients alluded to. Though as we will see it matters to practice this state irrespective of our circumstances, this doesn't mean we ignore our circumstances. To increase our odds of healing, general lifestyle reform as an act of love towards ourselves is essential. Finding how to reform your lifestyle and live more lovingly in your body is one of the mysteries I hope you'll be inspired to attend to in reading this book. Wherever we intervene in the HeartMindBody continuum serves as an act of love that affects us in the depths of our being.

When we change what we eat, how we sleep, whether we exercise, the amount of play in our lives, and how we feel, cascades of biochemical and electro-magnetic changes happen in our bodies. As Terry Wahls, M.D. said, "Life is a series of self-correcting chemical reactions. Therefore, once you have optimized your cell chemistry, the body will often begin to heal itself in remarkable ways, even when scientists don't understand the exact nature of what was wrong in the first place." [1]

My health at one point had declined so precipitously and responded so unfavorably to both conventional and complementary medicine that I eventually knew I had no choice but to learn how to make these "self-correcting chemical reactions" in my body by changing the feeling tone in my heart, simply to function. Just like the cancer patient suddenly inspired to trade fast food for a daily dose of broccoli, sprouts, and raw beets, ill health inspired me to trade in what I humorously came to think of as *Divine Deficit Disorder* for a more nutrient-dense inner diet. I would learn that letting my heart be moved by *something* is one of the most powerful self-healing practices available. Symptoms had to knock very hard and for a very long time to get my attention seriously enough to realize that living in that state of heart known through ancient cultures is not a luxury rarely afforded to the lucky, but is an opportunity, waiting for us all.

Our United States National Academy of Sciences developed for us a DRI (Daily Recommended Intake) of vitamins and minerals needed to survive. In the presence of illness, our nutritional needs increase. I think we should have a DRI for inner feelings of joy, love, compassion, and bliss. If you are attempting only to preserve health, you'll need a modicum of such feelings. If you are ill, or trying to heal, or wanting to live richly irrespective of circumstances, your baseline needs are going to sharply increase.

Bring all resources online

When I gave a talk to a Chemical Sensitivity Disorders group, many of the attendees arrived wearing oxygen tanks or masks. Multiple Chemical Sensitivities is an issue I am keenly sympathetic to having had it to a degree myself for years. A whiff of perfume or gasoline would cause me to feel nauseated and unable to focus for the rest of the day. I was sharing many insights about the HeartMindBody connection to this audience whom I had been advised was savvy, educated, and science minded. One attendee raised his hand and asked, "I want to use mind-body medicine, but how does this apply to me when the onset of my disease was pinpointed to a heavy mercury burden?" Obviously the first step in unlocking healing from an illness caused by a heavy mercury burden is to *remove the mercury*. But this man had pulled back his mask to ask the question, letting me know that he was still sensitive to fumes and scents, and even now without the mercury burden he was still not completely well. We don't want to forfeit any avenues to healing, particularly our Inner Molecules of Medicine. There were still untapped resources for him to bring online.

This exploration of Unlocking the Heart of Healing does not hold sole allegiance to the outcome of reversing illness. Radical health does not always mean our body heals. As we will see, we do best to live in *continuous creative response* to our circumstances. Though I enthusiastically share stories of many people who did recover from diseases or conditions that should have been impossible to reverse, healing includes finding peace and a sense of inner freedom when a disease doesn't reverse. I have had patients tell me that when a loved one dies, they spend months lamenting what could have been done differently or better, feeling sick over opportunities missed, and blaming themselves. Healing our dis-ease can be more important than healing disease. The freedom inherent to heart-based healing includes freedom from needing an outcome to be a certain way. Read the stories that follow for hope and inspiration, but not as a cause for disappointment or guilt if what worked for one person doesn't work for you.

The most important thing we can heal is the feeling state in our heart. We must heal cynicism, hopelessness, purposelessness, and joylessness. We must increase our ability to live with dignity, grace, joy, gratitude, and contentment, even as our bodies decline and eventually die. Healing includes the wheelchair-bound person who comes to a new inner freedom and finds satisfaction, enjoyment, and meaningfulness within the constraints of his or her circumstance. It includes the cancer patient who is close to death, but considers the final months of life her most rich as she speaks the things she never before dared to say to loved ones and savors a new sense of connectedness and awareness of the miraculousness of all of life.

I have spent my share of time feeling hopeless in the face of disease, as anyone who has lost someone dear to them or is personally facing a chronic or terminal illness may feel. Ultimately, whether a disease is reversible or chronic or fatal, there may be an unusual healing or new quality of life and heart that may be available that you have never imagined. There may be a new way to live in the context of disease that is rich and beautiful and well. The gap between what makes you tick and what makes you sick may be smaller and more easily bridged than you think. Open your mind and heart and shake up tired and unexamined old habits. It's time to Unlock the Heart of Healing!

Key #1 Open Your Heart

Vaporize Disease

Your heart has an electromagnetic field of five thousand millivolts, as compared to the brain, which emits only 140 millivolts. Remember, when Voyager transmitted signals from Saturn to Earth it used only a ten-millivolt battery. If Saturn to Earth takes ten millivolts, then with five thousand to work with, heart-to-brain communication, or communication from your heart to that of another person, should actually be a "no-brainer."
T.S. Wiley with Bent Formby, Ph.D.
Lights Out: Sleep, Sugar, and Survival[2]

The way is not in the sky, the way is in the heart.
Buddha

When I was in my twenties, not yet a Hughes, and only several months into private practice as an acupuncturist, a mentor introduced me to the board members of an organization I would be working with. When I walked into the room he said, "This is Bridget Hargadon. She's a shaman. Everyone she touches gets well." Yet only nine years before, my mother had spoken to me from the desperate compassion of a concerned parent hoping to motivate change and said, "You are like a black hole: you suck the life out of everyone around you." Her words (offered in a genuine spirit of constructive criticism about my pervasive pessimism) were true of that decade in my life.

I offer the two contrasting statements to show how markedly different an impact we have on those around us and on ourselves depending on what mood and state of consciousness we are living in. My life circumstances were no better or worse as a black hole, or as a shaman. But by coming to the freeing realization that I could live in an elevated state of heart irrespective of circumstances, my experience of life, my perception of life, my healing or harming impact on others, and my own health were radically different.

The chemistry of immortality

A key to my "shamanic" success with patients is that even 17 years ago as a beginning acupuncturist I held an absolute certainty that my patients would get well. To this day I am genuinely surprised if a patient doesn't heal in some way. In my 20s I had no real experiential foundation, nor large ego personality fueling my early utter conviction. What I had is what I call "intentional naïveté." I allowed myself to be naïve enough to believe that miracles were the natural consequence of the system of medicine I was using. When it comes to healing, I recommend a large helping of intentional naïveté to everyone. Cynicism erodes belief, and belief has a strange and powerful way of influencing outcome.

Specifically, I learned from the internationally recognized scholar, Taoist Master, acupuncturist and herbalist Jeffrey Yuen, Ph.D. that the ancient oral tradition of Chinese Medicine alludes to a state of heart that can vaporize disease. I took this literally. For those interested in Chinese medicine, Yuen's exact statement was, "Strengthen the organs that are necessary to deal with phlegm: lungs to expel, spleen to transform, kidneys to dissolve, and then the instance of what they call spontaneous healing, miracles, when the heart vaporizes. So like a science fiction movie, one day the cancer is just miraculously gone—vaporization of phlegm. That comes from the heart. See if you can open your heart to hope as well as open the heart of your client."[3] At the time of this teaching, Jeffrey Yuen was Memorial Sloan-Kettering Cancer Center's Integrative Medicine acupuncturist. He was delivering a talk to acupuncturists on Chinese Medicine and Cancer Care. Recognizing a state of heart as a powerful adjunct to cancer care stood out to me as the most powerful statement of his two-day talk. It became my mission to better understand and help my patients find that state.

As I began to see more and more evidence of this mysterious state at work, my intentional naïveté slowly gave way to absolute, experience-based conviction. There is unquestionably a state of the heart with the power to heal disease.

In both ancient Chinese and ancient Hawaiian healing traditions, as well as traditions such as the African Kalahari !Kung and other indigenous tribal people, there is mention of this mysterious healing state of heart. In an article called *The Power of Laughter,* Keith Varnum, author of *How to Be a Miracle Maker: Find Joy, Love, and Abundance*[4] describes it beautifully. When I asked him where he learned what follows, he shared that this was passed on to him via oral transmission from his Hawaiian Kahuna shaman over 40 years ago.

Varnum writes, "The ancient Hawaiians assert there are two chemical reactions within the human body that can accomplish Reconnection with Source Oneness. The first is the 'sacred tear' beneath our sadness and hopelessness. Beneath that tear lies the second chemical reaction, said to be more powerful than all the healing agents known to humankind. It comes 'out of the blue' with the power of a jackhammer, shattering the seriousness of the entire human estate. A power instantly freeing and balancing to all the body's chemistry. This is the power of laughter. When it comes in this manner, it comes through the 'na'au' (gut level) and will pierce the hopelessness of any situation or attitude. It is not a power to be taken lightly, for the ancient Hawaiians say it holds the chemistry of immortality and will instantly heal any terminal disease. It's said to be the 'laughter of God' which shatters the ridiculousness of hopelessness."[5]

The chemistry of immortality, instantly able to heal terminal disease, may sound to some like wishful thinking. But the discussion of similar phenomena across cultures and through time points to the profound, illness vaporizing changes in our body that are possible when our heart swells with authentic laughter, deep love, and an unshakable belief in the miraculous. For many, entertaining the possibility that a powerful healing state could follow a transformational change of the heart will awaken many layers of cherished and safeguarded cynicism. But not only have I seen the chemistry of immortality miraculously reverse disease and rapidly heal injuries, I have experienced it myself.

Rapid wound healing

The phenomena of Rapid Wound Healing has been demonstrated and documented around the world. In places including Southeast Asia, India, Iran, and Iraq, practitioners put themselves in an ecstatic trance at the time of religious festivals and then puncture or impale themselves with objects such as metal rods, spears, hooks, or skewers. When the metal implements are later removed, practitioners experience little to no bleeding and the points of entry close and heal with surprising speed. A friend of mine who is now a well-known healer had observed such acts at a street festival while traveling in Indonesia and said it permanently altered his understanding of the mind-body connection and what is possible when it comes to healing. As he described to me what he had seen, I wondered to myself who would be crazy enough to try such a thing. Later I would be wildly grateful for the example. I never imagined I'd be faced with an injury that would require me to apply such unusual principles.

One night as my then three-year-old son stood next to me peering into a hot oven, the oven-safe glass dish I was removing exploded. With a loud "POP!" 400 degree glass projectiles shot in all directions. By some unaccountable miracle my son was untouched. Five shards of scorching glass hit my eye and fused instantly. This wasn't something that could be rinsed out or removed with tweezers. My husband rushed me to the emergency room.

If you ever need to be seen at an ER *quickly* and the waiting room is packed to capacity, showing up at the reception desk with glass jutting out from your eye works wonders. You get hastily whisked back ahead of everyone. And, if you want carte blanche to all the Valium and Percocet you could dream of, an eye full of glass does the trick. Nurses were producing handfuls of it, purportedly to get a leg up on the agonizing pain they promised me was coming once the shock wore off. They were convinced I had lost my reasoning capabilities from shock when I repeatedly declined the drugs; they were sure I was out of my mind.

What they didn't know was that I *was* out of my mind and in a powerfully altered state. Only the altered state I was in was one where healing defies all reasonable expectation, much like the rapid wound healing seen in other cultures. In the weeks prior, I had been in a bit of a spiritual crisis. I "knew" that the mind has an extraordinary ability to heal the body. I "knew" that a feeling that comes from the heart can initiate powerful biochemicals of healing, and I "knew" how to get there. Feelings from my heart triggering the lessening or healing or reversal of illnesses had happened to me numerous times. But I kept slipping into thinking that those times were flukes, or dumb luck, and certainly not teachable or duplicatable. I would describe these miracles in lectures or with patients, but my belief was tentative and my confidence wobbly so my words didn't pack a punch.

The moment the glass hit my eye and bizarrely missed my son, I *knew* that this event was no accident. I was absolutely certain that this event occurred so that this time, I would own it–own that a biochemical reaction initiated by the heart can heal the body, even of a wound like glass in the eye. I never considered the possibility that anything less than a miracle would occur when the glass hit. I knew this was not bad luck, nor cause to sue a manufacturer. I use this brand of glass in the oven still today.

Without my thoughts engaged in generating terror, the adrenaline requisite with the event instead fueled a feeling of incredible power and excitement that welled up within me. I would later realize the adrenaline had been an *essential component* in the inner alchemical transformation that took place. It's not that we need to "calm down" or be fearless in the face of terrifying challenges. It is how artfully we engage our HeartMindBody connection to heal in the face of terror that influences outcomes.

I practiced holding a tone of love and wonder in my heart even as my circumstance tempted me with panic and worry. Though through my clinical work as a hypnotist I knew many mind-body techniques to control pain, I did not need to use any of those; in the profoundly altered state I had reached through my heart, there was no pain. There were a few times while the doctor was working on me when fear would begin to creep in. I was talking out loud as it happened, "Maybe I should have taken that Valium...NO! I'm in the hands of a gifted doctor and my body is miraculously healing as he works." I'm sure the doctor thought I could benefit from a referral to the psychiatric ward afterwards. I wasn't worried what he thought; I let the adrenaline enhance my ecstatic connection with a profound force that was clearly at work allowing me to be free of pain and filled with a sense of miraculousness. I let my heart burst open with amazement, gratitude, and wonderment.

I never let fear or panic constrict my body. I am quite sure that if I had engaged the very real possibility of permanent visual damage, my body would have tensed, circulation would have been impaired, and my eye could not have gotten the fresh oxygen, nutrients, and other necessary biochemicals it needed to rapidly heal. Fear is one of the most formidable

5

roadblocks to healing, and when I feel it, I remind myself of the acronym Forgetting Every Available Resource. With remembrance of hidden resources, hidden resources such as a practiced inner feeling state that opens the heart, the elevated state of fear transforms into an enhanced power to heal.

It took the doctor 45 minutes to extract the shards. It required the dexterity and steady hand of a neurosurgeon. In order to avoid tearing the delicate ocular tissues, he was running the side of a needle along the surface of my eye, delicately wedging it underneath each shard and then gently prying them out one by one. To discern whether any very tiny shards were present, he would put dye in my eye, then peer at it through a huge magnifying lens under a black light. He irrigated my eye several times as well.

During the 45 minute procedure, my thoughts roamed to those traditions throughout the world where accelerated healing is known to accompany spiritual trance. By opening my heart to be moved by something greater than me and by focusing my thoughts and feelings towards awe and wonder in the very moment I could have been sick with panic, I knew with a swell of gratitude that I was experiencing this effect.

When the doctor was finished he sent in a second doctor to verify that he had successfully retrieved all the glass. In retrospect, I'd wager a guess that what this doctor really wanted was a witness to a miracle so unusual that he wasn't quite sure he believed what he'd seen. The second doctor stood there, mouth gaping, looking back and forth between my chart and me. When she finally spoke, she said, "This is the strangest thing I've ever seen. From what you've gone through, your eye should be red, irritated, bloodshot, and with many lesions across the cornea. Instead, I can't tell which eye it was without looking at your chart. It's as if your eye healed instantly as each shard was removed." Because I had unlocked the mysterious chemistry of immortality in my heart and thereby changed what was possible for my body, *it had*.

Be Divine Receptive

Be not discouraged, keep on, there are Divine things well envelope'd. I swear to you there are Divine things more beautiful than words can tell.
Walt Whitman

The most beautiful and profound emotion we can experience is the sensation of the mystical. It is the power of all true science.
Albert Einstein

In *The Body is the Hero,* Ronald Glasser remarks, "Antibodies do not simply or magically appear in our children's bodies; they are produced, and it is how they are produced that is one of the major evolutionary achievements. A mixture of mystery and chemistry, it is a combination of physics and grace down to the molecular level, where despite our sense of importance and dominance, our lives are still preciously maintained." [6] If we understood the minutiae of the 100,000 biochemical reactions we experience per second in our bodies, that mystery, chemistry, physics and grace might all be easily accounted for. My experiences have allowed me to release my death grip on science as an explanation for everything and to allow my heart to be moved by something much greater.

When my dear friend read an early draft of this book she excitedly shot me an email that read, "Too euphoric to talk about this. Will comment later." Later, she told me the book had touched and moved her profoundly and deeply and yielded useful tools for change. But when it came time to make those notes in the margin, she wrote, "too religious sounding for me" next to my repeated use of terms like "holy" and "Divine." She is not unusual. Many people I know have had an uncomfortable or painful experience associated with religion and are quick to lump all things "Divine" in with that prior experience. To compound the situation, numinous experiences do not blossom forth from the Frazzled American Lifestyle, and without direct personal experience, it is easy to regard such reports warily and cynically. This marks a huge loss for our culture. Having a numinous experience and an authentic sense of awe and wonderment changes everything. As I often point out lightheartedly yet seriously, we are suffering an extreme case of Divine Deficit Disorder.

Reverse Divine Deficit Disorder

Being Divine-receptive does not mean being new-agey or religious. It means allowing

7

your heart to be moved by something that is unknown, and bigger than you, the contemplation of which "turns on" the holy reverence and sacred awe circuits in your heart and brain. Emily Dickinson knew something about this. She advised, "The soul should always stand ajar, ready to welcome the ecstatic experience."

Cynicism, or feeling unworthy of a holy experience, or considering such a state too good to be true blocks these circuits, and at a great price. Duke University's Center for Spirituality, Theology and Health is one of many research based institutions looking at the ways faith heals. *Which* faith we adopt doesn't appear to matter much. Allowing ourselves to be moved by *something* seems to be the key. I'm with Ziggy Marley, who sings, *Love is my religion.[7]* When we awaken the type of love that elevates us to a new plane of consciousness, the whole game changes.

For the person who just plain dislikes any reference to expressions that include the term "Divine," I would call it: being moved by whatever the thing is that keeps your heart beating and blood pumping and that unfolded you from a tiny DNA blueprint, that once apprehended in its vast mysteriousness, can overcome you with feelings of awe, wonder, and unspeakable joy. Whatever that unnameable thing is without which you would not be able to keep your body running because of the innumerable processes it miraculously coordinates for you in each nanosecond. That thing that facilitates the processes that allow us to heal wherever and whenever it can. That mysterious force that even allows us to exist in this universe in the narrow spectrum of conditions we require in the first place. As a mother who has borne a child, I marvel at this frequently. I'll look at my son and think, "Wow, all I did was take it easy, eat organic food, and swallow vitamins, and in nine months I got something as miraculous as him?" To me, the coordination of intelligence necessary staggers the mind.

In his 1932 piece called *My Credo*, Einstein wrote, "To sense that behind everything that can be experienced there is something that our minds cannot grasp, whose beauty and sublimity reaches us only indirectly: this is religiousness. In this sense I am religious." He later wrote to a young girl, "Everyone who is seriously involved in the pursuit of science becomes convinced that a spirit is manifest in the laws of the universe—a spirit vastly superior to that of man."

Science says we are electrons, protons, atoms, molecules and cells clinging together in our uniquely differing functional forms by vibrating fields of energy. Albert Einstein described, "All matter is energy." While receiving the Nobel Prize in 1917, Max Planck said, "There is no matter as such. All matter originates and exists only by virtue of a force which brings the particle of an atom to vibration and holds this most minute solar system of the atom together. We must assume behind this force the existence of a conscious and intelligent mind. This mind is the matrix of all matter."

What is the mind behind the matrix? What is it that causes the Fibonacci spiral (a spiral whose growth factor is the mathematical "golden ratio") to show up repeatedly in nature in the form of a nautilus shell, the petals on flowers including the Shasta Daisy and Black Eyed Susan, the spiral of our ears and spiral galaxies? What is it that causes what Leonardo Da Vinci called the "Divine Proportion" also known as the "Phi ratio" to show up repeatedly in the human body? The phi ratio, 1.618, shows up in the ratios of our navel to feet versus our navel to top of our head, our elbow to index finger versus our shoulder to elbow, and even the height of a double helix versus the width of our DNA.

When we stop thinking of humans as the most important force in existence and allow the possibility that there are awe-inspiring forces at work in the cosmos, we set in motion the conditions to free ourselves of Divine Deficit Disorder and reconnect with a sense of holiness in all things. In *Field Notes on the Compassionate Life,* Marc Ian Barasch refers to the Hubble Space Telescope as the "Humble." As he describes, "It's been a corrective lens for human astigmatism." [8] Considering or apprehending whatever that humbling miraculous thing is that allows for the miracle of life in the cosmos and being moved to tears by it is a universal, rather than religious opportunity.

Researcher and neuroscientist Mark Robert Waldman, co-author of *How God Changes Your Brain* describes in his 2010 TEDxConejo talk[9] that while there may not actually be evidence for things like God and compassion, meditating on them "builds a better brain." Brain scans his team gathered at the University of Pennsylvania show such brain changes in vivid color. Waldman makes the distinction that meditating on what he calls a "Big Idea" (your single most meaningful value, whether it be God, peace, compassion, or love) will grow dendrites that are helpful in the brain. Conversely, meditating for even a second on something negative releases stress neurochemicals that harm the brain. Negative things may include the concept of God for those people who have a negative reaction to it. As Waldman points out, "No matter how you think about it, God is going to change your brain."

In Waldman's lab, researchers showed that it didn't matter if a Buddhist focused on Pure Consciousness or a Franciscan Nun focused on Closeness to God, the positive effect on the brain was the same. Though the healing state of heart the ancients referred to is difficult to capture in words and can never be fully expressed in language as it refers to a state where we transcend what is known, familiar, and speakable, needing a way to speak of it, I came to call it Open Heart Consciousness. Focusing on Open Heart Consciousness is my Big Idea that is meaningful to me. Whatever yours is, be it love, compassion, joy, laughter, or other, when you read my shorthand for the Big Idea, feel free to substitute yours. The effect on healing in general and on the brain, no matter what we call it, will, *hooray for diversity*, be the same.

A healing state is a heart-based feeling state

An enhanced healing state often arises from a heart-based feeling state. To make medicine requires that we learn something about resourceful feelings. Just mulling things over or practicing from the mind and body without the heart isn't enough. We must allow ourselves to be moved by something greater than ourselves. Ralph Waldo Emerson said, "Let us take our bloated nothingness out of the path of the divine circuits." [10]

After hearing me speak about letting our hearts be moved by life, a woman called me a few days later and said, "I used to drive by varying religious institutions and cringe at the thoughts of all the suffering related to those places. But suddenly after hearing your talk, this realization welled up in me that I had become completely disconnected from spirit. Suddenly, everywhere I looked I could see beauty. It seemed like I was moved by *everything*. The next day, I drove past a church and I couldn't help but smile a huge smile. I drove past a synagogue and found tears welling up in my eyes. I realized that however they were going about it, these were all places where people were attending because they were hungry for that same heart opening that had just happened to me. I wept at the beauty of it."

Now *that's* what we're talking about.

Healing energy following a change of heart is experienced in different ways for different people. To account for the way it bubbled up like a searing heat for them, the Kalahari !Kung call the healing energy liberated through trance and dance "Boiling Energy." [11] Though I have never experienced healing energy as bubbly, in other ways the descriptions by the !Kung read strikingly similar to both my own and my patients' experiences. Let us overcome Divine Deficit Disorder and not be limited by names, but broadened by concepts.

Find the Unio Mystica

To put it simply, a person who has experienced the ecstatic state (samadhi) cannot possibly call into question its intrinsic value and desirability. The experience of blissful ease in the nondual state of consciousness, wherein all sharp differences between beings and things are "outshined," inevitably changes how we look at the whole spiritual enterprise and the world's sacred traditions, not to mention how we view everyone and everything else.

Georg Feuerstein

The Yoga Tradition: Its History, Literature, Philosphy, and Practice[12]

What we perceive as "realistic" in the realm of our personal health often falls far, far short of what is actually possible. I had been diagnosed with a paralysis severe enough to prevent me from walking or talking at six months of age. Yet I walked, (though clumsily, and with a slight limp) and talked, close to the expected ages. Then I was supposedly headed for a wheelchair a second time after receiving the diagnosis of multiple sclerosis at 17 years old. Despite accumulating these and other disease processes from the earlier mentioned list that should have made graceful athletics simply impossible, there was something else in store for me. Though I was distinctly non-athletic for the first 23 years of my life, that would all change in an instant.

It may have had something to do with the fact that I was traveling for two weeks in Costa Rica with my friend Frans Johansson. Anyone who knows Frans, an internationally recognized innovation thought leader, can attest that it is impossible to hang around him and not be in a profoundly transformation-receptive state. Founder of The Medici Group and author of *The Medici Effect: What Elephants and Epidemics Can Teach Us About Innovation*[13] and *The Click Moment: Seizing Opportunity in an Unpredictable World*,[14] Frans has a way of blowing creativity lids open in a whirlwind of optimism and joy that transforms whomever his client may be to a new, elevated state. I happened to bathe in his larger-than-life loving optimism and charisma for 14 days straight.

Frans knew I was obsessed with learning to dance salsa, yet I was morosely close to tears over my ineptness and perceived limitations. He simply did not believe dancing was impossible for me. His adamance that anything is possible and his non-stop ebullience pierced my certainty and slowly crumbled my dejectedness. In a bizarre moment that made no sense except in Frans' paradigm, a stranger grabbed my hand in a Costa Rican nightclub and whirled me around for hours causing every head in the place to turn. Heads turned because moments before I had been a gawky, gangly, partially paralyzed woman with two left feet. With no rational explanation, I was dancing with grace and ease. This proved to me in one shocking moment that what we are and aren't capable of has little to do with what diagnostic tests, rationality, or our faculties of reason say is possible. Defying any prediction that a doctor looking at my brain scan could have made, I was doing "the impossible." Audrey Hepburn discerned an important distinction when she observed, "Nothing is impossible. The word itself says, "I'm possible!"

Having a moment of transcending the "impossible" limits of my body was one of the extraordinary moments of my life. I was hooked. Once I overcame my own limited vision of possibility for myself, I've been able to dance ever since. For a period of years, I went salsa dancing three nights each week. That I danced at all shocked me. What would happen next would be even more shocking.

Salsa requires total presence, total focus of mind, coupled with a loose, free body. To dance with a paralysis required that I surrender all trying and let something magical happen. Otherwise, the harder I tried, the more my paralyzed side tightened up. I would later think of the meditative state that allowed me to dance as "No Mind." The surrender into No Mind allowed me to access Open Heart Consciousness, that mysterious state where the impossible becomes possible. When those inner gates opened up, I gained access to abilities that should not by any normal assessment of reality have been available to me. I would simultaneously shed limits and gain a physical intelligence that in an ordinary state was simply not possible. When that happened, I could dance at an extraordinarily high level. When it didn't, I was clumsy and tight. It wasn't any fun when that happened, so *I saw to it that I surrendered into the meta-normal state of Open Heart Consciousness almost every night.*

The miracle of dancing at all was a total joy to me. But that was just the start. Over time I found there was something beyond that: an "unknown factor," the magic and elusiveness of which drove all us salsa dancers in a continual quest. When a magical night "hit" as they seemed to do (contagiously ripping through us like wildfire when they did), we were suddenly transformed by the ability to extend our senses, our reflexes, our stamina, and our ecstasy far beyond the usual constraints associated with living in a body. It was electrifying. We would dance in such synchrony it was as if we were a unit, in a mind-meld, a heart-meld, fused with all of creation, free of the usual illusion of being separate from one another in time and space. For a time we were unified with the pulsing, vibrating intelligence of the quantum soup, in a distinctly non-sexual, yet profoundly ecstatic way. Though partners had to take care to grip my hand extra tight since my grasp is unpredictable, I was completely unaware of being physically limited in any way during these times.

Ultimately neither skill in dancing nor physical ability were requirements for this sort of transcendence as I well knew. But because novice dancers often held back, too tense, concerned with steps, and self-conscious to allow it, they would miss the opportunity to whirl with us sweaty, Latin-styled dervishes. This deepened the mystery to those who could see that something transcendent and magical was going on but who had no idea how we got there. Most watching us would chalk it up to lucky good skill and move on. They definitely wouldn't have guessed that my brain scan shows the left lobe of someone who should be in a wheelchair. You can't impart magic to a soul that doesn't hunger for magic.

At a glance, it was easy to discern who was dancing in this transcendent state. We sought each other out like magnets. Plenty of dancers had skill sets that matched or surpassed ours, but even if polished and light on their feet, something about the way they moved looked clenched, heavy, and weighted. It was as easy to see as if they had a cold or flu, only this was a spiritual sickness-of never having opened their hearts, their minds, their bodies, and their energy to be elevated and moved by something bigger than themselves. I came to think of the experience of communing with something unknown where the impossible became possible as a Unio Mystica, *Mystical Union*. (Mystical union: the merging of the individual consciousness, cognitively or affectively, with a superior, or supreme consciousness.)

The Unio Mystica wasn't something that would just sneak up by lucky accident. As a spiritual adept from any tradition knows, hunger in the heart coupled with sincere dedication and practice are the foundation. Whether a Divine spark then lights in your heart is part of the Great Mystery. The Divine energy surrounds us like a plasma, and yet many people never figure out how to let it into their bodies and hearts even once in their entire lives. The human drama distracts many, who assume circumstances need to be a particular way to know bliss. Others only ever know the Divine energy through physical pursuits and athletics and forever push deeper into those pursuits until aging closes that gate.

For me, feeling the mystery and power of something inexplicable through the physical pursuit of salsa ultimately spurred me to re-evaluate my entire life. I came to the conclusion that the only life for me was not one marked by an occasional glimpse of the miraculous all-oneness that depended upon a smoky, late-night venue, loud music, and other people, but rather was one marked by and steeped in a moment-by-moment connectedness, and a deep inner merging into Open Heart Consciousness. Little did I know at the time that what I was learning about for the sheer joy of it would so markedly alter my inner biochemistry it would later literally save my life.

Shedding Illnesses Like Old Skin

Through that salsa dancing time period of several years, I shed illnesses like old skin.

Though the transcendent state was experienced for only an hour or two here and there, the effects would linger for days and weeks. I laughed and laughed and loved and loved and lived all of life in an open, expanded state. Spontaneous healing became so commonplace in my body I took it for granted. Prior to that time in my life I had collected illnesses as if an impassioned hobbyist and I went on to collect many new illnesses after I stopped dancing. For those several years salsa dancing, it seemed illness simply could not thrive in the Divinely mediated cellular matrix.

On what was to be the last night I would access Open Heart Consciousness through the vehicle of salsa, something quite extraordinary occurred. There were two professional dancers who in a rare treat for the rest of us were practicing their craft in a bar-turned Monday night salsa venue. I watched them transfixed. These two were lit from within with an unbelievable inner light, and were moving in ways I knew were only possible in the expansion of a radically altered state. The club was crowded, but I watched them intently for some time.

Finally, finding myself in a place of satisfied exhaustion from the late hour and prior long hours dancing, I began squeezing through the crowd to leave. Though I did not know these two professionals, suddenly, in perfect timing and fluidity with the music, the man artfully lunged toward me, grabbed my hand, and swirled me into their vortex. Without pause he was dancing now with two of us, executing all the turns, spins, and elaborate steps of salsa with tandem partners in perfect synchrony.

This time, I entered the transcendent state more profoundly than ever before. It was as if an electric shock jolted my body and catapulted me into a different plane of energetic frequency. The elevated supra-human state from which these two accomplished performance artists were dancing opened up, and I stepped into it. All fatigue evaporated, and my awareness expanded so far outward from my normal sphere of consciousness it seemed I *knew* things that should not have been available to me to know. From a state of complete relaxation I could intuit exactly what I needed to do to respond perfectly with my partners as if I too were an elite athlete performing at the top of my game. Their movements seemed to happen in slow motion. Executing a mind-numbingly complex series of movements at lightning speed seemed as casual and easy as sipping a glass of water.

I was a student of acupuncture at the time and a prominent sentiment in eastern traditions is that we are *all one*. Suddenly, the concept of oneness was not just an interesting idea or a caring sentiment. I could *feel* and *see* that everything was connected, one luminous shimmering connectedness that just happened to be breathing and talking and moving in many expressions of body at one time. I became exquisitely aware that every flicker of thought, feeling, and action from me had infinite rippling cascades of influence through this inseparable all-oneness.

The Alchemical Path

The boundaries of my heart and body similarly expanded outward, seemingly without limit, causing a rush of feeling that felt like some sophisticated sister to euphoria. My heart filled with love, awe, and a sense of miraculousness so profound that in contrast, my ordinary state seemed dull and blunted. I could suddenly see the many ways my own worries, anxieties, stresses, cynicisms, and other Divine-obstructing mindsets and feeling states served to constrict the flow of this energy which was there and available all the time. I could suddenly sense that it was my own doing that I walked around most of the time with the reducing valve of my consciousness clamped so tight that there was no way for a Numinous experience to arise. Suddenly all the ordinary pursuits and goals and aspirations of my life seemed distractive, hollow, and somewhat ridiculous by contrast.

Split second responses requiring not only an incredible athleticism, but also an incredible skill set had become instantly available to me. I had access to a cellular intelligence that was not normally my own, that was allowing me to execute physical feats that could only be described as extraordinary. I realized that my former attachment to the "linear path" (where we believe our results to be a direct result of our efforts) suddenly made no sense. Why would I struggle and strain to achieve, further tightening and constricting myself, when this Divine synergy opened up to something far greater than my usual efforts could produce? The appearance of this energy had to do with being in a completely free state of joy, unhindered by distracting thoughts and beliefs. It had to do with peak performance that flowed forth from the pure enjoyment of it, not from labored efforts driven by "shoulds." It came by a surrendering into a state of bliss, not by chasing after it.

There were many mysteries to explore, but now that I had tasted the "alchemical path," where inner changes of the heart and mind give rise to seemingly miraculous physical changes, the fundamental platform from which I would explore such mysteries had just undergone a serious makeover.

The shot of electricity had affected not only me. Suddenly the densely packed crowd drew back to make room for us. People began stomping the floor in time with the music and whistling and whooping for us in excited wonder. It was one of the most profound moments of my life. My friend who saw it happen and knew what kind of dancing I had been capable of before that moment later remarked that there were no words that could describe what she saw.

Call to Action

At the time of this experience I was both an acupuncture student in the clinical portion of my training and a Home & Hospital Teacher for students on medical leave from school.

Healing was deeply on my mind. The electricity shooting through me had been so great that I sensed that a moment of touching a sick person could evaporate illness. Yet I had been in the middle of a hot salsa club, and sick salsa dancers are like cats-they'll do anything to hide their infirmity. Amidst the great gaiety, something seemed all wrong.

It would be years before I realized just how many people around the world have used spiritual trance through dance for healing. Rarely if ever in an indigenous culture would a profound altered state be accessed simply for entertainment or solely for personal enjoyment, but rather would always be in the context of a spiritual or healing purpose, amidst much ceremony and community participation. Though for me an inner orientation of being Divine-receptive came later, even then, having the experience I did in the middle of a smoky bar, somehow felt like sacrilege.

I knew something profound and beyond the usual access of sensory perception had revealed itself to me, and that this was a most extraordinary gift of awakening. And yet I was not meant to worship at the altar of salsa. That momentary enlightenment I had felt under those particular conditions was a fleeting state, dependent on many specific variables, and was transforming and healing only for me. I sensed that the energy associated with Open Heart Consciousness was boundless, and could powerfully heal not only me, but others as well. I knew in that moment that the defining purpose of my life was to learn how we all can become better "receptacles for the Divine," and to more intimately know this mysterious miraculous energy. The side effect of becoming a better Divine Receptacle, I would later prove to myself, was often an unexpected or unusual or spontaneous *healing of the mind, body, and spirit.*

The spark in my heart had been ignited, yet I knew I had reached the pinnacle of what was available through dancing. Open Heart Consciousness is an inner journey, and I had taken it as far as I could in the context of athletics. Though salsa had provided the vehicle through which my heart and consciousness elevated to something very new, with my career booming, a husband that liked salsa but not nightclubs, and the need for a recreation that ended a little earlier than 3AM, it would be 13 years before I went to a salsa club again. Life would force me to find that inner state another way.

Unlock Extraordinary Human Potential, Irrespective of Circumstances

"Life as usual" is familiar and addictive and threatens to swallow us all up if we are not awake, and awake again, and yet again. Luckily, the mystical experience of the Divine is not something that is abandoned peaceably in favor of the American Frazzled, Busy, Time-Deprived Way of Life. Rather, its experience and then absence foments a quietly building restlessness that threatens to undo all possibility of satisfaction until life is realigned.

Bliss unlocks a strange catalyst for healing. While it is true there have been sickly saints

16

and pallid prophets and no one has outsmarted death, something about holy joy, divine bliss, and an Open Heart Consciousness frequently opens mysterious portals to healing. Curious researchers have pinpointed things like extra bursts of electricity firing in the temporal lobe of the brain and health-promoting genes that activate when people repeat a meaningful prayer or have a holy experience. I am glad researchers are looking, yet I believe the changes that happen in the body when we change the mood tone in our heart are much more substantial and far reaching than we are likely to ever fully account for.

To live in Open Heart Consciousness requires no particular external life circumstances. Though for years after my transformative experiences dancing I kept waiting for my own life circumstances to line up tidily, thinking that the transcendent state had something to do with having life "in the pocket," I eventually realized that Open Heart Consciousness is an inner state, it has to do with our inner thoughts and feelings, it is available to anyone, at any time, can be learned fairly simply, and is a state we must experience irrespective of circumstances. And though my experiences dancing were dramatic, and served well to wake me up to the connection between health and our inner state, it takes only a whisper of a feeling to change the cascades of biochemicals in the body, and only a whisper of a change in these biochemicals to spark potentially significant changes in our health. It is not necessary to have a fully transcendent experience to heal our hearts or experience an unaccountable healing.

For years after I quit dancing I felt sorry for myself that I was sickly, and used that as a powerful justification for losing track of Open Heart Consciousness. Living tight and constricted is an easy life posture to default to. Finally, I gave up waiting and instead opened the door and accepted completely that Open Heart Consciousness is an inner state I had to cultivate, even if I was very sickly, miserable, or even dying as I thought I was at one point. I soon found that unlocking that inner state unlocks extraordinary human potential. Once I learned this, I completely reorganized the way I think, the way I feel, the way I eat, the way I breathe, the way I move, and the way I spend my spare time. And though a variety of lifestyle improvements played into my profound personal experiences of unusual healing, learning how to live in a state of Open Heart Consciousness, irrespective of circumstances became the defining key to unlocking the powerful healing resources contained within my body. By letting the beauty of uninhibited dancing move me in my heart, I had accidentally stumbled onto the mysterious ancient knowing of how to vaporize illness by unlocking the heart of healing.

Heal Your HeartMindBody When Life Wallops You With the Hard Stuff

In the middle of difficulty lies opportunity.
Albert Einstein

Even the helpless victim of a hopeless situation, facing a fate he cannot change, may rise above himself, and by so doing change himself.
Dr. Viktor Frankl
Man's Search for Meaning[15]

There is suffering in life that can touch us beyond all consolation. How is it possible to heal in the context of a life touched by tragedy, hardship, and suffering? Even if it is not our own life, how can any of us be well with an awakeness and an awareness that even in this very moment countless people are suffering deeply without any hope for resolution or remittance?

A friend of mine named Stu was an engaging man who had what most people would consider an amazing life. He had a fulfilling career, a great family and a gorgeous waterfront home. One day, while swimming with his family, his whole life would change. Stu dove into shallow water from the side of their boat and when his head hit bottom he was immediately paralyzed from the neck down. Life as a quadriplegic challenged everything he knew about how to live. He no longer knew how to be "right" in his heart and mind in a body that no longer worked.

We spent sun-drenched days on his dock overlooking that incredible waterfront view, but even so, handsome as he was, interesting to talk with, still cherished by his loving family, Stu took no pleasure in the moment. The ability to savor and be moved by life regardless of the circumstances had been overridden by a circumstance that from his viewpoint was simply "too big." Cultivating the ability to bear the hardships and tragedies of our lives is one of the essential components of healing. For my friend, he could simply not find a way to bear a hardship of such magnitude. He was completely tormented by the harsh reality of his situation.

We spoke at length about meditation, the HeartMindBody connection, and about how to explore his inner landscape. We spoke of people who retreat to mountainside caves to meditate, purposely seeking to sit unmoving in lotus position for months and years at a time. We spoke of the fact that scientists were making discoveries relevant to quadriplegia at a rapid rate. As I saw it, if he found a way to find meaning, joy, purpose, and empowerment in his current situation, that alone would prove meaningful and rewarding. It was not out of the question that a discovery would eventually be made that could help him physically. Even if a discovery did not emerge, the spiritual pursuits would have their own great merit. There was no solace for Stu in considering these possibilities. His mental anguish was so great that the suggestions were summarily dismissed. He made it explicitly clear to me that he didn't give a rats rear-end about mental and spiritual pursuits.

I asked Stu if, as a child, he could conceive of the Internet. With mounting excitement I asked him if as a child he could have conceived of a robotic surgery, performed over the Internet, by a doctor in a different country? Someone I knew had just had their life saved by such a robotic surgery. I passionately hoped that by considering the incredible advances in modern medicine he would deem it worthwhile enough to have hope, and find in the present some glimmer of grace and peace.

Instead, my friend used his chin-operated wheelchair to drive himself off the end of his dock in the one act he could conceive of that would bring him relief.

The death of my friend was a harsh blow. Losing any friend is hard, but this one really shook me. The deep aching in my heart fueled me to collect all the stories and lessons I have learned about miracles, hope, healing, love, and finding peace, even as hardship, illness, and tragedy touch us, so that someone else suffering deeply may possibly be helped. Stu's death was one of the great impetuses to write this book.

Use your sacred gifts

Healing does not always mean curing or even changing illness, and healing does not mean avoiding death, but it does mean getting "right" in our hearts and "right" in ourselves regardless of our circumstances. This is something my friend was ultimately unable to do. I did not believe my friend could have used HeartMindBody practices to heal his quadriplegia. I did believe he could use such practices to heal his mind and his heart and live fully and satisfyingly. We must be congruently "well" simultaneously in our heart and mind to deeply experience true flourishing wellness. Reaching this state, counter to what most people believe, does not require our body or our circumstances to be or not be any certain way. Those that realize this and have flourished despite serious bodily handicap or hardship have contributed deeply to humanity; Helen Keller and Stephen Hawking are two who come to mind. Nick Vujicic, born with no arms or legs, and Claudio Vieira de Oliveira, born with an "upside down head" are two more. They have all overcome extraordinary hardship and gone on to inspire and touch the hearts of many, many others.

Our exploration in this book is about getting right in our minds, our hearts and in ourselves, irrespective of circumstances. For Stu, to truly be well he would have needed to transcend cultural definitions of what it means to be a man, to be a productive member of society, or to live a life of value. He would have had to let go of the things he could no longer do and find a place for himself within the unique limitations of his incredibly difficult hardship.

I think of Stephen Hawking as one of the best role models for transcending limiting cultural beliefs of what constitutes a "good man" or "manly" contribution to society. When we are right in our heart and in ourselves, we change electromagnetically, biochemically, and interrelate differently in the time-space continuum. Sometimes, in this changed place, we may be surprised that our body heals things we did not think could heal—even if healing means being filled with a deep and abiding peace in a body that still doesn't move. Hawking has so extraordinarily outlived the life expectancy of a person with ALS that doctors have decided he must never have had that disease, but some lesser-known variation. I'm not so sure about that. What he has is a radically different orientation to his circumstances, and a life purpose that fills the long stretches he is alone with himself. His scientific questions and their potential solutions tug his attention more than his lamentations.

I do not fault my friend for the choice he made and any of us can appreciate the hopelessness and helplessness that would accompany the contemplation of never moving our body again. Still, there are multiple orientations we can choose in the face of extreme circumstances.

Technology races along

Years ago, *Nature* International Journal of Science featured an article on the new BrainGate technology, a silicon chip that interfaces with the brainwaves of quadriplegics, allowing them new freedoms including navigating computers, television, even playing video games through their thoughts alone. John Donoghue, the inventor of the technology, invented it after a childhood experience of degenerative disease where he learned firsthand the hardship of confinement to a wheelchair.[16]

Another development currently aiding paraplegics (not yet quadriplegics) are exoskeleton robotic suits manufactured by companies like Ekso. Paraplegics wearing the robotic device are able to get in and out of chairs, and walk. Though the cost for such suits is currently around $100,000 and so is not generally accessible, like all technology, yesterday's stars cost a fraction of their original cost today. More affordable solutions will come into play as human genius and innovation continues to be stirred to help lessen the suffering of others. Stem cell based interventions and blue LED light are showing incredible promise. At King's College in London, paralyzed mice have walked. In 2014, Polish surgeons used nerve-supporting cells from the nose of a paraplegic man with a spinal cord injury to repair the completely severed spinal nerves. The broken tissue grew and that patient can now walk with a frame. Technology continues racing along.

Unseen blessings

Whether or not my friend could have regained movement capabilities, unseen blessings inherent to the situation are there to be discovered. It has been said of Stephen Hawking that were he not confined to a wheelchair and instead had to expend energy on things like mowing the lawn and other routine life activities, he would not have the time or reserve of energy for the high level thinking that he does. We need more people thinking deeply, caring deeply, speaking, and teaching from an enlightened viewpoint about the issues and challenges of our world. We need prayer and love and the ripples they create in the quantum field. These are things many people don't take the time out of their harried schedule to do. If your circumstances provide you time that the harried have not, use that sacred gift.

One person who did just that is Joni Eareckson Tada. I learned of Tada from two of my patients who knew her through their church while she still lived in Maryland. They both attest that she is one of the most heart moving people either of them have ever met. Tada too was in a diving accident in the Chesapeake Bay, not far from where my friend had his accident. She too became a quadriplegic, at 17 years old. While grappling with her anger, depression, suicidal thoughts, and religious doubts, she taught herself to paint by holding a paintbrush with her mouth. Thirteen years after her accident, Tada founded a Christian ministry that has grown into an internationally recognized organization and center. Three years after that, she married her beloved husband. In 2010 she began treatment for breast cancer, yet still she carries on with her worldwide ministry. Her numerous books and website (www.joniandfriends.org) tell her story in far more amazing and inspiring detail than I can do justice to here. Tada speaks all over the world delivering a message of hope.

I tell Tada's story not to insinuate that there is any right or wrong way to handle hardship. I tell her story to illuminate that the exact circumstances one person may perceive as agonizingly unbearable may be the call to a life's work for another. Deeply moved by the suffering inherent to her particular hardship, Tada delivers fleets of wheelchairs to paralyzed children and adults around the world.

Guard your heart

There is a passage in Proverbs 4:23 that advises us, "Guard your heart above all else, for it determines the course of your life." It does not say your heart will be right as long as life is sweet and your circumstances and physical body are perfect. We have to guard our heart above ALL else, especially in the face of the most grisly and ghastly circumstances.

If you have experienced paralysis, loss of limbs, rape, stabbing, shooting, near-fatal car accident, chronic pain, or any of the other conditions of life which might invite you to decide life is unbearable, know that it is possible to change and heal your HeartMindBody. Become a collector of stories of hope and overcoming hardship.

One book so profoundly rich with creative problem solving in the face of hardship that every few pages found me in tears of awe and inspiration punctuated by hoots of laughter is Kristine Barnett's *The Spark: A Mother's Story of Nurturing Genius* [17]. Barnett's story of the transformation of her son Jake from profound autism to a paid researcher in quantum physics at age 12 and a current contender for a Nobel Prize demonstrates that following our "spark" can birth miracles.

I love autistic author, speaker, and feedlot cow activist Temple Grandin and the movie bearing her name[18]. Her inspiring story of overcoming her own hardship to benefit the lives of cows and other people touched by autism has me teary-eyed as I write.

For a compelling account of how rich a life can ultimately be even after shocking hardship and despite being in a wheelchair (in her case often a wheeled gurney) with excruciating pain—the two things that tend to most easily convince people that life is unlivable-I love Cynthia Toussaint's book *Battle for Grace*[19].

Another famous person with a great story of overcoming pain, disability and hardship who comes to mind is Arthur Boorman who is known for his YouTube video gone viral and appearance on Shark Tank, but for me is a little closer to home—Art teaches yoga at my gym. My friend sent me his YouTube link one day and said, "You've got to watch the video of this guy who teaches yoga! Then you have to take his class!" Disabled veteran Arthur Boorman's under five minute YouTube video (with over 10 million views) is incredibly moving and inspiring and I highly recommend viewing it if you need an inspiration boost. Obese, in constant pain and unable to walk nor avoid crashing over at any attempt to hold a yoga pose at the start of the clip, Art ultimately transformed himself into a vigorous athlete and teaches others what he learned. Retrain your brain and body to begin to think and feel in the same ways such inspiring people have done, even as they walked a road as difficult and painful as yours may be.

I take inspiration from the Dalai Lama's words, "I find hope in the darkest of days, and focus in the brightest. I do not judge the universe." Anyone can be cheerful when times are good. What we're investigating is how to remain "right" in our HeartMind when life wallops us with the hard stuff.

Allow Your Heart to Break Open

Life isn't about waiting for the storm to pass. It's about learning how to dance in the rain.
Vivian Greene

The soul is a newly skinned hide, bloody and gross. Work on it with manual discipline, and the bitter tanning acid of grief.
Rumi
Rumi the Book of Love translated by Coleman Banks[20]

I've become suspicious of the unblemished life. Maybe the heart must be broken like a child's prize honeycomb, for the real sweetness to come out.
Marc Ian Barasch
Field Notes on the Compassionate Life[21]

The first yoga class I took at 22 years old would be the last I'd take for more than a decade. The moment the skillful instructor guided us to soften our belly and breathe fully and deeply, I burst into tears. To my great embarrassment, it took everything I had to hold the wild torrent of emotions back. Though there were close to 70 people in the gymnasium and I was toward the back, the instructor noticed exactly what was happening and came over to coach me to keep breathing even more deeply, and to let what amounted to years of trapped emotions free themselves from my body. I panicked at the sensation that to me felt like complete loss of control, and instead clenched the emotions yet more firmly back. I didn't know at the time that living with upset emotions trapped in the body is like living in a vice. As I armored against the challenges of life, my body was becoming more stiff and hardened with each passing year.

Nowadays I'm much better at not acting as a bad feelings warehouse. But I do note the often small, subtle ways I still may be hardening my body and heart. A patient was once lamenting the struggle she had with certain relationships in her life. "I wish I could just delete that person" she quipped, "you know, like how you can just delete a friend from Facebook when they piss you off!" I realized there are small ways we may be deleting people, especially our closest loved ones, from our hearts. One thing I've noticed is that if I'm subtly smiling less or joking less with a loved one because of an upset that has been resolved but that I haven't yet

23

let go of, I'm the one that pays the price. My tightened or hardened heart makes it that much harder for me to experience Open Heart Consciousness! Forgiveness is a gift we give, that frees both people involved.

A hardened body and hardened heart that learn to soften are great treasures. A broken heart that learns to break even more fully open to love can be even more precious.

When grief breaks us

Shortly after I met my friend Janice, she went through what could easily be characterized as a living hell. In a period of only a little more than a year, she lost two sons and her husband to illness and tragic accidents. Her grief was unthinkable. Yet, how she handled it moved me deeply. Though I didn't fully appreciate the distinction at the time, what Janice had managed to do was to allow her grief to *break her heart open* rather than to break her heart. She reached out deeply to her remaining family, friends, and synagogue community. Her shockingly keen awareness of the fragility of life fueled for her an even deeper love for those with whom she dwells, and an even greater cherishing of the beauty of living.

With the loss of her husband came a marked change in lifestyle. Rather than frantically going back to work to maintain the lifestyle she was accustomed to, Janice simplified, using her spare time to volunteer at a shelter for battered women. Though she had never been battered, she knew intense pain and suffering, and the women she ministered to felt the power of her deep love strengthened by her losses. Her very presence healed. In turn, those women gained a new perspective: that their suffering might be the root of a great strength. Though I watched all of this with wonder, I would soon learn that there are many ways to respond to grief, and not everyone responds with such grace as Janice, including me.

Grief injures the lungs

As a young student of Chinese medicine many years ago, I had dutifully memorized the mind-body correspondence "grief injures the lungs." However, there are certain things that can only truly be grasped through experience. My understanding of what this association means increased exponentially when my beautiful exotic duck Poochie died.

All of life is precious, and when we open our heart to a creature, human or animal, the feelings of love we have represent our capability for universal love, and are no less important if they happen to focus on an animal. Any connection we have that deepens loving feelings is a great blessing. Such loves are the experiences that open us toward a vaster, more unlimited love.

24

Poochie was the name our young son gave to our exquisite Welsh Harlequin duck. Her feathers were white, intermingled with iridescent purple, blue, and green. While our other ducks are tolerant of people but not very tolerant of being touched once full-grown, Poochie would sit in my lap for hours, nipping mosquitos out of the air and nibbling at interesting specks on my arms and neck. She would sit on the top steps of our porch waiting for me every morning. She laid enormous eggs with yolks the size of a chicken's egg. I love all my ducks, but Poochie had extended herself to me in a unique way. She had wiggled into my heart in a way that was deep and rich. I spent many hours with a sense of love and wonder just being with her.

One day I noticed Poochie was acting strangely in the yard. When I got out to her, I realized she could not get up. I gently picked her up to determine what was wrong, and noticed she was panting heavily. Suddenly, she sighed out a long breath and her head drooped forward onto my shoulder. With no explanation, my extraordinary duck was dead.

My grief welled up in a wave of despair. I couldn't believe that my precious pet was gone. I sobbed and sobbed. I paced the house throughout that day with a maelstrom of thoughts fueling my grief. With each thought of the things "I'll never get to..." I sobbed more. I'd never hold her again, never sit by the fire pit with her again, never admire her beautiful plumage again, never eat one of her extraordinary eggs again, "never, never, never..." my mind reiterated. Adding to the despair was our remaining duck. At the time we had only two ducks, and ducks, regardless of gender, pair-bond for life. The surviving duck ran back and forth across the yard in a panic, quacking at the top of her lungs, craning her neck, looking around frantically for her friend for 10 hours straight.

That sent me into many rounds of, "She'll nevers" on top of my, "I'll nevers." She'll never have her friend again, she'll have nobody to sleep with, nobody to hunt bugs with, she'll never get over it, how will she ever survive without her best friend, she might die of grief...on and on I went. Shock and adrenaline caused the awful image of Poochie's head wilting against my shoulder to replay in my mind over and over. I wracked my brain frantically for something I could have done differently that would have prevented her mysterious death. I agonized over imagined and real inadequacies I determined I had as a duck caretaker.

Though I'd been healthy that morning, with an immune deficiency in my medical history, my immune system has never indulged upset emotions without protest. By the end of the day I developed a deep, chest racking cough. It would take me a month to get rid of that cough. With a start, I realized what had happened. As the ancient Chinese texts had foretold— my grief had injured my lungs.

I reflected on this closely that night. Assuming the association was correct, I didn't want my lungs injured, and I sure didn't want to participate in injuring them any further. But what did it mean? Nowhere had I seen it spelled out what to *do* to prevent grief from injuring lungs. If protecting my lungs meant suppressing or denying feelings for my now-deceased pet, I didn't want any part of it.

Suddenly it dawned on me. I was grieving in a way that was driving my heart deeper and deeper into sadness and despair. I began to appreciate why in some parts of Asia a person is appointed at funerals to make sure no one becomes too extreme with their grief. There was a way to grieve that could lift my heart into awe at the fragility of life, and fill me with wonderment at the miraculous experience of having ever bonded with a duck. The actual pangs of my grief came in short bursts, but I was prolonging each burst into a long, unrelenting wave of sadness with my thoughts. When I turned my thoughts to the things I was grateful for, to the miracle that I had ever even known such a duck, those pangs of grief, rather than break my heart as they had been, began to *break my heart open wider*.

A few days later, a patient called for an emergency appointment to deal with the sudden, unexpected death of her best friend. She couldn't stop thinking about how tragic and unfair the loss was. When I told her the story of Poochie, she replied, "I know you are right! I just can't seem to be able to give myself permission to be happy. I can't even wear my favorite tie-dye shirt!" Together, teary-eyed, we pondered this new, strange inquiry that my friend Janice intuitively had understood. We pondered how to be with loss while still retaining the ability to be moved deeply, to feel ecstatic joy, to wear tie-dye, and to sob so our hearts could break open even wider to beauty. I later learned that Rumi had known something about this. "Cry out!" he said. "Don't be stolid and silent with your pain. Lament! And let the milk of loving flow into you." We could cry out while letting the milk of loving flow in through the newly opened cracks in our hearts.

Let grief carve your heart open to love

When a mutual friend had a recurrence of a cancer that was very possibly going to be fatal, one of my best friends texted me saying, "This irrespective of circumstances thing is really hard..." I texted back, "This is when we sob so that our hearts break open, but not break down. Then from that poignant space we find our holy joy irrespective of this painful circumstance for *her* benefit. She needs it from us more than ever..." A few days later my friend replied, "I get this, this is *so different* from when we went through her cancer the first time. I didn't have that bit of wisdom the last time around. I am available to her in a way I never was before understanding these distinctions...I don't *want* her to die, but if I get hung up in that, then I'm not really there with her *now* with all my heart."

There was a story I once read in *Science of Mind* magazine about a girl who arrived home late from first grade. As she related to her mom, her friend's doll had broken her arm. She explained, "I had to stay with her and help her cry." When we share our sacred tears together, and help each other to cry, we allow an opportunity to be moved with a sense of profound treasuring of the preciousness of life. As Saint Theresa of Avila once observed, "...the hollow vessel her tears had carved in her heart was overflowing with love." [22] Through loss and tears, our hearts are carved open to overflow more deeply with love.

Key #2   Practice a Feeling Mantra

Make Inner Molecules of Medicine

If man knew that he never ceases creating even for an instant, he would realize through the Presence of God within himself, he could purify his miscreations and thus be free from his own limitations.

Godfre Ray King
Unveiled Mysteries[23]

The order of the universe may be the order of our own minds.
Fred Alan Wolf

Evidence even exists that every one of our thoughts affects every one of our cells **instantaneously.**
John Douillard
Body, Mind, and Sport: The Mind-Body Guide to Lifelong Fitness, and Your Personal Best[24]

Hippocrates said, "Natural forces within us are the true healers of disease." To truly unlock healing, we must discover and maximize those natural forces. The most important though generally neglected tool each of us possesses for healing is the ability to *make* medicine in our body. Though we don't often think about this inner ability, our body is already making medicine all day long. Silently and invisibly, it makes insulin, serotonin, dopamine, endorphins, DHEA, oxytocin, relaxin, nitric oxide, and many other biochemicals–some of which we may know by name and could even buy with a prescription. By using the HeartMindBody connection, we can actually change the levels and quantities of substances our body is already making: our Inner Molecules of Medicine.

If I offered you a thousand dollars right now if you could raise your levels of adrenaline and cortisol, I bet you could figure out how to get yourself sufficiently stressed out, upset, and anxious to do it. I bet you even know what it feels like when those particular biochemicals are elevated, just thinking about it now. Our Inner Molecules of Medicine change levels in response to what we think and feel as well. Most indigenous tribal cultures through the ages have known something about this, and have used rituals, music, singing, dancing, trance, prayer, whirling, or hypnosis to facilitate a powerful inner state of healing. We will explore how meditation practiced in a way that changes how we feel increases the inner biochemicals that heal.

I use the term "biochemicals" because most people can relate to ideas of internal ever-fluctuating levels of insulin, serotonin, and the like. But many forces are also ever-fluctuating in our bodies as well, including electromagnetic, vibrational, crystalline, mineral, radioactive, and other known and unknown forces. When I use "biochemical," I mean *all* of the minute processes in the body that may change. When a person has an unusual or spontaneous healing, one or more of these factors has likely changed, causing rippling changes that in turn trigger other changes, potentially all the way to our DNA, as we will see.

In *Love 2.0*,[25] Barbara L. Fredrickson discusses the use of reliving a past emotional event as the key to successful method acting. The reason that reliving an emotional event from our own life works for actors is that through reliving an event, the cells in our body remember that event, and our current state is informed and reformed by that memory. The more an actor practices touching into the feeling of that memory, the more easily they get into that state. Through rehearsal, the actor "becomes" the role they are practicing. We can use that secret to unlock new possibilities for our health.

There was a 1995 study called "The Physiological and Psychological Effects of Compassion and Anger"[26] that is compellingly interesting. Using an immune system indicator known as Salivary IgA, subjects were shown to have increases in immunity after experiencing feelings of compassion, and decreases in immunity from feelings of anger. That alone is amazing. However, there was something else I found even more intriguing than their incredible results: *how* they consistently induced states of anger and compassion in the lab.

These researchers originally attempted to induce anger in their subjects by showing video footage of war, and to induce compassion by showing footage of Mother Theresa. The trouble was, the emotional states these videos stimulated in the subjects turned out to be inconsistent at best. For instance, some subjects responded to images of war with sadness, with fear, with grief, or with hopelessness, rather than anger.

Ultimately, the researchers had a brilliant idea. They simply instructed their subjects to *think about something that made them angry* or *think about something that made them feel love and compassion.* By these means, they achieved consistent results. Every research subject in their study was able to effectively use their imagination to access feeling states, which then consistently affected their immune response. This is incredible! The ability to use the mind to physiologically change the body is at the heart of all inner alchemy practices, and is the foundation of making Inner Molecules of Medicine. (The transformational practice of inner alchemy recognizes that if I live in a transformational state in my heart, my body can't help but change. When the glass shards were in my eye, as long as I practiced Open Heart Consciousness, the adrenaline *helped* rather than detracted from the healing. Inner alchemy powerfully engages our HeartMindBody connection and is not only inherently rewarding in and of itself–it "feels good"– it also increases incidences of the "impossible.")

It is worthy of note that the subjects did not think about healing themselves or increasing their immunity. Don't make striving to heal your goal. Make striving to feel good, irrespective of circumstances, your goal. Focusing on a feeling until you feel different unlocks the mysterious ability of the body to make Inner Molecules of Medicine. If you train your focus on those things that cause you to feel an uplifted mood in your heart, your body may then surprise you with its healing capabilities.

We are not stuck with "ourselves"

Did you know that people with Multiple Personality Disorder (now called Dissociative Identity Disorder) often have different diseases medically documented to alternate between being present or not present in their bodies, depending on which personality is in charge at the moment? There have been cases documented where a person's eye color, allergies and hives, eczema, handwriting, voice pattern alterations–greater than even an excellent actor could achieve–and other biological patterns change instantaneously with each differing persona. This to me is astounding. If such traits aren't fixed, what really is fixed? When we consider that the molecules that we are comprised of are organized and held together by those vibrational fields Max Planck called "the matrix of all matter," it is easier to imagine the flexibility of such traits.

Perhaps the best thing we can do for our health is to practice the moods, feeling tones, expectations, and assumptions of the most vitally well person we know. When I find myself getting too tight and constricted and living in too limited a sphere of consciousness, I'll readjust my posture, facial expression, thoughts, and mood. In a short time, I *feel* different. As Dr. Mosaraf Ali says, "Mind over matter is matter undermined." [27]

I think of the practice of using the imagination to find a feeling memory as akin to a meditation, or a mantra, only it is a feeling meditation, a *Feeling Mantra*. While most people typically think of a mantra as a sound tone used repetitively for focus, spiritual growth, and transformative change, a Feeling Mantra uses a feeling tone or mood tone in the heart used repetitively for transformative change. The meditation I espouse does not require taking a break from life for silent sitting (though that has great value, too) but rather is practiced in the midst of life, and has to do with filling your heart, focusing your mind, and finding a particular feeling. These practices are undertaken as a discipline, amidst our duties in life, in the spirit of the Taoist and Zen belief that, "meditation in action is a hundred, no a thousand, no a million times greater than meditation in repose." Actively practicing a particular feeling that changes biochemistry and unlocks a new possibility for health through inner alchemy is one of the most valuable practices we can take on.

If you can think lemons, you can make Inner Molecules of Medicine

Imagine for a moment in as much sensory detail as you can what it tastes like, smells like, and feels like to bite into a lemon. Imagine a thick juicy wedge, and what the juices taste like as it explodes in your mouth and rolls down your chin. How does it feel as the little "cells" of the lemon explode, releasing their juice? Can you smell the lemon? How vibrant is the yellow? Spend a moment right now imagining this experience.

I want you to notice as you imagine biting that lemon whether your mouth changes in any way. Does your mouth water? I have guided a "lemon biting" meditation many times in talks and workshops, and almost invariably, if participants relax into the daydream, they report that their mouth waters or their lips pucker.

This is incredible: With a few fleeting thoughts, most people can create a noticeable and reproducible change in the physiology of their body. If you can make your mouth water by "thinking lemons," you now understand the basic mechanism by which we make medicines.

In his book *Psycho-Cybernetics*, Maxwell Maltz sagely shares the following, "Feelings cannot be directly controlled by willpower. They cannot be voluntarily made to order or turned on and off like a faucet. If they cannot be commanded, however, they can be wooed...Remember that feeling follows imagery."[28] Feeling follows imagery, and wooing the right feelings through imagery liberates the Inner Molecules of Medicine in our bodies. Our job is to become experts at wooing the right feelings.

Because of my fascination with the HeartMindBody connection and all the ways we can engage it for healing, I carved time out of a booked schedule to train and become nationally Board Certified as a Clinical Hypnotherapist. I had been to a stage show by a famous hypnotist years before and had been simultaneously disgusted, frightened, and amazed by the hypnotist's influence over a group of 20 volunteers, several whom I knew casually. It was horrifying watching the unscrupulous hypnotist skillfully hypnotize these people so deeply that they squawked like chickens and rested their heads in men's laps. I was certain I could never be hypnotized—I would never turn my will over to someone like that! I wondered if that meant I was effectively barring a door to the HeartMindBody connection for myself. I knew if an unethical hypnotist could achieve what that stage show performer did, in the right hands, hypnosis had a profound place in healing.

Years later when my clinical hypnosis trainer asked for a volunteer on the second of eight long days of training, I practically jumped out of my seat. I had to see what it was like for myself in the safety of a clinical, as opposed to a stage, setting.

Clinical hypnotists, unlike stage show hypnotists, prefer that their clients are not hypnotized so deeply that they don't know what is going on. Rather, a clinical hypnotist wants the client to simply relax much more deeply than is usually possible, and from that place, access a resourceful state to engage the healing resource of the HeartMindBody connection. It took our trainer about 90 seconds to get me there by prompting me to remember a past such state. I couldn't believe it. I was sitting there staring at an Exit sign as he instructed me, and suddenly I was flooded with a feeling of euphoric wellbeing that had to do with remembering a favorite memory. He had me choose an "anchor" to help me re-find this state. At the time, I chose pressing my thumbnail into the palm of my other hand. Later, I didn't need any particular anchor; I could find this state in an instant. At the time, I was so afraid I'd "lose it," that for the rest of the eight days of training I repeatedly dug into my palm with my thumb until it left a mark, reliving and remembering that state over and over again.

Now, after successfully teaching Feeling Mantra Meditation to hundreds of people, I know you don't need an exit sign to stare at, you don't need to gouge your palm with your thumbnail, and you don't even need a hypnotist. What you do need is the willingness to "practice" a feeling state over and over again until it is easy to find.

I think of Feeling Mantras as meditation practice rather than as self-hypnosis though both meditation and self-hypnosis have shared elements. One of the most important of the shared elements is facility with using our imagination. Most people aren't particularly practiced at using their imagination, and so they may think of it as "hard." I once had a patient who told me her "imaginer is broke." I asked her, "Where in your grocery store is the lettuce?" When she described to me the far right aisle, on the left, she was successfully using her "imaginer." Any time you see something in your mind's eye, imagination is at work. Using your imagination intentionally is a skill gained through practice, just like any other skill. We do best not to forfeit the development of this skill. As Albert Einstein said, "Imagination is everything. It is the preview of life's coming attractions." Knowing firsthand how much my imagination has enhanced the coming attractions in my own life, I wholeheartedly recommend learning the skill.

Cleanse your brain of limiting beliefs

There is a self-hypnosis exercise that gives me a good chuckle and is a great warm-up practice for imagination exercises. As told by Bernhardt and Martin in *Self-Mastery Through Self-Hypnosis*, some children with difficulty reading were taught to self-hypnotize themselves in the following way. They were instructed to imagine lifting their brain out, hosing it out with a garden hose to remove things that interfere with learning, and then putting the clean brain back in. Next, they were to picture themselves on a movie screen, "reading fluently and without effort—with pleasure." [29] Then they were instructed to walk into the screen and into that body, fusing it to their body as they became this person.

The kids were instructed to imagine this for five minutes, twice a day. Compared to a control group that used no self-hypnosis, these kids at two months had gained 1.6 years in improved speed, accuracy, and comprehension in reading. The control group had gained only four months. We have used this meditation at our house not only for improving learning and reading fluency, but any time we need better working brains. Though we haven't used it to blast things that interfere with loving from our hearts, I imagine the effects would be the same.

Take your brain out now and hose it down. Get rid of any gook that keeps you in your old familiar ruts, or makes it hard to learn new things. Blast away the old beliefs that keep you living predictably, and start off with a clean slated brain that can dream up something inspiring and new. Any habits of depression, anxiety, hopelessness, worry, pessimism, or other unhelpful inner states that are not currently useful—give them a good strong cleansing blast. Put that pristine brain back in place, ready to receive creative inspiration and to become a radical tool of healing. See yourself on a movie screen exactly as you would be in optimal health, living in a state of Open Heart Consciousness, where miracles and magic are commonplace. Step right into that image and shimmy with joy as it fuses to you. Take a moment to identify and savor what that feels like now.

Our imagination is our most powerful asset. It's free, and we can use it whether we are bed-bound, wheelchair bound, or simply bound by the constraints of our limiting thoughts and beliefs.

As Paracelsus sagely stated in the 15th century, *"The spirit is the master, the imagination the tool, and the body the plastic material."*

Use the Power of the HeartMindBody Connection

The Indian guru said to me, it all comes down to deciding to be "ever blissful."
Richard Bandler and Owen Fitzpatrick
Conversations With Richard Bandler[30]

Using conservative estimates, there are 100 trillion neuron junctions in the brain. (Some scientists are now saying that there are closer to two to the trillionth power connections among brain cells.) This means that there are more possible mental states than there are atoms in the universe-which makes it seem even more unlikely that anything should be impossible for us.
John Douillard
Body, Mind, and Sport: The Mind-Body Guide to Lifelong Fitness, and Your Personal Best[31]

A local author was volunteering her time working with prison inmates when she discovered John, the husband of my friend, who was serving a life sentence. This published writer was taken with John's story and found his writing to be powerful and compelling, and so encouraged him to write his life story. To suddenly have a meaningful purpose while serving time was like a gift from the heavens, and John threw himself entirely into the project. Within a few weeks my friend asked me for some advice. To tell his story properly, her beloved husband was touching into feelings and memories he hadn't thought about in 40 years. And the more he thought about them, the more angry, sad, depressed, and stressed out he became. They began to wonder together if the telling of the story was worth the cost.

Much like with imagining biting lemons, or thinking of something that makes us feel compassion or anger, our bodies cannot entirely tell the difference between an event that is happening, and an event that we are imagining or reliving in our mind. As John became keenly aware, simply thinking about past events caused cascades of stress chemicals: cortisol, adrenaline, and many others to pour through his body. It was impacting his mood, his perception of the current events of his life, and his sleep. Without a fast intervention, I knew it would deeply impact his health. Our bodies are amazing pharmacies, stocked with more elaborate and complex medicines than any brick and mortar pharmacy on the planet. And John was getting a prescription filled, only it was an accidental script for the abundantly cascading chemicals of distress and disease. He needed to be able to move into those deeply distressing inner places in order to tell his painful story with authenticity and feeling. But he needed to be able to get out fast, and spend an equal or greater amount of time in a "medicine state" to nullify any damage incurred while writing.

Have you ever had an experience like John, thinking about something that previously made you angry, or sad, or anxious, and suddenly you feel angry, sad, or anxious all over again? That is because the body responds to an event in our thoughts as if it is actually happening in real-time. The moment we lapse into one of these daydreams about a past event, the body gears up to deal with it as if it is happening now. A myriad of biochemical and electromagnetic events fire off in response, and depending on what we were thinking about, those biochemicals and electromagnetic impulses serve as powerful agents of change—for better or for worse. If our "accidental meditation" revolves around something stressful, as John's did, our body may flood with cortisol, adrenaline, and many other molecules of ill health, as his did. If our accidental meditation centers around something that fills us with a sense of love, gratitude, or makes us laugh so hard our belly hurts, we immediately bathe our cells in a complex biochemical elixir of molecules that heal. In fact, the cascades of biochemicals generated by our feelings are some of the most powerful medicines, or, if we are not mindful, powerful forces of harm, on the planet.

It ends up being quite useful that our body doesn't distinguish easily between an imagined, and real event. By harnessing the power of our imagination, we gain access to a whole inner pharmacy of substances that heal. When I ask audiences if they can think of some of the medicines our body can make, many are able to cite serotonin, dopamine, and oxytocin. Researcher Sue Carter of Chicago's Psychiatric Institute says that "A *single* exposure to oxytocin can make a *lifelong* change in the brain." [italics mine]. Often forgotten are the pain relievers, immune complexes and antibodies, stimulants, relaxants, mood elevators, and mood stabilizers our body makes every second. Just as our body is quick to make stress biochemicals when we are stressed, what do you think it will make more of when bathed in a deep and abiding sense of bliss, holy joy, and Open Heart Consciousness? I knew John needed to learn to use the skill of the Feeling Mantra.

Most people have had an experience in life whereby they felt a great joy, a deep awe, a feeling of love, gratitude, or an intense belly laugh, even if only for a split second. Perhaps you have had an uplifted feeling while listening to music, or a feeling of lightness while swimming or lying in the sun, or a peaceful relaxation while spending time with a friend. As the researchers who had their subjects "think about something that made them feel compassion" found, it doesn't take a grand ecstatic experience for the body to make Inner Molecules of Medicine. It is through our small moments of reflection on the richness of life that we unlock this state. By choosing a past memory as the basis for a Feeling Mantra, we can begin to powerfully change our inner state.

Just like John found when he relived old memories of bad times and his body felt the surge of upset, when we relive (or even imagine or invent) memories of times when we felt good, our body experiences a surge of Inner Molecules of Medicine. As Kelly A. Turner Ph.D. describes in *Radical Remission*,[32] meditation has been associated with increases in melatonin, immune function, and virus antibodies, as well as increases in telomerase activity—which allows immune cells to live longer; it increases regional brain gray matter density, which is associated with empathy and memory, and decreases brain density in areas associated with anxiety and stress. And these are only a few of the physiological and biochemical changes associated with meditation.

When medicine-generating feelings become our habitual daydreams, and our habitual meditations, we enter into a zone where healing and transformation become much more possible. When I described this to John over the phone, he asked, "Is it really that easy? If it is that easy, it's like the obvious was staring at me all along." Yes. It's that easy. What is complicated is all the ways we undo ourselves, all the ways we fire up our Molecules of Misery, and all the ways we block the flow. This is what spiritual teacher Swami Satchidananda was referring to when he said, "I'm not a Hindu; I'm an Un-do." We have to undo certain habits to set ourselves free.

Don't peg inner states on outer circumstances

Most of us know it is good for us to be grateful, but are you grateful right now? And most of us know it is excellent for our health to breathe slowly and deeply, but are you breathing meaningfully, right now? Knowing something and living it in your cells, in your moment-by-moment awareness, are two fundamentally different things. I consider the most valuable help I can give my patients and students to be the unflagging repetitive reminder that no matter what, they may choose an Open Heart Consciousness and a rich inner holy joy irrespective of circumstances, and live in it right now. The savoring of a memory of a past time when we spontaneously felt joy, awe, gratitude, or laughter unlocks the feeling, and the feeling informs and flavors our present moment in the here and now.

Ultimately, we're not after a way of being that involves wandering around in a permanent daydream reliving the highlights of our past. The daydream unlocks the feeling, and then with that feeling floating in our cellular matrix, creating all of the little biochemical, electromagnetic, and other changes it does, we can be present to and enjoy life as it comes. Eventually the daydream is unnecessary as the new state percolates on its own.

Unlocking Open Heart Consciousness is an intentional practice whereby we shift our daydream from one that dwells extensively on our worries, concerns, likes and dislikes to one that dwells on our celebrations, loves, generosities, gratitudes, heartfulnesses, kindnesses, humorousnesses, and playfulnesses. It's an intentional act of getting our favorite feeling song "stuck in our head" (and our heart) to blot out the annoying refrain of a song we can't stand that otherwise keeps popping up. It is intentionally capitalizing on the way the brain makes and sustains neural pathways so that the feeling song the brain keeps singing becomes a song we are uplifted and moved by. This in turn impacts all those around us. As Lao-tzu said, "Music in the soul can be heard by the universe." We want to get that soul music running on auto-pilot.

When I ask patients and audiences to choose a past memory of a moment of an uplifted feeling (one not confused or conflicted by later events that occurred like break-up, loss, or betrayal) some people easily choose a memory while others squirm uncomfortably and struggle to think of one. Some of the moments people have chosen and shared with me are as diverse as the moment they first held a child, the moment of *receiving* an unexpected kindness, the moment of *delivering* an unexpected kindness, the moment an enormous whale unexpectedly approached a tour boat and made eye contact, the feeling of zipping down the road in a red convertible with the roof down, the feeling that comes while listening to a favorite song at full blast, and the feeling of satisfaction from an important accomplishment that involved overcoming fear and engaging new abilities. With time, most people can find one moment to recall, even if fleeting. If not, they can imagine what such a moment would feel like. Remember, when it comes to real-time experience versus thoughts in our imagination, our body responds either way.

Let a wiggling monkey wiggle your heart loose from old habits and stuffy conclusions

There are no rules on finding a Feeling Mantra. One of my students was having a grand time practicing a meditative feeling state based on a memory of a moving moment shared with a loved one. He felt he was changing profoundly from the practice. But after three weeks, he told me his meditation had suddenly "stopped working." He was deeply distressed. He no longer felt anything when he revisited this memory, and he feared meditation would not "work" for him. He reflected on this for a few days and then solved his own problem. When he checked in with me a few months later, he'd been meditating ever since. As he described, he had decided to lighten up and have some fun. An image that had come to him was one of monkeys wiggling inside people's clothing! He had no idea where the idea had come from, but he had been belly laughing several times a day thinking about it ever since.

If I have a churchgoer struggling to settle on a memory to use for a Feeling Mantra, I'll ask them to sing me a few bars of their favorite hymn. It is extraordinary to watch the change that comes over them. By a few seconds in, they are usually misty-eyed and glowing. The kind of memory which has the power to change our physiology that potently is the ideal. But in the case of the person transformed by spiritual hymns, the person has been singing that song in the context of love, joy, gratitude, and awe on a weekly basis for possibly their entire lives. They've had some time to anchor the feeling, so the body biochemistry changes like the flip of a switch. Don't worry if the memory you choose does not have such a profound immediate effect, or if you don't feel much of anything when you review your chosen memory. It takes time to install an inner medicine switch.

Eventually, as the body, mind, and spirit change, direct experience replaces imagination as the focus for meditation. The practice is meant to transform consciousness and awaken the heart and not meant, as Chogyam Trungpa warned, as a "spiritual materialism" [33] in which one uses the practice to escape the human predicament rather than be opened and moved by it.

Many ancient and modern spiritual traditions assert that our true nature is bliss. Once we develop the habit of touching into bliss, it becomes easier and easier to perceive all of the thoughts, presumptions, moods, habits and expectations that occlude it. Once aware, we can delve more deeply into dissolving those obstacles. If you are not currently experiencing bliss regularly, begin to pay attention to the subtle thoughts and moods or expectations that are occluding it for you.

One patient told me, "Well I could feel bliss if I won the lottery and bought this cute house that's for sale." I asked her, "What does it feel like when you think about that?" She lit up and smiled a huge grin enthusiastically answering, "Juicy! Fun! Exciting!" "Well," I responded, "What the hell do you need the house for? You have the feeling right now!" I didn't mean to sound like an idiot, but consider it. Why on earth would any of us postpone feeling juicy, fun and exciting waiting around for some house? Why would we saddle ourselves with that condition? The experience of inner bliss is as possible, or impossible, in a hovel as it is in a mansion. If the feeling depends on conditions like mansions, it is not the authentic state that is always free of conditions. Bliss consciousness does not evaporate if our conditions take a turn for the worse. In what ways might you be delaying bliss now, waiting for something in your circumstances to change?

We so often peg our inner states on our outer circumstances, but we have the standard-issue biochemical and electromagnetic ingredients within us to feel bliss right now. Meditation trains the body how to get there, and then we get to enjoy the benefits of our training efforts for the rest of our lives. Otherwise, we're always pushing bliss just out of arms' reach as we wait for the right house/job/spouse/child/body/health or an infinite number of other conditions that we think we need, and then use as the justification for not acquainting ourselves with, and delighting in, bliss *right now.*

In *Daring Greatly,* Brené Brown shares the wisdom of her six-year-old daughter Ellen who knows something about finding the kind of resourceful feelings we use as the basis for a Feeling Mantra. Ellen says, "(A) picture memory is a picture I take in my mind when I'm really, really happy. I close my eyes and take a picture so that when I'm feeling sad or scared or lonely, I can look at my picture memories."[34] Find a memory of a moment in your life where you spontaneously felt love, or joy, or laughed from your belly, sang a moving or uplifting song, or, like Ellen, were really, really happy. Daydream about that memory until you feel different right now!

Choose What Your Cells are Eavesdropping On

Our cells are constantly eavesdropping on our thoughts and being changed by them. A bout of depression can wreak havoc with the immune system; falling in love can boost it. Despair and hopelessness raise the risk of heart attacks and cancer, thereby shortening life. This means that the line between biology and psychology can't be drawn with any certainty. A remembered stress, which is only a wisp of thought, releases the same flood of destructive hormones as the stress itself.

Deepak Chopra

Ageless Body, Timeless Mind[35]

Each of us holds the keys to a pharmacy containing a dazzling array of healing compounds: our own brain. We are capable of secreting the chemicals that enhance our immune function, make us feel pleasure, and insulate us from pain...Consciousness, acting through the body, can generate the molecules required for healing. Our brains are themselves generating drugs similar to those that our doctor is prescribing for us.

Dawson Church

The Genie in Your Genes: Epigenetic Medicine and the New Biology of Intention[36]

When the biochemistry and electromagnetic fields of the heart, body and brain change, all 100,000 biochemical reactions we experience each second are influenced in untold ways. What we commonly call miracle healings may be perfectly accounted for if we knew what those hundreds of thousands of biochemical, electromagnetic, radioactive, crystalline, mineral, and field changes amounted to in sum. In *The Life We are Given*, George Leonard & Michael Murphy speak to this when they write, "Imagery practice can give rise to metanormal powers and consciousness by the recruitment of many somatic processes. Through such recruitment, countless cells are somehow enlisted by mental images, so that as an integrated whole they support extraordinary functioning."[37] I believe this is how Mother Theresa, who took little food and almost no sleep over many years, was able to carry on with what could be regarded as a grueling work schedule for so long. She was running on a different kind of juice.

Also in *The Life We are Given,* authors George Leonard and Michael Murphy discuss the resolution of allergies through placebo interventions that capitalize on the mind-body connection. Their comments highlight just how extraordinary it is when our body coordinates healing when touched by the mind. They write, "Allergies involve interactions among trillions of cells and virtually all of the body's organs; getting rid of them requires precise alterations of the nervous, hormonal, and immune systems. That men and women do get rid of them simply because they believe in a sugar pill has caused medical people to marvel at our abilities for self-transformation. Placebo effects have forced researchers to see that the mind can touch *just the right tissues* and shift the functioning of *just the right cells* involved in the change, rebalancing the body all the while as it breaks its familiar patterns." [38]

The good news is, we don't need to be tricked by a sugar pill. The mind-body connection has been so well documented that we don't need to be fooled to believe in something that works. We just have to learn how to engage our HeartMindBody connection to make inner medicine, then *take the medicine in a regular dose.* Living in feelings that uplift us works wonders, but you can't expect one dose to get the job done. As my colleague Dianne Connelly, Ph.D. and author of *Medicine Words: Language of Love for the Treatment Room of Life,*[39] often says, "Change is not a one-walk dog." We don't wonder why we have to take the dog out several times a day, it's just the way it is. So, too, goes personal change.

That said, practice doesn't need to fill every second. In a paper presented in an American Physiological Society session at Experimental Biology in 2006, Lee S. Berk of Loma Linda University reports that just the *expectation* of mirthful laughter boosts our endorphins and human growth hormone. As Berk states, "Mirthful laughter diminishes the secretion of cortisol and epinephrine, while enhancing immune reactivity. In addition, mirthful laughter boosts secretion of growth hormone, an enhancer of these same key immune responses. The physiological effects of a single one-hour session viewing a humorous video have appeared to last up to 12 to 24 hours in some individuals." [40] I can't think of a single medicine with that kind of potency, that long-acting, that is free and without side effects. The next time you feel a little down or off, how about doing whatever it takes to facilitate a dose of mirthful laughter? YouTube brims with funny comedy clips. Humor is at hand if we reach out for it.

Thoughts prompt feelings prompting biochemical cascades

Our thoughts prompt feelings. Every feeling we ever experience signals the body to create what I think of as "signature" biochemical cascades. As we move in and out of a variety of feelings throughout the day we are intentionally or accidentally triggering cascades of biochemicals, hormones, electromagnetic signals, neurotransmitters, and more. I remember when I used to get depressed a lot in my teens and twenties, I'd think to myself, "Ugh, here comes that awful feeling again..." There was a particular signature configuration of biochemicals, neurotransmitters and hormones that I had gotten very adept at firing off through my thoughts and feelings and in which I was prone to dwelling. I thought I was the victim of those thoughts and feelings and that they had hijacked me. I had not a clue that I was providing for them, and that I could adopt a new level of consciousness.

A Buddhist friend mercifully taught me that when my feelings of intense anxiety and depression arose, to think of them like the waves of an ocean. If I watched the waves long enough, he pointed out, even a wave as violent as a tsunami always drops back into the sea. He was right, and my emotions gradually became increasingly more peaceful. Without "me" to amp them up and egg them on, the chaotic emotions slowly dissipated. It was none too soon for my mind and body health, for those emotions were having a potent impact that cascaded deleteriously through my physiology. As Deepak Chopra describes in *Creating Health*, "We do not in fact have a body and a mind but a bodymind, one seamless web of intelligence that expresses every flicker of intuition, every shift in the configuration of an amino acid, every vibration of an electron."[41]

Access your inner apothecary

If we are habituated to be stressed, worried, and tense, the signature biochemical cascades we are releasing invariably involve cortisol, adrenaline, and a myriad of stress related complexes. If instead we become more practiced at accessing resourceful states so that we can tap into our "Inner Apothecary," we then create cascades of those ready-to-be-activated biochemicals of healing, the Inner Molecules of Medicine. The medicine our body is capable of generating is of a far higher order than any manufactured medicines.

An apothecary is an old-timey word for pharmacy. In the old days, the chemists in an apothecary mixed individualized potions and liniments for their patients. They were not like current pharmacists who are only legally allowed to provide the standardized formulations that are profit-making enough to make it through the cogs of the Big Pharma machinery. Though safety and standardization were the goal, individualization was lost. Our inner resources share much more in common with an apothecary than a pharmacy. Our body is even more skilled, more deliberate, and more precise than the most gifted compounding pharmacist.

Within our inner apothecary, an action as simple and commonplace as laughing (mirthful or otherwise) can initiate a high level inner process of cellular coordination active all the way to the level of the DNA. In *The Genie in Your Genes: Epigenetic Medicine and the*

New Biology of Intention, Dawson Church points out that indeed, "genes may be activated by memories, feelings, thoughts, and other aspects of the internal environment–some genes in *under two seconds.*"[42] Research by the Institute of HeartMath, Dr. Kazuo Murakami, and others have shown that laughter can reduce blood sugar, up-regulate immunity, and send biochemicals of joy and relaxation throughout our entire body. Murakami, a 1990 winner of the Max Planck research award and author of *The Divine Code of Life: Awaken Your Genes and Discover Hidden Talents,* demonstrated in his lab that diabetic subjects who laughed with a stand-up comedian for an hour before eating, processed a meal very differently from a group of subjects who were bored by an hour-long lecture before eating the same meal. Not only were their blood sugar readings different, but at the level of the DNA in the laughing group, 23 genes that regulate blood sugar, 18 of which also control immune response, were up-regulated. The bored group did not receive that benefit.[43] This was critical info while I was losing 90 pounds, because it meant my mood or *feeling state* mattered as much as what I ate.

As Deepak Chopra describes in *Creating Health,* "You cannot experience the faintest mood without your heart cells sharing it, and at the same time your lungs, kidneys, stomach, and intestines. These organs participate in your mental life as fully as your brain does."[44] We possess inner medicines with the ability to reach every microscopic crevice of our body. It looks like magic next to any crude pharmaceutical preparations. Do you know what prescription to order, and how to get it filled? Unlocking resourceful feeling states is the most powerful key.

Just like one dose of mirthful laughter changes the body for 12 to 24 hours, a Feeling Mantra or Open Heart Consciousness are "initiating factors" that get a biochemical cascade going. Our cellular intelligence handles the rest. The body knows how to make the medicine, and it is manufactured in the perfect dose, titrated exactly second by second, with no side effects, and no complicated dosing instructions or efforts required by us, personalized in minute ways to meet our exact needs. The medicine is profound in scope, and lasting. In short, a medical miracle.

The problem is, if we do manage to access a peak or resourceful feeling state, we may not be particularly good at sustaining it for long. I suggest wallpapering your house with sticky notes that say *Love* or *Bliss* or *Open Heart!* to remind yourself that feeling good is a choice. It is not a circumstance. It is not available only under certain delectable conditions. It is a choice that frees us to a new level of heart, mind, and body. As Richard Bandler remarks in *Conversations with Richard Bandler,* "Until you learn to saturate your own neurology with your own chemicals to feel good for no reason, it's very difficult to make it in life, because otherwise everything that happens in the world is going to matter too much."[45]

When something goes wrong and we think about it over and over again, and retell it, relive it, and ponder the indignity, the injustice, and the awfulness of it, if we think about what could have been different, and so on, we are placing an order for a specific type of refill from the apothecary. The apothecary is going to crank the cortisol cascade, and crank the adrenaline cascade every moment we spend in the replay. Remember, even though the event is happening in our imagination, the body doesn't know much difference. As Doc Childre and Howard Martin with Donna Beech describe in *The Heartmath Solution*, "Even if we pause for a few hours to give ourselves a little break from the onslaught (of stress), our body chemistry has been altered as surely as if we'd taken a drug. It can't just snap back into place again. After ten shots of whiskey, no cup of coffee is going to make you sober. You have to wait for the effects to subside—without drinking (or in this case, stressing out) while you wait!" [46]

When something goes wrong, garner your best resources for problem solving. Allow elevated states of anger, upset, fear, disgust, grief, or worry to stir you to unlock the biochemistry of creativity, the biochemistry of success, the biochemistry of awe, the biochemistry of gratitude, and the biochemistry of love. Use those biochemistries to find solutions to whatever you can. Cultivate the ability to stand amidst the challenges and hardships of life with an ember of bliss glowing in your heart.

The last time that something good happened, did you think about that over and over? Did you retell that again and again? Did you ponder the amazingness, the gloriousness, and the inspiration of it? Did you memorize the feeling so you could revisit it like a prayer, or a feeling meditation, that unlocks medicine from your very cells? Did you savor that feeling and allow the deliciousness to wash over you, cleansing your mind and heart? As Charles Fillmore once said, "Ten thousand cells are listening to every word we say."

The migraines are the sticky note

A patient named Karen was surprised when I taught her to meditate with a feeling as the focus, using the impending pressure and pain of her migraines as her reminder to practice. A local neurologist sends me his migraine patients for mind-body treatment and acupuncture after ruling out a brain tumor because as he once told me, "Conventional medicine has little to offer a migraine patient besides med management." While some patients with migraines are reacting to food triggers, imbalanced hormones, or have a more complicated presentation, Karen's problem turned out to be surprisingly simple and straightforward.

As the Feeling Mantra for her meditation, Karen chose a moment when her infant son was nursing and she began to sing to him for the first time. As she described to me with a voice wavering with wonder, he had stopped what he was doing, lifted his head, and gazed at her directly in the eyes. His astonished delight at the sound of her voice so moved her that she felt the same expansive, joyous feeling in her heart telling me about it years later as she did on the day it happened. Amazed that remembering that moment could have any impact at all on her migraines, much less avert them, Karen commented, "When I think of that moment, it transports me to a different place. I understand that my biochemistry changes if I'm tense and worried about the headache about to come on, versus getting tears in my eyes remembering such a moving memory. But when you've had a symptom like migraines for such a long time, it's hard to believe that just by changing thoughts that it could go so quickly." But go it did, and after only three acupuncture sessions to release held tension in her neck and shoulders, I discharged her. Now if she feels something like a headache coming on, she relaxes and remembers her treasured memory with her son. The twinges of pain are Karen's sticky note reminder to practice.

I know my day goes a whole lot differently if I consume a serving of gratitude and a dose of unconditional love upon rising versus swallowing a dose of irritation and resentment. That doesn't mean life doesn't provide an invitation to be irritated and resentful; those invitations have a tendency to come up. It's that we don't want to keep drinking them into our consciousness. Drink delight when given the choice. As horror survivors Corrie ten Boom (imprisoned in the Nazi Holocaust), Viktor Frankl (also a Holocaust survivor), or Brother Yun (a prisoner treated brutally in a Chinese Maximum Security prison) would tell us, being violently beaten by captors, starved, humiliated, smeared in feces, in severe pain, or sleeping in swarms of mites and fleas day after day for years are not reasons for drinking venomous or hopeless or miserable thoughts. They have come back from such circumstances and informed us, there is always a choice, irrespective of circumstances.

If you are feeling like your circumstances are so challenging that it would be impossible to drink delight, take some time to read about some of these people who have been challenged by extreme hardship and found a way to preserve their sense of love and gratitude. We want a happiness hangover, where we can't seem to shake the good feelings. Corrie ten Boom described a strange giddy joy she felt even as she walked through the awful Nazi concentration camp with death and horror all around. Brother Yun spoke of the rapture, and awareness of the Holy Spirit he felt even as he was being beaten nearly to death by his Chinese captors who considered him an "enemy of the state" for the crime of "confusing the Chinese people" because of his underground Christian missionary efforts in China.

As Richard Rohr describes in *Simplicity: The Freedom of Letting Go*, "Cosmic or spiritual joy is something you participate in; it comes from elsewhere and flows through you, and it has little or nothing to do with things going well in your own life at that moment. Thus the saints would rejoice in the midst of suffering, which to the rest of us is unthinkable."[47] Our thoughts shape our experience and our cells eavesdrop on our thoughts. Think now about something you are glad happened. Irrespective of your current challenges or suffering, think about it now, again, until you *feel* different.

Change Me

Not to kill the emotion, but to turn it in toward the Divine is the right way.
Sri Aurobindo

Meditation is no ordinary concentration; it is the highest form of spiritual concentration.
Swami Adiswarananda
Meditation & Its Practices[48]

Meditation is the breeze that comes through an open window.
Krishnamurti
Think on These Things[49]

There is no substitute in life for regular experiences of joy, humor, and delight. A life full of squashed dreams, dreary and uninspired work, or too much stress to allow for fun are going to increase the odds of ill health. Sometimes the best thing to do for healing is to institute more fun and meaningful pursuits.

That said, we all have challenges, hardships, and suffering. Practicing a Feeling Mantra even while we face hardship is the most important thing we can do. One of the most common thing frazzled patients say to me in the treatment room is, "I need a vacation." Unfortunately they often find they are just as frazzled on and after vacation as they were before. Joy, humor, delight and peace are inner states that must be cultivated in the context of life. As inviting as the thought of lying on a beach for a month may sound, we always come back from vacation to ourselves. Learn how to create an inner vacation in the context of a full life, and you've got it made.

In a poem called *Slicing Potatoes,* Sufi poet Rabia wrote,

It helps,
putting my hands on a pot, on a broom,
in a wash
pail.
I
tried painting,

but it was easier to fly slicing

potatoes.[50]

Begin to live in the inquiry of, how can I fly while raising a family, making a living, tending my house, dealing with hardship, and slicing potatoes?

Let yourself be happier

Number five of Bronnie Ware's *Top Five Regrets of the Dying* is "I wish I had let myself be happier."[51] Isn't that amazing? The number five thing people wish they had done differently while reflecting from their deathbed is to have let themselves be happier. If we want the circumstances of life to line up a certain way, then we forego happiness waiting for that always out of reach thing. What does it take to let ourselves be happier right now? What parts of the human drama can we let go of to make room for true happiness, which requires no particular conditions? We are accidentally meditating (focusing repetitively) all day long, but is our focus on that which opens our heart to a divine-receptive state and floods our bodies with the biochemistry of healing and our Inner Molecules of Medicine? Knowing what a numinous experience feels like, I can't imagine why anyone would meditate on anything else. But we do, I do, and we lapse into our unexamined meditations all day long. Reminders can never come too frequently.

When we let ourselves be happier, we let our body make the Inner Molecules of Medicine it knows how to make. When we meditate (focus repetitively) on those happy feelings, we give our body the chance to make those medicines all day long. Any time we do something joyful, or dwell on something joyful, we are bolstering our healing reserves. A quote often attributed to Antoine De Saint-Exupery says, "The tide recedes, but leaves behind bright seashells on the sand. The sun goes down, but gentle warmth still lingers on the land. The music stops, yet echoes on in sweet, soulful refrains. For every joy that passes, something beautiful remains." Take the time to revisit the lingering warmth, and sweet, soulful refrains of such joys from your life in your mind's eye and let yourself be happier, right now.

Throw your arms skyward and yell "THANK YOU!"

When I was 21 years old, I read Paramahansa Yogananda's *Autobiography of a Yogi*.[52] I remember being completely awed by the way Yogananda transformed himself through a practice of meditation and prayer. At the time, I thought his dedication was noble and incredible, but for me impossible. Twenty years later if I'm not living in Open Heart Consciousness at least two thirds of each day, something is very wrong. If I don't feel like

49

throwing my arms skyward and yelling *THANK YOU* with tears welling in my eyes at least a few times a week, something is definitely off. If my human struggles and hardships catch me in upset, it is only a short time before I remember that there is no therapy, no solution, and no resolve that can "treat" a problem that is ultimately all one problem: insufficiency of trading my Human Drama for Open Heart Consciousness and bliss. It is my thoughts about how things should be that occlude it, not any malfunctioning in my standard-issue inner Bliss equipment. The details of our dilemmas may distract and engage us, but all problems are iterations of the same problem: forgetting to choose a heart elevated state, here, now, no matter what. If we allow ourselves to become embroiled in our problems, we never get to the daily practice of the real work.

There is a unique healing path marked by joy, love, and a grateful heart available to each of us. As Quaker Lucretia Mott once said, "The light is available yesterday, today and to eternity. What is thee doing about it?"

Adopt the inner hygiene of feeling good

When the great Neuro-linguistic programming trainer Richard Bandler was asked about the "chemistry" of people liking each other in *Conversations With Richard Bandler*, he remarked, "If you feel really good on the inside, so that you are really happy on the inside, so that you are really shining on the inside, so your internal dialogue sounds really good and your pictures are really wonderful, then people will want to be around you. If you exude joy and vibrate joy, people will want to be around you. It's the most important thing. I mean people will dress up. They'll get their hair done. They'll do everything to look good, but they'll forget to take the steps to feel good. If you feel really good when you meet people, they'll like you; it's just that simple."[53]

If you have a daily regimen of external hygiene practices you wouldn't skip, do not underestimate the importance of the inner hygiene practices of feeling good. Take a moment to do an inner hygiene practice of feeling good now, and savor a Feeling Mantra, again, now. We don't often give ourselves permission to relax and daydream, but to do so consistently until Open Heart Consciousness awakens and runs in the background, informing our thoughts, our mood, and our biochemistry, is the most important self-improvement task any of us can undertake.

Change *me*

It can be awfully difficult to live in Open Heart Consciousness when life is unmercifully hard. However, until we know how to feel filled with a sense of meaningfulness, have a tear of gratitude in our eye, and feel waves of love in our heart, particularly when life is unmercifully hard, we don't really have it. Anyone can feel good when life is clipping along fine. The challenge is to learn to live so fully in Open Heart Consciousness that the challenges of life don't shake it, but rather open us to further heights and depths of heart and mind. And while we can spend a lifetime (or many lifetimes according to some) improving our circumstances, we can't wait around for the circumstances to tidy up before we get to the business of making inner medicine in our body through a divine-receptive feeling state. As Sri Gyanamata prayed, "Change no circumstance of my life. Change *me*."

Living in Open Heart Consciousness, irrespective of circumstances does not mean we condone circumstances that are evil, bad, hurtful, or wrong, and it does not mean we like it if our personal circumstance is one of great suffering or hardship. It does mean that we take whatever corrective actions we can, and then still figure out how to drop deep into our heart.

One of my friends was horrifically abused by her mother as a child. We're talking whipped, beaten, and chained to a tree with no food or water. The next door neighbor knew what was going on but was so fearful of repercussions, *she never called the police*. Living in Open Heart Consciousness doesn't allow for us to turn our back and brush our hands of other's misfortune. It means our heart is even more keenly attuned to the plight of others so that we are empowered to overcome our own hesitancy and take the loving action that matters. No one working with the inner alchemy of healing could turn their back on a child chained to a tree. Open Heart Consciousness is not a one-note feeling where we try to be positive and loving about everything. Rather, we let ourselves be moved by our circumstances and respond from the state of consciousness that knows with laser clarity exactly what to do.

Had I heard a story such as this from my friend 20 years ago, I would have been absolutely sick over it. I would have crawled into bed devastated with heartbreak, depressed with sorrow for my friend and the plight of humanity, and fearful that such evil could exist. Now the hurt in my heart moves me to become an even more vocal champion for living in Open Heart Consciousness, *because* inhumane things happen. We need one another to hold a vision for and presence of humanity's highest self.

As Buddhist astrophysicist Trinh Xuan Thuan remarked to Ricard Matthieu in Matthieu's *The Quantum and the Lotus: A Journey to the Frontiers Where Science and Buddhism Meet,* "Not attacking aggressors with violence doesn't mean that we can't use all the other means—nonviolent but determined resistance, dialogue, political and economic firmness-in order to combat evil and reduce overall suffering. In fact, the worst caricature of nonviolence I can think of is the naiveté and complacency of Western heads of state as regards despots in general—and Chinese leaders, in the case of Tibet. Here we find a laxity and credulity that are absolutely indefensible, in terms of nonrespect of human rights and international law."[54] When we are operating from Open Heart Consciousness, we don't

51

disregard human rights violations, but we allow our hearts to be moved, and take right action from that place.

Because I no longer question circumstances, and like Sri Gyanamata, seek not only to change the fact that horrifying circumstances do occur but to *change me,* I can change my perspective and see the possibility of a blessing in my friend's hardship. I can choose to see her not as permanently damaged by such early treatment, but as resilient and able to find a gift. My friend had such a vision for herself long ago. She did seek help, rallied from her hardship, and devoted her life to protecting human rights. She is now one of the most exquisitely gifted psychotherapists I know. I once tentatively asked her if she had found any gift from the early horror. She surprised me with her clear answer. She said she had become so subtly attuned to reading the moods and cues of her violent and unpredictable mother that it had given her exquisite insight into reading others. She described being able to "see into" her patient's minds and hearts, a sensitivity she was quite sure she would never have developed so keenly were she out playing ball all afternoon instead of alone and tied to a tree. She felt like information often came to her almost psychically, but she had a suspicion that it was linked to her enhanced ability to pick up and interpret subtle cues of tone, posture, and facial expression that more happy-go-lucky children who's safety had not depended on reading such things might never have learned to perceive.

I can think of all of the extraordinary people through history who were shaped by torture and abuse and from this perspective I can wonder, "Who would Corrie ten Boom and Viktor Frankl be without the concentration camp? Who would Nelson Mandela be without 27 years in prison? Who would Brother Yun be without his Chinese torturers? Who would Maya Angelou be without the rape? Who would Mother Theresa and Gandhi be without their paths of poverty and difficult service?" Greatness may not hinge on hardship, but we can all benefit by relating to our hardship as a blessing, not a curse. Thornton Wilder penned, "I am convinced that, except in a few extraordinary cases, one form or another of an unhappy childhood is essential to the formation of exceptional gifts." It is up to us to relate to our hardships in ways that unlock those gifts.

Even so, as I write these words, a friend emails that a son of a friend who went to the Middle East to found an emergency relief group was kidnapped and is now identified as the next planned victim for a gruesome execution. It takes an incredible dedication to inner transformation to stay steady with a vision of love and a heart open to holy joy in the presence of such atrocities. As Thich Nhat Hahn wrote in *Being Peace,* "Each day 40,000 children die of hunger. The superpowers have more than 50,000 nuclear warheads, enough to destroy our planet many times. Yet the sunrise is beautiful, and the rose that bloomed this morning along the wall is a miracle. Life is both wonderful and dreadful." [55]

In each moment we have a choice. Here, now, in this moment, I can choose Open Heart Consciousness. And here, I can choose it again. And in this moment now, I choose yet again. Now, I choose anew. After some practice choosing, a momentum gets going. Our body gets used to things and it likes familiarity. It likes to run things on autopilot and not use all its attention to sculpt every little bit of each moment. So if we get a momentum going, and do it enough times that it becomes familiar, and then comfortable, we can forget about it as eventually it runs in the background, or at least close at hand, for the rest of our lives, through our hardest times and our easiest times.

To overcome old ways of being and adopt something new like living in Open Heart Consciousness, we have to practice. I'm not kidding when I tell my students and clients to either set phone alarms, or wallpaper their home, car, and work with sticky notes to remember their meditative Feeling Mantra. For at least a month or until we remember without prompting, we need reminders to practice *all day long*. Though it only takes about 12 seconds of a feeling state practiced about 10 times a day to rewire the biology of our body (that's 120 seconds, or *two minutes* a day!) if we don't actually remember to practice, nothing changes. Set those computer reminders or alarms and paper your dashboard, refrigerator, shower, and bedroom with reminders now! Dr. Amit Sood once quipped, "The mind has a momentum problem."[56] We want to put this problem to good use. Get your reminders in place and remember your Feeling Mantra for 12 seconds now to help get that momentum going.

Dye Your Heart With Love

Kabir, the fifteenth-century Indian poet-saint, said that he didn't wish to simply dye his clothes the saffron color of a holy order; he said that he wished to dye his heart with Divine love.

Lama Surya Das
Awakening to the Sacred[57]

I was honored when Sara, a renowned meditation teacher, scheduled a consult with me. She was so skilled a meditator and teacher that she had been ordained in a centuries-old meditation tradition and was regarded highly by many of its most advanced adepts. Sara was changing the lives of her students every day, and yet she requested my help for a persistent case of depression. Some reports cite numbers as high as one in every three Americans taking anti-depressants, and Sara counted herself among their ranks. Her powerful inner practice of releasing and dissolving thoughts and emotions that interfered with being present in the moment had changed her life profoundly for the better, but had not given her relief from a chronic, nagging sense of depression. She had no particular "reason" she could pinpoint as a cause to be depressed, she just couldn't seem to shake the feeling.

In some meditation traditions, dwelling on the past is thought to potentially fuel dissatisfaction with the present and a desire for things to be different. As I explained to Sara, for our purposes we were *borrowing* the feeling tone from a past memory, to *increase* our contentment in the current moment, so that our inner bliss was not dependent on circumstances! I gave the Dalai Lama as an example; I don't think anyone would disagree that he is downright contagiously jolly, despite incredible challenges and hardships that he and the Tibetan people face. It is that inner jolliness we are after. I had a guess that because Sara had decades of practice disciplining her mind, she would be able to put the power of her HeartMindBody connection to use fast and powerfully. I was not disappointed. After only the most rudimentary instruction to find a Feeling Mantra, she was off and running.

I told Sara about spiritual teacher and peace activist Peace Pilgrim who set out on her 40 walks back and forth across the United States with one of her primary objectives inspired by 1 Thessalonians: *to pray without ceasing.* She professed to master her objective on the very first walk. One of my personal objectives for Sara, for myself, for the patients and clients I treat, and for you readers, is to *live in Open Heart Consciousness unceasingly.* This could also be stated, *to pray, (or meditate) with sincere feeling, such that we are moved in our very cells, unceasingly.* The prayer or the meditative practice is not primarily an exercise of the mind, but of the heart. The transformation changes our very consciousness. With practice, anything becomes a habit. Making Open Heart Consciousness a habit is one of the most powerful things we can do for ourselves and our health.

Though Open Heart Consciousness transcends religious categorization, finding the inner alchemical state whereby our hearts, minds, and bodies change is not new and has been explored in the context of many traditions. Adepts of different spiritual and religious traditions have referred to such alchemical states as: Divine Communion, Walking with God, Aligning with the Tao, the Unio Mystica, the Light of God, the Love of God, the Holy Spirit, Christ Consciousness, Kingdom of God Consciousness, Great Spirit, Great Mother, Brahma, Allah, Heavenly Father, Divine Mother, Tian Yin (what Chinese Mystics call the Voice of Heaven), the Beloved, the Zone, Infinite Mind, the Inner Game, Samadhi, Nirvana, Nature's Mind, The Field, The Matrix, Entraining with the Quantum Field, and Enlightenment, to name a few.

Personally I have been inspired and moved by many spiritual and religious traditions and practices. There is much to be gained by contemplating the experiences of anyone transformed by a spiritual path. Though my experience of Open Heart Consciousness *feels* like a spiritual or devotional state, it does not require any particular set of beliefs. It is something we must come back to over and over again with great regularity, until the feeling runs in the background, *unceasingly*.

As Sara learned, a Feeling Mantra has as a point of focus a feeling memory. The moment she understood that and focused her mind on something that changed her feelings, she felt better right away. With surprised delight, Sara realized that depression didn't necessarily mean something was wrong in her brain, but it did mean that her brain had been conditioned to provide the biochemicals that gave rise to that particular feeling. With practice focusing on a new Feeling Mantra she could recondition her heart, body and brain. Soon (literally within only a few weeks), she found herself naturally defaulting to the new state. Suddenly, the ancient meditation tradition she had practiced and taught for decades took on a new richness and texture. Sara had done more personal and spiritual practice than most people ever commit to, and with this subtle adjustment to her inner feeling state, all her decades of work clicked to an even deeper level.

Differing styles of meditation are not mutually exclusive. We can learn, grow, transform, and take inspiration from any of a multitude of living traditions. A new level of heart and consciousness is available for any of us, even if we are already very far along a particular path. I'm amazed for myself how I can continually drop even more deeply into love, and continually expand more fully into freedom.

From Sara's eyes now shines a most beautiful and compelling light. She reminds me of the Dalai Lama with her wise and kind twinkling eyes, and effervescent boundless good cheer. No antidepressant had been able to give her that.

Get the knack of changing your inner feeling tone

A friend once told me after being moved by one of my talks, "I taught the exact meditation and imagery skills you are teaching to a college sports team *25 years ago*. Their performance improved incredibly using the technique of feeling themselves execute the perfect shot. *Why on earth haven't I been using what I know on myself?*" We have to overcome inertia to change. Make the effort now.

A Feeling Mantra is practiced repetitively until the cells of the body "catch" the memory. Striving and trying are best replaced with relaxed savoring. In *Meditation: The First and Last Freedom*, Osho says, "Meditation is such a mystery that it can be called a science, an art, a knack without any contradiction...A knack is not a science, it cannot be taught...A knack is the most mysterious thing in human understanding."[58] To develop a knack for something requires practice until you "own" it. Take a moment to savor your Feeling Mantra again now. Remember the moment in as much detail as you can—the sounds, smells, sights, feelings, your body posture, your facial expression, and any other detail you can recall. Practice "getting the knack" of changing your feeling state using your imagination. While sustaining a feeling for 12 seconds is enough to change our body and brain, in the beginning, it may take longer to find the feeling. So, give yourself the time to relax into the daydream. Remember, practicing 10 times a day can bring about significant and permanent change.

In teaching meditation to audiences, Deepak Chopra describes that if you touch into the space of silence even once for a moment, it is like dipping a white cloth into red dye—the red may fade easily, but it is now there. If you dip the cloth into that dye every day, eventually you will have a red that is so vibrant that it will not fade. The same can be said for a Feeling Mantra or Open Heart Consciousness. Touch into that space every single day. Eventually it becomes a part of the fabric of your life. Dip the fabric of your inner self deep into the dye by remembering your Feeling Mantra yet again, right now, for however many seconds or minutes it takes to start to feel your biochemistry change.

Henry David Thoreau advises us, "To affect the quality of the day, that is the highest of arts. Every man is tasked to make his life, even in its details, worthy of the contemplation of his most elevated and critical hour." Truly, what art is more important? Thoreau lived at Walden Pond for two years and two months to cultivate an elevated inner state. Will you invest 120 seconds a day?

Choose the Alchemical Path

(O)utside of the sphere of practical human concerns, nature is full of nonlinear phenomena. Highly complex processes can emerge from deceptively simple rules or parts, and small changes in one underlying factor of a complex system can engender radical, qualitative shifts in other factors that depend on it.

V. S. Ramachandran
The Tell-Tale Brain[59]

"Rabbit's clever," said Pooh thoughtfully.
"Yes," said Piglet, "Rabbit's clever."
"And he has brain."
"Yes," said Piglet, "Rabbit has brain."
There was a long silence.
"I suppose," said Pooh,
"that's why he never understands anything."

Benjamin Hoff
The Tao of Pooh[60]

In *The Scalpel and the Soul,* Dr. Allan Hamilton tells the story of how he was met mysteriously by an African tribal leader he was looking for, just as he had become hopelessly lost and unable to find the remote village to which he was delivering medicine. Though Hamilton and his guide were not expected, the tribal leader had set out to find him after *dreaming* that the men were lost. The dream had specified precisely when and where to meet them. As Hamilton summarized, "To the impoverished and disenchanted mind, such events would seem coincidental."[61] There are mysterious forces available to help us; may our minds not be too impoverished and disenchanted to receive the help.

One way of being impoverished and disenchanted is to underestimate or underutilize the power of our HeartMindBody connection. Usually this stems from adherence to linear thinking which says that my efforts in life produce my results, so if I work hard I'll succeed, and if I do nothing I'll fail. Isn't that what so many of us are raised to think? I used to work myself into a frazzled state of exhaustion trying to justify to myself that the mathematics of this equation were just part and parcel of the way things were. It was some time before I switched over to alchemical consciousness, which says *if I live in resourceful feeling states, the*

57

alchemy in my brain and body, and the quantum field, give rise to untold and unexpected results.

Find the High-Five Vibe

My friend Justine frets all the time that she can't figure out what she's supposed to be doing with her life. She feels stuck and weary with her current job, and holds onto hope that if she could just find her calling, her life would improve. She ruminates that she is not making any meaningful contribution to humanity. In the meantime, she is exhausted and miserable year after year.

I see her situation another way. If Justine would learn how to feel joy, be playful, and find meaning in her current work, the first thing that would happen is her creativity and productivity would increase, and thereby her work would become easier and more satisfying. The team she leads would experience better morale, and would get their jobs completed more efficiently. If she created a "high-five vibe" at the office, she would probably find she enjoys her work more than she thought she could. That is when the magic would start to happen.

When we are living in the high-five zone, people are attracted to us in a way that is often inexplicable. My guess is that opportunities would open up for my friend that neither she nor I could dream of from our current vantage point. I've seen this happen, and the opportunities that arise are often far more incredible than anyone involved could conceive of or create through rational, analytical, linear plans for change. This is the way of the alchemical path. People call it "good luck," but it is really about good feelings, practiced irrespective of circumstances. The alchemical path focuses on feelings first, and the challenge of how to feel good even if the circumstances are really bad, and then lets outcomes be shaped and guided by the alchemy that ensues from those good feelings.

In *Faust*, Goethe noted that, "...the moment one commits oneself, then Providence moves, too. All sorts of things occur to help one that would otherwise never have happened. A whole stream of events issues from the decision, raising in one's favor all manner of unforeseen incidents and meetings and material assistance, which no man could have dreamed would come his way." [62] But Justine keeps waiting for her circumstances to be right, never committing to feeling good no matter what. So she forfeits her access to unforeseen incidents, to unforeseen meetings, to unforeseen material assistance, and to Providence. I, like Justine, have a deep impulse to make a meaningful contribution to humanity. Most people do. But I've come to believe that our inner work contributes much more than our outer work. I truly believe it's not what outer work you do that matters, it is how you do it that matters. All types of jobs are necessary for life to carry on. Find the high-five vibe and alchemical path no matter how humble your work. A deeply loving heart is the greatest contribution to humanity.

Whether we live with a linear or alchemical orientation to our health can be a matter of life and death

I once was looking over the intake form of a new patient and noticed that her sister's death at 46 was attributed to cystic fibrosis. I remarked that that was an amazingly long life for someone with CF. The patient described to me that though her sister experienced extreme trouble with her lungs throughout her life, no one could discover what was wrong with her and so she got on fairly well. It wasn't until a new gene was identified as a CF gene that doctors were able to test and finally give her a diagnosis at 46 years old. Two months later, she suddenly died.

Not knowing her grave diagnosis and assuming she just had "weak lungs" and not a fatal condition had allowed for the magic of alchemy. Her body beat the odds for 46 years. This woman had no reason to think she should die early, so her body had mysteriously gone about finding a way to sustain life. Once diagnosed, reason and rationality asserted an incredible force, more powerful than the force of awe at knowing that her body was amazing. Because the linear path was clear—that there was no reasonable way she should still be alive —her body rapidly complied.

Sick people draw calamity

During a time period when I was 90 pounds overweight and miserable, a photograph captured me glaring at my infant son with a scowl. I was *not* in the space of alchemy and miracles. I was plodding along, working the linear path like a disciplined devotee, and wondering why every domain of my life kept blowing up around me. Nice people aren't supposed to have so much bad luck! My baby had a list of symptoms a mile long, he was losing weight each week, and he screamed inconsolably day and night. The longest sleep interval I'd gotten in four months was 15 minutes. I was about out of my mind and close to a real breaking point from sleep deprivation, and my health was totally tanking. In *The Awesome Science of Luck,* Peter Ragnar says, "When your luck goes sour like an old sock, you carry a vibrational stink that ruins everything you touch. Like a sick plant that draws insects, sick people draw calamity."[63] I was his poster girl. I was the Grand Poobah of Calamity, clearly reeking of vibrational stink.

One day my mom, who had been helping day and night with the crying baby, realized that though I had spent years cultivating a new level of heart and mind, when I was confronted with no sleep and no hope, I had reverted right back to the habits she'd known so well when I was a teenager. In a moment of "cutting to the chase," she sternly clipped, "You are a mess. You need to reread THIS," and handed me a copy of the book *The Secret*.[64] I looked at it with a feeling of deep revulsion. I knew the book, and the movie even better. When my husband and I ran an addiction program at a county Health Department years before, we used to play the DVD during an educational segment for the clients. It was so well-loved, our copy "walked" out with a client desperate to learn the message. The message in that movie–that our emotions attract the good or bad things in our life–seemed like a distant memory. Reluctantly, I flipped through the book. "Bullshit," I muttered.

The next day, I dragged myself out of bed long enough to take a trip to the library. My solution for how to deal with a wailing infant who eight pediatricians had told me was "fine" was to play DVD's to entertain him day and night, while I lay limply on the sofa nursing a case of deep exhaustion and chronic sinusitis. When I got to the immaculately organized kids' movie section at the library, I couldn't believe it: there was a copy of the DVD of *The Secret* misfiled between *Barney* and *Dora,* and seemingly staring at me. "No way" I muttered, and brushed passed it to grab my kid movies. But it commanded me like a force field. I just couldn't walk away. "Hell's bells," I grumbled, and grabbed *The Secret,* too.

I do not embrace every premise presented in *The Secret,* but trust me when I say that to a drowning person, it was a lifeline. I watched it seven times that week. I took notes on every author who spoke in that movie, and ordered everything they wrote through the library. When Louise Hay's DVD *You Can Heal Your Life* came a few days later, I watched that seven times, too. I knew I couldn't trust my own brain to think helpful thoughts, so I had to feed it other people's helpful thoughts like a medicine, only on an even tighter dosing schedule. Until I was reworked and rewired, I couldn't trust myself for even a moment to be alone with my own brain.

That week the polarity of my luck changed. I must have sufficiently cleansed myself of the vibrational stink. Only the week before, the eighth in a line of pediatricians we'd seen told me, "If you weren't so anxious, your son would be fine. All he has is a simple case of colic!" Now, in a state charged with hope and new possibility, answers seemed to stream at me from every direction. I read about elimination diets, and figured out that my son had celiac disease, which we later confirmed through testing. I found a Yahoo group for autism, and the moms on the forum helped me identify what it meant that my son was covered in eczema and only having a bowel movement once every nine days, though he was a breast-fed baby who should have been going nine times a day. They helped me determine the meaning of the cradle cap that had caused a crater-like indentation in the top of his head; what to do about it, and what to do about the thrush he'd had since birth. For the first time in four months, my son smiled, made eye contact, and slept. The behaviors that had looked like autism to me, including lack of eye contact, hitting himself repeatedly in the head, arching his back so frequently it looked like a tic, and screaming, slowly faded away. Soon after, we found several helpful doctors who were creative, out-of-the-box thinkers, and who helped us rather than dismissing our concerns.

Trade your cynicism for wonder

The next week, I read an obscure mention of a very obscure prescription that could be compounded for chronically infected sinuses. The prescription was developed by Dr. Jacob Teitelbaum, a native to our area and author of nine books. I had heard glowing reports of Dr. Teitelbaum many times from patients of mine who had seen him while he was living in Maryland. The spray was available only through a compounding pharmacy about 40 minutes from my house. It eventually curbed the chronic sinusitis that three ENT's told me would require surgery.

A few weeks later, our new pediatric ophthalmologist sent us to the same pharmacy for a compounded prescription for my son, who had developed a chalazion cyst on his eye that morphed into a granuloma the size of a grape. Because I consider 40 minutes away far, I called in advance on the day of pick-up to make sure the prescription was ready before driving there. It wasn't. Weirdly, each day I called again, and each day the prescription still wasn't ready. I hadn't learned to trust in anything alchemical, and definitely not something like a mystical magnetic power of the universe aligning things behind the scene. So my response was to get increasingly frustrated. Though pick-up for the sinusitis spray just weeks before had been without incident, this time I critically remarked to my husband, "These people are a bunch of buffoons!"

Too freshly rid of my negative vibrational stink, and still expecting the worst, still more cynic than mystic, I was incapable of conceiving of synchronicities being attracted to any new good luck vibrational fragrance. I had not fully embraced the possibility of an invisible web of intelligence that might conspire on my behalf. The fourth time I called, the pharmacy affirmed my script was ready. I confirmed, "You mean it is ready now, right? Ready so I won't have to wait when I get there, right?" When I got there and learned they had not even started filling the prescription, I was livid.

Because of the now four times botching of my prescription, I had 30 minutes to hang out at the front desk, where the head compounding pharmacist and owner of the pharmacy was making an unusual appearance. Though my sinus infection had cleared, my nose was still not right. "What would cause the sides of my nose to itch like crazy?" I asked him on a whim. "Oh, that is demodex folliculorum, the organism that causes rosacea, chronic sinusitis, and granulomas" he replied. My husband had just been diagnosed with rosacea, so with one succinct response, he'd nailed the three things our family was currently grappling with, including my son's granuloma for which I was there to pick up the prescription! The ophthalmologist hadn't mentioned this organism, and I had done Internet searches for "itchy sides of nose" numerous times, and never seen reference to what turned out to be a microscopic, but normal, resident of the skin that only caused problems when out of balance with the rest of the skin ecology. *"What do you treat it with?"* I practically hissed. "Tea tree oil" he replied. Once I knew *what* to do an Internet search for, I found a voluminous supply of answers to my many questions.

I left that pharmacy in a state of awe at all the tiny details that had to line up for that information to come to me. We had been chasing around to ophthalmologists, dermatologists, and ENT's to solve what we thought were three separate problems, all of which soon resolved using a $7 bottle of tea tree oil. I left with an irrefutable belief that the Divine Intelligence of the universe is much better at taking care of me than I am at taking care of myself, if I let it. I had angrily assumed I was dealing with ignorant idiots. Now, I believe an exquisite ordering of time and space had been orchestrated on my behalf. *I* was the ignorant idiot. I have learned that when things "don't go my way," I do best to quietly smile to myself, get myself in an elevated heart space irrespective of circumstances, and wait and see what pans out. My way has limits. The Divine Intelligence is limitless. Rumi said, "Trade your knowledge for bewilderment." I say, trade your cynicism for wonder. And trade it again and again and again.

Surf in the wake

Leave room for magic and the miraculous. Don't always try to figure things out to the dot and nail everything down rationally. In *Wholeness or Transcendence?* Georg Feuerstein says, "The rational consciousness is the matrix of scientific materialism, virulent ethnocentrism, terrorism, and existential neurosis. It is a deficient form of consciousness, giving birth to deficient social and cultural manifestations. Far from being the summit of human accomplishment, the rational consciousness is an evolutionary cul-de-sac." [65] Live in the alchemical state of Open Heart Consciousness, a place of hope, creativity, and unseen possibility. Cultivate the ability to be playful and feel love even amidst your most challenging circumstances. When we stop struggling against our problems or relying solely on our limited linear efforts to solve them, some of the struggles of life may smooth over in unexpected ways. The alchemical path engages good feelings and an attitude of working with the flow of life.

As Albert Einstein said, "The most important question a person can ask is, 'Is the Universe a friendly place?'" Don't just assume the Universe is friendly. Assume the Universe is your most beneficent best friend! The way I think of it, the Divine Intelligence is the motorboat. My job is to be the dolphin and stay close to the boat where the surfing is great in the wake. Too far out of the zone, it's a drag!

Live Large and Bring It!

(N)either mastery nor satisfaction can be found in the playing of any game without giving some attention to the relatively neglected skills of the inner game. This is the game that takes place in the mind of the player, and it is played against such obstacles as lapses in concentration, nervousness, self-doubt and self-condemnation. In short, it is played to overcome all habits of mind which inhibit excellence in performance.

W. Timothy Gallwey

The Inner Game of Tennis: The Classic Guide to the Mental Side of Peak Performance[66]

God gave us endorphins for a reason: to stop doing the things that aren't working.

Richard Bandler & Owen Fitzpatrick

Conversations with Richard Bandler[67]

When our son was six and showed up for his first belt test at a new martial arts school, we had not realized how rigorous this school made their belt tests. My son had already spent an hour that afternoon grappling at another school, where in the process of giving everything he had to his match, he had gotten his jaw knocked visibly out of alignment. Now, halfway through the belt test, my son's spirit visibly withered as he gave in to exhaustion, pain, fear about his jaw, and uncertainty over whether he had enough reserves left to make it through the grueling test. How often in the face of illness do we wither, exhausted and depleted of reserves, and not sure how much more effort we can make?

Master John, who loves our son and saw he was at a breaking point, yelled, "COME ON CHUCKY, BRING IT!!!!!" The nickname, based on the horror movie Chucky doll, was a point of pride for our son, because it was meant to reference his fierceness and invincibility packed into a small body. Suddenly, my son pumped his fist in the air and let out a wild whoop, then completed the test like he was on fire, finishing first in the class. When it comes to healing illness, how do we get to the place where we can pump our fist in the air and *bring it*?

When we "bring it," we want to draw our power from the mysterious source that is available when we transform our consciousness. We don't want to dig into second and third winds fueled by coffee and adrenaline. A patient of mine recently told me that while he hadn't slept more than 4.5 hours per night in the past two months, he's never felt more powerful in his life. He was pumping his fist in the air over a huge work project he was in charge of, but in all likeliness, as evidenced by how irritable he also felt and how haggard he looked, he was mistaking being jacked up on adrenaline for being jacked up on Open Heart Consciousness. For my six-year-old son, there is still much to learn about living large and finding peak performance and Open Heart Consciousness in the context of competitive sports. If he occasionally uses willpower to transform his state, he will learn important lessons about the HeartMindBody connection. But as we mature, it is essential that we learn to chronically tap bliss consciousness rather than chronically tapping adrenaline and willpower, or there is a cost to our health. To win the "inner game" of consciousness transformation, we can't be overly motivated by winning the "outer game," or we will miss the whisper of wisdom our body gives when we are becoming habituated to pushing too much.

In *The Inner Game of Tennis: The Classic Guide to the Mental Side of Peak Performance,* author W. Timothy Gallwey describes a moment before a tennis match in his first tournament competition. As he stood there with shaky knees, nervousness, and compromised focus, he considered both the worst possible outcome and the best. He concluded that neither outcome would much impact his life in any way, and asked himself *what he wanted most*. He was surprised at the answer. He realized he cared little about whether he won or lost the upcoming match; what he cared about most was that he figure out how to *win the inner game*. [68]

Winning the inner game has to do with getting our thoughts, feelings, and focus right under pressure and challenging conditions. It involves overcoming the mental and emotional obstacles that interfere with living large and playing our best. With his intention in mind, he found a new enthusiasm and inner certainty, and felt relieved of the pressures to "win." In this new place, he played with *all his energies at his command*. Though he "lost" that match, he had won the inner game.

Unlocking the heart of healing is an inner game. When we approach this game as Gallwey did, with no attachment to outcome, and only a sense of wanting to defeat our inner opponents in our consciousness, energies are always freed for healing. As inner energies become available through increased relaxation and peace, through thoughts and feelings that elevate our heart and change our mood, and through a sustained focus on the things that increase our hopefulness and appreciation, our body can use those resources to heal.

The will to live and the will to heal

A woman came to me for help in relieving extreme tendonitis in her elbow. Her doctor had told her that with tendonitis as severe as hers, her only hope of healing it was to refrain

64

from using her arm completely for four months, which, he had pointed out with a furrowed brow, still might not work.

When our first acupuncture treatment was complete, she asked me for some help getting off the treatment table. Usually patients use a step stool to navigate the several-inch gap between where their feet dangle and the ground. This woman was worried that to use the stool she'd need to steady herself with her recuperating arm. Instead, I wrapped my arm around her waist to steady her so she could make the hop off the table. The next thing I knew, I was on the ground on top of her.

Somehow this woman had lost her balance, and in her extreme effort to not use the arm, had simply crashed over into a heap instead of reaching out to catch herself. Never expecting even the remote possibility of such a thing happening, I had not braced myself for that kind of weight, and so down we both went.

Miraculously no one was injured, and her arm sustained no damage. However I am certain, that had her doctor been consulted, he would have made exception to his recommendation to refrain from using the arm, *if* the arm was needed to prevent a potential break to the hip or neck. When the troubles and challenges of life come at us like a tornado, instead of being swept down and thrown in a heap, we sometimes have to flex our muscles a little and shout, "I am tough!" while pumping our arm in the air fiercely for added spirit. Just as there is a "will to live," there is a "will to heal." Without it, we're not really plugged in to the juice that is behind all healing, and we are not playing the inner game. This woman, though diligently following doctor's orders, was not plugged into the juice. She was the consummate victim, letting life toss her around like a rag doll. Rather than setting out to beat her doctor's grim prognosis and show him the power of her body to heal, she instead thought of herself as so fragile that a moment of imbalance was enough to take us both down.

I used to live in a similar state of consciousness and would get sacked by every malady that came along. I thought that successful people who pumped their fists in the air victoriously were just cut from a different cloth than me. Now I pump the air because I know it pumps up my Inner Molecules of Medicine. There is no better medicine than the biochemistry of success that comes from living large. It is a chosen state, like Open Heart Consciousness, that we choose irrespective of circumstances. Once we get some practice choosing such a state, a momentum gets going, making it easier to find it again. As Patricia Neal said, "A strong positive mental attitude will create more miracles than any wonder drug."

I remember when my grandmother was 86 years old, she fell and broke her hip. I had always heard that hip fractures in the elderly kill, and I observed firsthand what that meant. My grandmother was so overwhelmed with pain, hopelessness, and trepidation over a lengthy rehabilitation that she just gave up. Though otherwise healthy, and despite our daily bedside ministrations, my beloved grandmother died within several weeks of that fall.

When the challenges of life have overwhelmed your will to live or will to heal, don't rely on the thoughts and feelings that your defeated biochemistry is generating. Seek out stories of hope, inspiration, recuperation, and regeneration until you have a tear of inspiration in your eye and a genuine desire to pump your fist in the air. Feed your heart and brain that which rekindles your authentic hope, enthusiasm, and heroic capability. Instead of thinking, "My life is over as long as I have this ailment," or, "I could never bear to spend the rest of my life immobile and with chronic pain," dare to ask yourself, "What mysterious blessings are hidden in this hardship? Which priorities and values will I rearrange in the face of these interesting circumstances?" and, "How will I live large and unleash the biochemistry of success in my cells, despite a circumstance that invites me to give up, fall over, or die?"

Find Freedom at the Heart of Everything

The Buddha often said that wherever you find water, you can tell if it is the ocean because the ocean always tastes of salt. By the same token, anywhere you find enlightenment—whatever improbable or unfamiliar shape it may have assumed—you can tell it's enlightenment because enlightenment always tastes of freedom. Not comfort. Not ease. Freedom.

Martha Beck
Steering By Starlight[69]

Be empty of worrying.
Think of who created thought!
Why do you stay in prison
When the door is so wide open?

Rumi

Many years ago in the first months of knowing Brandon, who would later be my husband, I was so taken with the recordings of motivational speaker Anthony Robbins that I played them wherever we went. Brandon not only tolerated this, but got a speeding ticket once because he, too, was so excited by what Robbins was saying. One day I decided we would do an exercise that Robbins suggested, which was designed to facilitate more deeply knowing and understanding your partner. The exercise seemed simple enough.

Each person was to take a list of "Life Values" and rank them in order of personal importance. The only other instruction was that neither person was to judge or criticize the other's list. We were simply to use any newfound awareness to appreciate and understand each other more deeply.

I went to work ordering the provided list, and easily placed "Love" in the first position. I went down the line, stopping to puzzle over the value "Freedom," which had little significance to me. "Freedom from what?" I wondered, and placed it last.

Now you might guess what happened. This new boyfriend of mine placed "Freedom" first, and ranked "Love" *after* that! I was so shocked I didn't know what to do. Because the instruction prohibited grilling your partner, I toned it down and instead attempted to wheedle him to explain it to me. One of his degrees was in philosophy and he was part-way through a Master's degree, so I didn't take the hidden paradigm behind his ranking lightly. Perhaps my thinly disguised haranguing inspired his ensuing silence. He wisely intuited that any explanation he gave would be "wrong." The absence of a clear explanation launched me into a silent series of wild musings that questioned whether such a man was marriageable.

I wondered whether he was some kind of rebel without a cause. I wondered whether this obsession with freedom would result in a man who would one day scream, "I WANT MY FREEDOM," and waltz out on me in response to presumed trespasses against his precious needs to be free. I wondered whether he suffered delusions of oppression. I finally decided that he just didn't know what he was talking about. He ACTED like somebody who ranked Love first, so I chose to trust in the actions.

What is it with these guys?

In the meantime, this notion of "Freedom" burned in my mind for years. For 10 years my ears pricked up whenever the word was mentioned. I could make no sense of how freedom could rank higher than love. One day we attended a small private lecture with Dr. Joe Dispenza, a chiropractor and author of many books, including *Evolve Your Brain*,[70] *Breaking the Habit of Being Yourself*,[71] and *You Are the Placebo*.[72] I listened, riveted, as he described how we can change our DNA by changing our thoughts and feelings. I related to every word he was saying. But three times Dispenza said something that irked me to no end. He thrice repeated, "Freedom lies on the other side of pain." While entertaining thoughts of my chronic pain patients who would surely disagree, I thought to myself, here we go with that "Freedom" thing. WHAT IS IT WITH THESE GUYS???

Curious to resolve the Freedom mystery, I delved into Dispenza's book *Evolve Your Brain*.[73] At the lecture, Dispenza had been standing directly in front of me, in fact only inches away. I'm trained to look at the way people move their bodies and for clues that reveal nuances about their health. Dispenza was vibrant and healthy. But after reading his book, I was so shocked by his story that I decided if such a thing as freedom was capable of being on the other side of pain, Dispenza was the world authority on it.

While competing in a triathlon, Dispenza had been hit by an SUV and smashed to the pavement. He suffered multiple fractures and compressions in his spine. After being raced to shock trauma, he was informed that he would need emergency surgery that would place several rods through the entire length of his spine. As a chiropractor who knows how such rods would impact his life, he declined. The emergency team was insistent, voicing concern that he was delusional from shock. Without the rods, they grimly informed him, he would be paralyzed from the chest down the very moment he attempted to stand and put weight on his spine. After consulting with multiple specialists who all agreed that the rods were his only choice, Dispenza again declined, and signed himself out of the hospital.

What happens next inspires my deepest awe. Refusing to accept defeat or feel sorry for himself, Dispenza tapped into the genius that often arises of necessity. With the assistance of friends who provided him full-time care during his healing, he devised a slant board by which he could elevate himself several degrees each day to increase pressure on his spine as it healed. He employed extreme self-care: he ate an entirely raw foods diet, meditated and practiced self-hypnosis three hours a day, and *felt* the joy of being healed before it was actually so. He mentally restructured his spine, and stared at pictures of healthy spines. He had friends and family lay their hands on his spine for two hours every day. Finally, when he was able to position at 60 degrees on the slant board with no pain, he started swimming. All the while he lived by his belief, "Our thoughts matter. Our thoughts literally become matter." Dispenza returned to a full life free of pain in 10 weeks.

I reflected on this for some time. Most people fear pain and in its presence tighten up against it, resist it, and repeatedly think, "This is awful, if only this would go away. I can't live with this." Of course such thoughts and the fear that the pain will be unbearable help them to feel even more awful, and become even more constricted. The more constricted they become, the less likely it is that blood can circulate properly through the site of injury to heal.

Dispenza's recovery is nothing short of miraculous. He used his focus, his emotions, and the power of his mind to find freedom, freedom on the other side of a very emphatic and attention seducing circumstance of pain. At the beginning of his recovery, this didn't mean he was necessarily free *of* that pain, but he chose to be free *from* that pain. As Dispenza well demonstrated, freedom is an inner state, not an external condition.

True freedom is free of *every* condition

It is not unusual for a new patient to somberly report to me at their first visit that they have a disease diagnosis that is considered uncurable and irreversible. The well-meaning physicians they have consulted have assured them that they must live with the illness for the rest of their lives. From the clinical viewpoint of their doctor it is true, there is no other possibility. Over the years I have seen patients with many, many diagnoses. Often I have partnered with patients who reversed the exact illness the new patient has been condemned with. As I describe the successes of other patients and what they have done, I often observe that this new patient may begin to set their jaw, stiffen in their seat, or fold their arms across their chest. Though the body language may be subtle, it is clear to me that the message of hope is not being received as an exciting new possibility.

At that moment, I'll ask the person to notice if they are experiencing an inner sense of resistance. If they say yes, though I don't need them to share the specifics with me, I ask them to discern what thought, feeling, emotion, or belief might lie behind that resistance to the possibility of living well with, or free from, this diagnosis. At that moment, many will burst into tears. Much of the time, they confess that they are simply too terrified to hope.

In *Conversations With Yogananda,* Swami Kriyananda describes the moment he exclaimed to Yogananda, "You are getting better, Sir!" after a prolonged illness. "Who is getting better?" he replied. When Kriyananda clarified, "I meant your body, Sir," Yogananda asked, "What's the difference? The wave belongs entirely to the ocean from which it protrudes. This is God's body. If He wants to make it well, all right. If he wants to keep it unwell, all right...It is wisest to be impartial. If you have health, but are attached to it, you will always be afraid of losing it. And if you fear that loss, but become ill, you will suffer. Why not remain forever joyful in the Self?" [74] True freedom is free in *every* way, and is free of *every* condition for remaining ever joyful. We don't need to be well to be free.

Freedom is knowing that we can live with grace and blessings in any condition. When we cultivate that inner freedom, a disease process offers an opportunity to hope with gusto, and to live with the excitement that anything is possible. We aren't devastated if a disease process doesn't lessen or reverse. But we surely don't constrict and constrain our life force from giving it a juicy go by preemptively hardening ourselves with fear, doubt, or hopelessness. In some ways, it matters little whether the disease reverses or not when this place of inner freedom is reached. However, with our vital energy available and engaged while we relate to our body with curiosity and creativity, as Dispenza and many others have demonstrated, the incidence of miracles increases exponentially.

A parking pass to freedom

Understanding that freedom is a choice is not always the same thing as practicing the choice of freedom. Life has a way of putting our principles to the test. One such test happened for me three days before I was due to speak about healing and the HeartMindBody connection before an audience of 90 people. Life would make sure the principles I was about to teach were well grounded in reality.

Six months prior, on an outing in Baltimore, the parking slip required for street parking had slipped slightly down on my windshield when I slammed the door shut. Not noticing the malpositioning and the fact that the time on the ticket was now partially occluded, I went on my way. Upon returning, I found a $14 parking ticket.

Had I known what was to follow, I would have paid my ticket cheerily with a big smiley face attached to the payment. Instead, on principle, I sent my parking pass by registered

70

mail with an explanation of the error and naively waited for justice to prevail. Several letters soon came advising me that my case was pending and there was nothing more to do. Then, as it came time to renew my registration, I received a final notice that advised me that the case had been decided and I was guilty as charged. Now, I was informed, in addition to the $14 due, I suddenly also owed several hundred dollars in late payment penalties, fines and fees. I was informed that my registration had been flagged and could not be renewed until I settled the debt. Countless hours on the phone and in lines at the DMV got me nowhere. Finally, realizing another day of court visits and more DMV lines lay ahead otherwise, I angrily and indignantly paid the hundreds of dollars and went home to prepare for the talk scheduled for three days away.

At that point, my hair-trigger immune system took the opportunity to remind me that such a state comes with a price. Many people don't realize that viruses and bacteria are within us all the time, and when our immune system is functioning well, it keeps them in check. For me, a bit of stress is enough for my already challenged immune system to become overwhelmed and succumb quickly to illness. I came home from the DMV feeling so angry, so violated, and so *screwed* by a rigged system that my glands started to swell and I felt fluish within the hour. I found myself standing at the crossroads of my very justifiable outraged emotions, and the opportunity to be free.

With a talk scheduled in three days, I could *not* be sick. I knew that returning to health required a choice of freedom from my upset. For the next four hours, every time a thought of anger, violation, helplessness or upset surged in my mind, I met it with the thought *"and I can still be free."* My mind was like a wild stallion, bucking against my attempts to tame it. My bitterness at the waste of time, the waste of money, and the corruption inherent in the parking ticket system threatened to overtake me, yet I kept meeting the thoughts with *"and I can still select freedom, irrespective of those things."* As a bad feeling would edge in and tempt me to engage it, I thought to myself *"I can't afford you. You are too expensive."* I knew those feelings were like fertilizer to illness. I would bring myself back to my Feeling Mantra and trade those illness fertilizing thoughts and feelings for Open Heart Consciousness.

I knew I was on track because the sick and achy feeling was beginning to recede. But I was in a battle for my health and my greatest opponent was *me*. I wanted to blame the City of Baltimore, but it was my own thoughts and feelings fueling the illness. As the end of the fourth hour approached, I knew I had succeeded. In place of the seething anger, I started belly laughing at the absurdity of the situation. I actually felt genuinely thankful for the experience and the accelerated learning lesson it had provided. I felt glad that someone's salary would be paid that week by my fines. Furthermore, I knew that the lesson was profoundly valuable and I would tell the story at my talk. As I marveled that I had indeed figured out how to truly be free, a great euphoria came over me. All traces of flu gone, I realized that though we may never be free of the *invitation* to suffer, we can still *be* free. Freedom is a state of heart, a state of mind, a state of consciousness, and a choice. It is something we choose, practice, and master. *And it feels great.*

While an unfair parking ticket is low on the scale of hardships life has to offer, I share the story precisely because we are all capable of extreme reactions to the small bumps of life. Most of the time, I observe people failing to associate such reactions with any price, and so they rant or vent with no thought to the inner consequences, rather than using such opportunities as a training ground to cut their teeth on living free. When I notice how many people are trapped or suffering, not realizing they are forfeiting freedom as a choice, I wonder as Rumi wondered long ago, "Why do you stay in prison, when the door is so wide open?"

Though I didn't know it at the time of the parking ticket episode, years later when Dr. Dispenza wrote *You Are the Placebo*,[75] he revealed that he, too, had to bring his attention back to healing his spine when he jumped repeatedly to thoughts like never walking again, stressing over whether to sell his chiropractic practice, and whether he'd spend the rest of his life in a wheelchair. By disciplining his mind to focus on the outcome he desired, the power of his thoughts and feelings supported what could be considered a miracle. The choice of freedom in the face of hardship works for situations big and small.

I later learned that *freedom* and *love* were once the same word: *freogan*; an Old English word. I now put "Freedom" right up there with "Love." Life provides us opportunities for pain, for suffering, and for miseries of multiple varieties. No one escapes the invitation to suffer. But Freedom is available with a flick of the attention. From the space of non-duality, "nothing" is ever on the other side of "anything." Rather, as I have directly perceived while in a transcendent state, everything is a oneness, a wholeness, and in unity–perfect with no effort. On the path to such integration, where seeking is traded for being, we have a helpful choice available in every moment. Though it may require of us that we learn something new: meditation, self-hypnosis, accessing Open Heart Consciousness, prayer, forgiveness, compassion, acceptance, or a Feeling Mantra, the fact is, freedom not only lies on the other side of pain. *Freedom lies at the heart of everything.*

Key #3   Change Your Mind

Set Your GPS Coordinates of Health

The casual expressions of speech we unconsciously use fundamentally shape our health. Within just two hours with patients on a recent morning, one had said, "I'm rotting from the inside out from all the anesthesia I've had." Another stated, "My health is like a train wreck." Yet another proclaimed, "I know my headaches aren't going to get any better, but maybe you can help me with the tension in my neck."

Our body is listening, and when we speak these things, we're giving our cells GPS coordinates. These patients were dialing in destination coordinates for "internally rotted," "train-wrecked," and "permanently saddled with pain." If you are tempted to think you don't do this yourself, I urge you to enlist someone close to you to note your habitual habits of speech, and help you identify ways you may unconsciously be programming a GPS destination that isn't really where you want to go. As Peace Pilgrim once said, "If you knew how powerful your thoughts were, you would never think a negative thought again."

It is up to us to see a future potential for our health, and then to maintain it much the way our car GPS holds the coordinates for our destination until we are there. As Michael Murphy and Rhea A. White describe of athletic performance in *In the Zone*, "(F)or example, he encouraged players to imagine a particular shot several hundred times until they saw it vividly. When the image is powerfully established, the athlete practices that shot on the court, bringing his body into alignment with his inner vision. Periods of physical practice alternate with periods of mental practice until the athlete clearly sees what he wants to do—and then does it to his or her coach's satisfaction."[78]

When we give the cells of our body a vision, a vision we have established powerfully, the cells have a chance to figure out a way to accommodate and come into alignment with that vision. We can begin to take more loving lifestyle actions and observe whether the gap between where we are and where we are going begins to close up, and readjust our loving lifestyle actions accordingly. People who go looking for answers tend to find them. People who resign themselves to the status quo tend to find more of the same. As the old Japanese saying goes, "Vision without action is a daydream. Action without vision is a nightmare."

When you enter a destination on your car GPS, the computer figures out the step by step calculation for how to get there. Similarly, when we enter in a biological GPS destination in our feeling imagination, the cells go to work figuring out how to get us there. It doesn't matter if you don't know "how" an improvement in health might happen. Don't worry about the how, that part is not "your" problem. The cells operate with an intelligence far greater than we could ever instruct them. Your job is being consistent in holding the GPS coordinates you want by imagining the future health destination you want, and touching frequently into a Feeling Mantra or Open Heart Consciousness.

In *Secrets of the Lost Mode of Prayer,*[79] Gregg Braden tells a story of a time during drought when he learned from his Native American friend to "pray rain." They didn't beseech the heaven for rain, and in fact they asked for nothing. What they did is *imagine how rain feels* while maintaining a feeling of gratitude for the opportunity to commune with the forces of creation. Hold your inner GPS true by *imagining how vibrant health feels, and sustain a heart tone of gratitude at the opportunity to commune with the healing forces of creation.*

Holding our inner GPS steady neither accepts nor rejects our current health circumstances. Being obsessed with healing can block the possibility of doing so as much as the mindsets of my patients at the start of the chapter who were blocked by their proclamations of persistent ill health. However, if you mindlessly and habitually keep envisioning the wrong destination, the cells will do an excellent job of transporting or maintaining you there. Sometimes it may not seem to make sense to hold a vision of health when the reality we are greeted with is a picture of disease, but as Swami Kriyananda describes in *The New Path: Life With Paramahansa Yogananda*, "It is a striking fact that, until my faith returned in all its former vitality, Lady Luck withheld from me further proofs of her favor."[80] Sometimes we have to charge our faith with possibility against all reason and evidence to the contrary.

Of course not all envisioned destinations are places at which you can arrive, just as all imagined health destinations may not be states you can attain. Don't forego dreaming of the moon just because only a few ever make it there. I see miracles happen in people's health every day. Challenge your vision of your own possible health destination a little.

One thing about a GPS destination is you actually have to get in the car and drive it to get there. Give your body some help getting to a new health destination by adopting a body-loving lifestyle. That said, there is no need for the driver to be obsessively fixating on the destination and filled with angst that we "aren't there yet." Destination change takes time, and that experience of time is going to be much different if we enjoy the journey. Let go, live in Open Heart Consciousness, and let your body take an inner journey of healing.

The inner journey of healing can have ruts, bumps, and glitches inherent to the ride. Errant thoughts definitely cause glitches. Sometimes we have not only an errant thought or two confusing our effective GPS programming, but a brain that has become wired to think worried thoughts over and over in a spin. One thing about a mind that spins is that just like a car spinning donuts, it keeps digging deeper ruts but never gets anywhere.

Move toward transformation

A woman named Dana once told me that to stop her anxiously spinning mind she was studying a particular spiritual path that involved chanting long phrases in a foreign language. She was experiencing only minimal success, and so was looking for ways to enhance her practice. When I asked her what the phrases meant and what her intended result was, she professed that there was no particular intended result besides stopping her racing mind, and she had no idea what the phrases meant. Dana wasn't chanting the holy phrases in a state of sacred reverence, she was simply using the chants as an interruption to her spinning thoughts. Most people just use television for that.

Had Dana chosen to chant certain simple holy sounds I would have had more anticipation of a satisfying outcome as the vibrational frequencies of particular sounds can heal. Many traditions recognize that sound tones can transform and heal; I teach the Qigong Six Healing Sounds and often find students close to tears or bright-faced and luminous in an expanded state of joyous rapture by what those simple sounds can do to transform our inner state.

Had Dana chosen to chant phrases with *meaning* that so moved her they brought tears of joy to her eyes I would know for sure she was on track. One mantra that is the backdrop of a song we love in our house is, "Wahe Guru, Wahe Guru, Wahe Guru, Wahe Jio" which translates to "O my soul, when I experience the indescribable wisdom of God, I am in ecstasy." Sentiments like that truly have the power to transform! As it was, without engaging meaning and lacking a connection to the practice, she was dedicating much time but was influencing her biology and heart very little, and her mental donuts kept spinning those ruts ever more deeply.

Any attempts toward meditation and self improvement are better than none, yet I wanted her to harvest a more abundant yield from her dedicated efforts. Arnold Schwarzenegger once said, "A pump when I see the muscle I want is worth ten with my mind drifting." The acts of lifting weights, meditating, or chanting are good. When we focus on our GPS destination while doing them, they are much, much, better

Any practice may transform us, if practiced transformationally. The details of the practice matter much less than whether or not the practice lifts and moves the heart and frees the mind. Ironically, while Sri Da Avabhasa was residing in India in the Ashram of Swami Muktananda, he had a holy vision of Mother Mary who in the vision taught him a form of the prayer "Hail Mary" and instructed him to get a rosary. Hail Mary became his mantra while doing Ashram duties. For Sri Da Avabhasa who was completely non-sympathetic toward Christianity and thought that the yogic path was the only true path toward awakening, a visitation by Mary and his subsequent practice seemed a cosmic joke. But he let the joke move him, and loosened his grip on the belief that only one path could light the way.

I can hear a chorale rendition of Ave Maria (Hail Mary) in my imagination right now that brings tears to my eyes. Those few melodic bars evoking such tender emotion serve as a powerfully transformative mantra for me. When one of my Qigong students asked how she would know which version of the Six Healing Sounds would be best for her to use, as several Chinese Qigong Masters had pronounced the tones slightly differently, I suggested that her body would know by the feel. Another student chirped, "It's like shopping for sound! We're shopping for the tone that brightens us up!" If you are considering singing or chanting as a healing path, shop for the sounds that brighten your heart, expand your consciousness, and fill you to fullness with a true sense of the Divine.

When it comes to any transformative practice such as meditation, prayer, or chanting, there is so much more that is possible beyond stopping a spinning mind. Stopping the thing we hate is a "moving away from orientation" whereby we never actually make a decision and stake a claim on what we *want* to move *toward*. In contrast, do we want, for example, a mind and heart made more receptive to and capable of deep love, expansive hope, true meaning, and full-bodied peace? This is a "moving toward" orientation. Once we know what we are moving toward we can choose practices to deepen such states. Truly, any practice is fine if done in such a way that our heart is stirred to greater love, our mind awakened to greater compassion, and our biochemistry awakened to the molecules of medicine that by their very nature leave our thoughts quieter and our body capable of a deeper joy and gratitude. However, such a "moving toward" orientation involves a clear and intentional setting of the internal GPS. When it comes to the journey of inner transformation, I think of it like a road trip. While it is good to leave room for spontaneous detours and side trips, if I'm going to fire up the car and burn the gas and the oil to go somewhere, I like to know where I'm headed!

Change how your body responds to disease

A research study published in the *International Journal of Neuroscience,* called "Voluntary Modulation of Neutrophil Adhesiveness Using a Cyberphysiologic Strategy," showed that a short and simple visualization exercise can change the effectiveness of our immune systems. Subjects had blood and saliva analyzed before and after a thirty minute rest condition for the Control group, and a thirty minute Cyberphysiologic strategy (visualizing immune neutrophils increasing their ability to stick to foreign objects) in the experimental group. Statistically significant increases in "neutrophil adherence" (specifically, mopping up bad guys) was demonstrated in the experimental group with only two weeks of visualization practice.[81] We have the ability to change the way our body responds to disease. The power of our mind to focus is one of our most potent tools.

One of my favorite examples of setting an internal GPS for healing is the sign Navy SEAL Lieutenant Jason Redman hung on his hospital room door after being injured by machine gun fire in Iraq that caused severe injuries, including a mangled face and missing nose that required 37 surgeries. He wrote,

ATTENTION
TO ALL WHO ENTER HERE

If you are coming into this room with sorrow or to feel sorry for my wounds, go elsewhere. The wounds I received, I got in a job I love, doing it for people I love, supporting the freedom of a country I deeply love. I am incredibly tough and will make a full recovery. What is full? That is the absolute utmost physically my body has to recover. Then I will push that about 20 percent further through sheer mental tenacity. This room you are about to enter is a room full of fun, optimism, and intense rapid regrowth. If you are not prepared for that, go elsewhere. [82]

-Lieutenant Jason Redman

That's a well set internal GPS for healing. It doesn't leave us scratching our heads wondering whether the guy might or might not heal. In fact, Redman did profoundly heal and went on to found the non-profit Wounded Wear, providing kits of clothing for other wounded soldiers with slogans such as "Scarred so that others may live free," to promote awareness of the sacrifices soldiers make and to minimize the stares that so many maimed and injured soldiers receive. Redman's book *The Trident* tells his inspiring story of overcoming adversity.

Intentions seek fulfillment

In training Olympic athletes, Russian researchers determined that groups employing 25% physical training and *75% mental training through visualization* (setting the inner GPS)

made greater gains in actual performance than subjects using 100% physical training, or groups using 75% physical training and 25% mental training. Setting our inner GPS through creative visualization truly unlocks our greatest resources.

Many patients come to our healing arts centers with cancer. One of the first things I teach my patients to do is to hold an inner GPS visualization of vibrant health. Next, I teach them to feel a Feeling Mantra or Open Heart Consciousness, irrespective of their health circumstances. Finally, I too move into a state where I can see and feel that outcome for them, and I place my hands over the area of their cancer. Francis S. MacNutt, Ph.D. has called laying on of hands "God's radiation treatment," and I would agree that sometimes hands used for healing seem to work mysteriously like radiation. An eerie number of patients I do these practices with experience changes in their cancer status that simply don't make any sense in terms of modern oncology practice. But to those who understand that feeling-based changes in the heart have the power to affect terminal illness, such possibilities are not so hard to believe. Skepticism is a distractive habit that eats up resources for putting information into practice. That thoughts and feelings have the power to heal has been so voluminously studied and demonstrated, it is no longer a discussion open to scientific debate. It's a wrap. It's up to us to wrap our minds and hearts around our own HeartMindBody resources and put them to good use.

Set your inner GPS coordinates of health and then enjoy the ride. Be open to intuition and inspiration as you travel along; a key may present itself in an unusual way to facilitate your travels. Setting your inner GPS should not be like bossing life around, but more like taking a vision quest to the mountaintop and being deeply and authentically moved and transformed by an awareness of a new possibility that allows you to take flight. Your thoughts, your inner GPS and your mindset are intentions, and as Deepak Chopra said, "Intentions automatically seek their fulfillment if left alone." [83]

Be a Person of Radical Health

Kids are great dreamers with an excellent ability to focus their internal GPS. And then there are cynical adults who would mock or belittle those dreams, or try to enter in the GPS coordinates we think are realistic or appropriate for kids. I say let 'em dream big. When my son was four he showed me a picture of the house he wanted to live in. Only it wasn't a house, it was a luxury hotel on 1,200 acres on the beach in Mexico. I'm not sure where he got his taste. I saw this as a fantastic opportunity and taped it on his dresser.

"You want to live there, huh?' I asked. "To live somewhere like that, you'll need to be a Man of Excellence. A Man of Excellence does the work he needs to do without complaining so I expect that from now on you'll brush your teeth cheerfully. A Man of Excellence knows the value of proper rest so I expect that you'll take pride in getting to bed at the proper time. A Man of Excellence is impeccable in all that he does." I was playing around and having some fun but I wasn't about to crush his dream—who am I to say whether or not he should or could "make it big" and buy that hotel? Though to me the place looked a wee bit ostentatious for a house, for all I know, for him, owning that hotel might play a role in facilitating a deeply meaningful contribution to humanity one day. Some of the most humanitarian people I know are wealthy beyond what many of us would be comfortable to dream. In the meantime, *having his sights focused on a future possibility helped our son live in a different way now.*

Are you dreaming so that your cells can conspire to "make it big" and attain radical health? Are your future dreams helping you live more lovingly in your body now? A Person of Radical Health loves and values their body and treats it as a holy ground, not a dumping ground. A Person of Radical Health values rest, recreation, love, and activities that fill and nourish the heart. A Person of Radical Health lets all that is good and sacred touch them and transform them and awaken the electrical, magnetic, and biochemical impulses that heal. Lock your sights on love, hope, healing, transformation, and peace.

As Johann Wolfgang von Goethe said, "The intelligent man finds almost everything ridiculous, the sensible man hardly anything." Don't let your intellect override genius nor let your cynicism override hope. George Bernard Shaw says, "Some people see things as they are and ask 'why?'; I dream things that never were and ask 'why not?'" Take a page out of a kids' book and shoot for the moon.

Let go of what is, and make room for what can be

Setting our inner GPS does not mean we barrel ahead toward one acceptable outcome with no regard to how the rest of the world is responding or to collateral damage collected along the way.

When my friend Karen found herself at emotional odds with her son and was permitted only limited contact with her grandson, she was frustrated, disappointed, and mad. The more she expressed her frustration to her son, the further he drew away, and the less he allowed Karen to see her grandson. As an afternoon to be spent alone with her son drew near, she asked me what she should do. Here was a case where setting a relationship destination on her internal GPS would be a help. But Karen wanted to use the time together to give her son a piece of her mind. As she protested to me, if she "set her GPS" sights on having a closer relationship with her son, and set aside her disappointment and anger over their relationship breakdown, she felt like that would be being inauthentic or untrue to herself. Rather, she felt she needed to lay her complaints out plainly on the table and resolve the issues point by point. She wanted satisfying answers given, and she wanted the situation resolved, fixed, and rectified. She felt that she had a right to be upset, given what she considered unacceptable behavior from him, and vowed to remain upset until he changed his ways. Yet intuitively, she knew he would withdraw even further from this approach.

The advice I gave to Karen was to get herself into Open Heart Consciousness with her son, no matter what. When I said it, she understandably scrunched up her face and said, "How do I do *that*?" I suggested she remember a time when she felt great love, connection and joy in her son's presence. I recommended that on their afternoon together, she come back to that feeling every time she was tempted to be angry and disappointed. Her son was perfectly aware of her anger, so drawing that feeling out at every visit as a sort of punishment or manipulative attempt to change the circumstance was not fulfilling her true objective-to be close to him. It was also not inspiring him to want to spend more time with her. She was trying to nail the issues down, to account for every upset point she had, and to get his agreement to act better in the future (signed in blood would be best), but in so doing it allowed no possibility for true healing to unfold out of good feelings shared together. She had to be willing to let go of what *is* to make room for what could *be*. She had to find peace in the present, a peace that was not dependent on his choices, whereby she could love him even when he was being "bad." She had to let go of the need to be vindicated for being right, and create a circumstance where true rightness—the closeness and connection she so craved—could develop.

When Lt. Jason Redman set his inner GPS, his will, tenacity, and refusal to accept any other outcome gave power and momentum to his body to heal. When Karen set her inner GPS to be close to her son, she had to find an inner willingness to move with the current of life and not fight so hard to wrestle the outcome she wanted out of the circumstance. You can't force love, but you can create the conditions that invite and nourish it. Instead of unwavering will and force, Karen needed to get to work building the good feelings that would over time more naturally result in her desired outcome. She had to learn to finesse, not force. Life asks of us to be artists with a depth of unique responses to our challenges, and not technicians with limited formulas for success when it comes to living fully. Karen later told me that it was hard to shift her attention back to the memories she had of times of closeness with her son, but she managed to do it every time her anger threatened to rise up that afternoon. As a result, she observed, they were able to laugh together for the first time in several years. By the end of their visit, the old warmth was flickering back. Over the next few months their relationship dramatically improved, and Karen was invited to spend one day a week with her grandson.

Engaging the inner GPS is a powerful tool when we set our destination well. Setting a destination well sometimes means looking past our immediate limitations, wants and desires to a bigger picture. In your own life, what bigger picture destination will draw you toward a vaster love, a greater peace, and a heart moved by all that is beautiful in life? Are you daydreaming a future destination now?

Rewire Your Neural Pathways of Emotion

Why is it easier to ruminate over hurt feelings than it is to bask in the warmth of feeling loved? Your brain was wired in such a way when it evolved, primed to learn quickly from bad experiences, but not so much from good ones. It's an ancient survival mechanism that turned the brain into Velcro for the negative, but Teflon for the positive.

Rick Hanson, Ph.D.
Hardwiring Happiness[84]

Sow a thought and you reap an action; sow an act and you reap a habit; sow a habit and you reap a character; sow a character and you reap a destiny.
Ralph Waldo Emerson

Great men are they who see that spiritual is stronger than any material force, that thoughts rule the world.
Ralph Waldo Emerson

Researcher Richard Davidson, director of both the Laboratory for Affective Neuroscience and the Waisman Laboratory for Brain Imaging and Behavior at the University of Wisconsin-Madison, has described the fact that our brain can learn states like happiness and compassion through cultivation. This learning is no different from the way that a person learns golf, basketball, or a musical instrument. Meditators in Davidson's lab have effectively increased activity in the left prefrontal cortex of the brain which is associated with happiness. They have also effectively suppressed activity of the right prefrontal cortex of the brain, which is more active with mood disorders. These changes were achieved through practicing happiness.

All skills are learned by practice because it is through practice that the brain develops neural pathways. Each time we think, do, or feel something, activity among neurons is stimulated in the brain. I once saw a video of the brain at work while a person was learning a new skill involving tapping a finger pattern. These two neurons that were near one another but not connected slowly began to "reach out" until in a sudden magical moment, they joined. It looked like two hands reaching toward one another to shake. They connected in the exact moment the subject mastered the complex pattern. Over time and with practice repeating the finger pattern, that one connection turns into a massive neural network. As that neural network grows stronger, the tapping pattern becomes easier to execute until the subject can do it effortlessly.

Many people may not realize that within our brains new neurons are born every day by way of a process called neurogenesis. While it was once believed that we are born with a static number of neurons that declined between birth and death, we now know that is not so. Even into old age our brain births new neurons every day. The brain instantly puts these new neurons into service of some sort. However, there is no executive function that makes a wise survey of our life to discern what best use we have for a new neural pathway. If it did, I'm sure I'd get new neural pathways supporting a greater love of exercise and a craving for spinach. This is *not* what happens. Based on what you already know, what do you think most influences these brand new baby neurons? What provides them the instruction for where to move into service?

The answer is *attention*. Whatever we are paying attention to, or practicing, is what our new neurons jump into the neural networking dance to support. If our attention is on the recurrent anxiety and worry that we've had all day, those newly birthed neurons immediately go about supporting greater anxiety. If what we've been doing is having a blast savoring the richness of life and languishing in our positive and resourceful feeling tone all day, our neurons link into and strengthen the neural networks that support continued positivity and resourcefulness.

One researcher contributing to this topic is Dr. Daniel Amen, who runs clinics all over the country and has published multiple books demonstrating the unique ability of the brain to rewire. Dr. Amen uses SPECT brain imaging technology with which he can tell whether a person is suffering from anxiety, depression, ADD, ADHD, bipolar disorder, or other non-optimal brain states merely by observing which part of the brain is misfiring. He found that the SPECT scan of a patient who receives proper treatment will show the brain firing correctly. Treatment may be through a medication, holistic remedy or modality, or even meditation and relaxation. Amen's most amazing finding is that *once properly treated, if the treatment is maintained for 6-24 months, brains often heal, and even after treatment is discontinued can sustain the change.*[85] Whereas previously we may have considered certain medications necessary for life, Amen has shown evidence that as the brain rewires and heals, there are cases where medications may be reduced or withdrawn while the brain maintains the positive benefit the drug conferred.

When we make Inner Molecules of Medicine in our brain and body through our thoughts and feelings, we too can permanently improve and rewire our brain. Meditators have been shown to have a thicker part of the brain called the *insula* than non-meditators. Meditators also show increased activity in the left pre-frontal cortex associated with happiness, and decreased activity of the right pre-frontal cortex common to mood disorders. We are not the victims of, but are to some large part *the creators of,* our own brain. The brain has no off switch, and thereby our mental and emotional states are always busy at work influencing whether we are bathed in a soup rich with Molecules of Medicine, or Molecules of Misery. The new term for the art of intentionally rewiring the brain is *self-directed neuroplasticity.* With this in mind, the brain truly seems more like a work of art, and we, the artists.

Henry David Thoreau said, "As a single footstep will not make a path on the earth, so a single thought will not make a pathway in the mind. To make a deep physical path, we walk again and again. To make a deep mental path, we must think over and over the kind of thoughts we wish to dominate our lives." Whatever we focus our attention on, we're going to get more of. Attention is a precious resource, and is limited. Give the sacred gift of your attention to those things that are worthy of that gift. Everything is participatory. What are you participating with?

Finding new neural pathways

My patient Sherry was faced with a cancer diagnosis and was doing as many holistic things to help herself as she could. She became particularly interested in exploring how to release her own stuck emotions. Grimacing, she told me, "I thought I dealt with this years ago in therapy." Yet when she thought back, she could identify "sick" feelings that arose in her gut when she remembered how lonely and abandoned she felt as a child. I was curious as to how she was setting out to "release" those feelings. The practice she had come to in the absence of any clear-cut direction to take was daily journaling. Yet she could tell by how she still felt that, "It wasn't working." I consider journaling a rich practice for anyone to commit to, yet I was concerned that her writing was wiring the neural network for "loneliness" ever more deeply into her brain.

Gently, I pointed out that loneliness is an inner state, not an outer condition. We can be surrounded by people who love us yet feel desperately lonely, and conversely we can be perfectly by ourselves, "traveling solo," and feel rich with connection to all of humanity. "Yes, that's what doesn't make any sense!" she exclaimed. "I was lonely, but surrounded by a family who was kind and loved me!" Slowly, a twinkling of understanding sparkled in her eyes. "You mean I was in part creating my own inner experience of loneliness!" As a child, Sherry had not been able to understand or make sense of the pervasive lonely feeling and so had looked to her circumstances as the "cause." She had not been able to find a way to change that pervasive feeling, and over time she had gotten better and better at "producing it." But with a wild realization of possibility, she recognized the gift that she could give herself now that she had not been able to give herself as a child: The gift of cultivating an inner state of connection.

By thinking back over her childhood with fondness, dwelling on the thoughts that brought a tear of gratitude to her eyes, feeling a swell of compassion in her heart, and acknowledging with a sympathetic realization that no one may have "gotten" her perfectly yet all were trying their best, she could draw forth a new set of truths from her experience. Instead of trying to "release" the emotions, she could use alchemy, and transform her inner biology by using the feeling of loneliness as the *reminder* to meditate on something more nourishing, more liberating and more *connected*. In a loving and artistic act of self-directed neuroplasticity, she could give herself the gift of inner healing that her parents had never figured out how to give her despite their genuine concern. As she "practiced" these new feelings, she could almost *feel* her neurons reach toward one another for that handshake connection as she mastered the new skill.

Eventually, new feelings wired into her neural pathways of emotion. Sherry was stunned to find freedom and release from a lifetime of feeling lonely. Once she found that freedom, she began combing through other memories that made her feel "sick." One had to do with driving past the building where her first husband was treated for cancer before he died. Another had to do with the memory of how she felt when her parents had died while she was still relatively young. She realized she could meet those memories with kindness and gentleness and still train her attention on her most cherished beautiful moments. She could savor her most treasured fond memories with her husband and parents, grateful that she had ever known them at all. She could feel grateful that such a loss had been important enough to ever make her feel sick.

With neurogenesis in full swing wiring new neural networks in support of the new direction of her attention, Sherry could soon think back over the span of her entire life and realized with relief that she could no longer find a single memory that made her feel "sick."

Dwell on What's Well

The minds of most human beings are like the sky on a partly cloudy day. The mental clouds may part for a time, and let in the sunlight of clarity, but unless those people deliberately seek out the bright spots and bask in their warmth, the clouds close in again, and hide behind mists of worldly karma the sunlight of clarity.

Swami Kriyananda (Donald J. Waters)
Conversations With Yogananda[86]

Fix your thoughts on what is true, and honorable, and right, and pure, and lovely, and admirable. Think about things that are excellent and worthy of praise.

Philippians 4:8

My friend Alan grew up in poverty in a foreign country. He had managed to get a university degree and become so gifted an artist that he'd been invited to live in another country as an artist-in-residence, though he had to decline because he couldn't afford the plane ticket. At the time, the only job he had been able to find in his impoverished country paid him a dollar a day and required an hour-long commute on a bus that cost him 35 cents. Yet he bubbled with peaceful joy and calm wisdom. When our other friend asked him how he stays so peaceful with so little, he said, "It's not that worried thoughts don't come to me, too. They come, and then I say a prayer deep from my heart, and then turn my attention back to all the blessings I have." He was teaching her how to *dwell on what's well.*

Called "differential focus on the good," many holocaust survivors, who beat what were considered impossible odds by surviving, were found to focus disproportionately on things like finding something small to eat or seeing a sunset. People who have the innate ability to be cheerful or find the good, irrespective of hardship, have been noted to engage an ability to hyper-focus on and sensationalize (engage the senses) on what is going well, and the simultaneous ability to de-focus or disregard or minimize what is not going well. This is reminiscent of the race car driver who only looks where he's going and never at the wall, or the Olympic athlete who only envisions executing the perfect performance every time, or the tightrope walker who never looks at the ground. It's just that sometimes we think we are doing the right thing by hyper-fixating on what is *wrong*. Even our most skilled and caring professionals might have us look at the wall or the ground in the name of good therapy, and be as surprised as we are when we crash.

Candace was a patient who came to me in the depressed phase of a serious case of bipolar disorder. She had been working with psychiatrists and psychologists for years, but still managed to fall into what she described as "the depths of despair" at fairly regular intervals, despite being on an impressive list of psychiatric medications. When Candace learned that I had once had the diagnosis of bipolar disorder myself but considered myself free of it for over 17 years, she very enthusiastically adopted a new regimen inspired by changes I had made.

Candace added a few vitamins based on research showing that activated B vitamins and larger doses of niacin may help. She reduced grains and gluten, and most importantly, she adopted a meditation practice in which she dwelled on a feeling of deep and holy joy in her heart for a few minutes a day. She took the practice on like prayer, spending those moments reflecting on the things for which she was grateful and allowing that feeling to wash over her heart and through her body.

For months Candace did phenomenally well. Her moods were steady, her spirits were good. Then one day she nearly dragged herself into my office—it looked like the electrical circuit breaker for her body had been shut "off." Her voice was slow and weak, her color was pale, and she sat heavily slumped. As I queried her on the events leading up to the crash, she was able to pinpoint an exact moment when she "went crazy," as she described it. Though she had been doing well and had not particularly felt a need for psychotherapy, she had "reported" to a scheduled appointment with her therapist because, as she explained, "that's what people with bipolar disorder are supposed to do." In the absence of any concrete problems to address, the therapist had suggested she write a list of all the people and events she had anger about and bring it to the next session so that they could work on forgiveness and release.

The moment Candace got home and dutifully began crafting this list, she was filled with overwhelming feelings of anger, upset, and dread. By the time she dragged herself in to me four days later, she was in the throes of a full blown depression, complete with helplessness, hopelessness, and an inability to get out of bed.

Luckily, Candace is smart and resourceful, and once she realized what had happened, she had a "release party" and burned the list. While trauma research shows that there is a place for "desensitization" of traumatic memories, for Candace, she had not made it to her return appointment with her psychologist in time to integrate the memories in a way that was desensitizing. The creation of the list had not furthered a sense of peace, empowerment or resolution. Instead, the act of dwelling on the perceived hurts and violations was experienced by her body as if she was reliving the pain all over again. Her body triggered a cascade of stress chemicals that walloped her as if the hurt or abuse were happening now.

Once Candace released her dark thoughts regarding a life filled with so many past hurts and violations, she was again able to regain a sense of peace and lightheartedness. Both things are true: her life is full of past hurts and violations, and it is full of present blessings and peace as well. Both statements are equally correct. However, when she focuses on the hurts and upsets, she feels so bad she can't get out of bed. When she lives in the awareness of her blessings, she creates exquisite art and music that touches hearts. Both ways of orienting to the circumstances of her life are true, but her experience is radically different depending on which "true" thing she dwells on. As Ernest Holmes says in *Words That Heal Today*, "The most effective way to displace a negative emotion is to find a positive one which absorbs it. Thus, hate is swallowed up by love and fear dies when enveloped in faith."[87] And as Thomas Bien advises, "Water the flowers, not the weeds."

Six months later it happened again. Candace loves her therapist and values her warm reassuring presence in her life. I don't blame her; I know her therapist personally and professionally, and love and respect her, too. Somehow, they both forgot how dwelling on her troubles had spun Candace into despair once before, because the therapist sent her off with similar homework. This time, the exercise was to write out the history of familial abuse in her life.

The therapist's intention was good. However, by the time Candace got to me she was again, in her words, "a wreck." There is no way to rewind history and erase the reality that Candace was hurtfully and wrongly abused as a child. When she relives it, remembers it vividly, and writes it on paper, her body experiences it as if it is happening now. Choosing not to dwell on hurts of the past is different from denial. In denial, we act like it never happened and repress our feelings. Denial is anti-acceptance, anti-meditative, and anti-transformative. In non-dwelling, we allow the hurts and tragedies of the past to shape us into the best person we can be. We allow our feelings to move us deeply to a better way. If we have been violated, we become champions for human dignity and rights. If we lived in chaos and terror, we become champions of peace. If we lived without love, we become champions of compassion and deep-hearted loving. *Without the experience of the one extreme, we would not so well know and passionately champion the other.*

Park the Mind

My fear grows fat on the energy I feed it.
Scilla Elworthy

Wisdom is the art of knowing what to overlook.
William James

Over time, Candace noticed that the longer she went without thinking about the traumas and tragedies of her childhood, the less hold they seemed to have on her. This is because neural networks take up precious real estate in the brain, and when our brain thinks we no longer need one, the synaptic connections slowly unlink, and new neural networks form in their place.

Nobel Prize winning neuropsychiatrist Eric Kandel found that unused neural connections begin to shrink in as few as *three weeks*. Remember, it is our attention that influences where newly birthed neurons go to service. This is why the strategy of non-dwelling has a distinctly valuable place in human healing. What we pay no attention to is eventually deemed boring by the brain. The brain then stops reinforcing that particular neural pathway. As Rick Hanson, Ph.D. describes in *Hardwiring Happiness*, "(L)ess active connections wither away in a process sometimes called neural Darwinism: the survival of the busiest."[88] It is our job to make our brain and heart busy with other things.

A patient of mine had taken some advanced level personal development classes and reported a technique with the opposite strategy, but similar outcome. In this training, they were asked to make a comprehensive list of every awful thing that had ever happened to them, much like Candace had done. Next, they were instructed to read the list to the other participants in the training. They were then instructed to read that list to others over and over until they became so excruciatingly bored with it that they never wanted to *talk or think* about those events again. In psychology, this is known as "flooding" or "prolonged exposure therapy" and is a way to reintegrate painful emotions with current awareness. As Wayne Dyer said, "You don't get killed by a snakebite, you get killed by the venom that keeps circulating through." Here was another means to free oneself from circulating venom.

What memory in your life captures your attention and hijacks your good feelings? What would help you get neurally bored with that memory? What if every time you thought of that event you used it as your reminder to practice a Feeling Mantra or Open Heart

Consciousness? That way, you pair the stimulus of the already charged state with a new elevated inner state. Eventually, like Pavlov's dogs who learned to salivate at the ringing of a bell, anything that reminds you of past trauma may now serve as a powerful trigger for an inner resourceful state.

Remember, whether you are making Molecules of Misery or Molecules of Medicine is determined by your focus. As Lissa Rankin, M.D. shares in *Mind Over Medicine*, "In addition to triggering the stress response, negative emotions also enhance the production of pro-inflammatory cytokines, leading to inflammation, which has been linked to certain cancers, Alzheimer's disease, arthritis, osteoporosis, and cardiovascular disease. Furthermore, negative feelings can contribute to delayed wound healing and infection."[89] Let's carefully attune our focus to the thoughts and feelings that heal.

Don't let the birds of sorrow build nests in your hair

In *Inner Skiing*, Timothy W. Gallwey and Bob Kriegel describe a simple exercise used to improve skiing: singing a song while taking a ski run. The effortless concentration that arises while skiing and singing is a result of what they call "parking the mind to music."[90] By distracting the mind, it is able to relax and release the anxious thoughts that interfere with peak skiing. When we park our mind to music, or anything else that helps it park, we recover a natural relaxation and halt the interference that a worried or anxious mind produces. Of course, parking the mind to Open Heart Consciousness or a Feeling Mantra while listening to exalting music would be even better!

Thinking about challenges beyond what is necessary for solutions rarely produces better outcomes. Instead, we produce more tension, more constraint, and less ability to handle challenges smoothly. As Eckhart Tolle points out in *The Power of Now*, "It's about realizing that there are no problems. Only situations–to be dealt with now or to be left alone and accepted as part of the 'isness' of the present moment until they change or can be dealt with. Focus your attention on the Now..."[91] And as an ancient Chinese proverb says, "You cannot prevent the birds of sorrow from flying over your head, but you can prevent them from building nests in your hair."

Stay in the present moment, flush the rest

One of the most exciting moments in my Qigong classroom happened when a woman named Tina with a schizophrenia diagnosis suddenly and deeply grasped the idea of self-directed neuroplasticity. The light bulb went off for Tina after viewing the movie *A Beautiful Mind*[92] one night after class. In the movie, John Nash (whose character is based on the real

90

John Nash, who is both a mathematical genius and schizophrenic) learned to reject his delusional thoughts and focus only on his rational scientific thoughts. He learned to ignore selected voices in his head, and in doing so was able to live more peacefully.

For Tina, this provided a new possibility that had her giddy with excitement. It suddenly didn't matter that the thoughts her brain produced were "crazy." It didn't matter that throughout the day her brain volunteered suggestions such as "You are stupid," "Everyone hates you," and "You are a terrible person." What she suddenly realized was that she could simply identify those *thoughts* as "crazy," and stay in the present moment as the thoughts passed by. She found that as she became better practiced at not engaging those thoughts, they popped into her head less and less. Her neural network began to drop a neural superhighway that had been grooved in place for over 70 years.

Not engaging thoughts does not mean denial or discounting, but it does mean not adding momentum to an upset by reliving it repetitively in our thoughts and feelings. It means giving our focus to what nourishes us, and not to what activates the biochemicals of distress and disease. It is realizing that we have a choice in every moment, and selecting carefully what we attend to. William James observed, "Our acts of voluntary attending, as brief and fitful as they are, are nevertheless momentous and critical, determining us, as they do, to lower or higher destinies."

There are creative ways for lessening the grips of a neural superhighway. An old time hypnosis strategy for releasing negative feelings is to see the feeling as a shape, insert the shape into a helium balloon, and let that balloon fly far, far away. Another is to focus on the image of the feeling you'd like to release in your mind's eye, and increase the brightness of that image until you can literally "white it out." Yet another time-tested technique is to mentally light a fire in your mind and let the flame consume the distressing thoughts. One more is to let unwanted thoughts float on a river and watch them float past and away. Perhaps the most entertaining method was pioneered by sports psychologist Aimee Kimball, Ph.D. with the UCLA softball team. They put a fake toilet in the dugout and instructed players to come in after each inning to "flush that inning away." All of these methods help us release the mental distractions that keep us from being free and present in the moment.

A technique I used to use before I knew the positive power of a Feeling Mantra was to wander around muttering to myself, "Cancel, cancel" while breathing slowly and deeply whenever anxious or worried thoughts would start circulating in my mind. No amount of therapy or psychiatric drugs over a 10-year period had helped me release chronic anxious thoughts. By interrupting their unceasing "run" cycle, the thoughts eventually faded out after a few months.

Begin to distinguish between the worry that comes from habit, versus worry requiring action or insight. When it comes to reflexive worry, I take inspiration from Corrie ten Boom who had experience parking her mind on her blessings and the grace of God amidst the horror of a concentration camp. She wrote, "Worry does not empty tomorrow of its sorrow, it empties today of its strength."

Sing in the angels

It is easy to worry when we are applying a logical, rational, linear, analytical consciousness to our health. But I know a woman who is 80 years old who was pronounced "eminently close to death" 30 years ago and yet is vibrantly healthy today. When Jane told me her story, I must say even I was startled, and I'm a deep believer in miracles.

Jane had been stricken with a virus called cytomegalovirus that did not respond to the treatments her caring doctor provided her. Jane was so ill the doctor said she should prepare herself for the end. In a last rally of hope, her husband took her to an acupuncturist. After a thorough examination, he too offered her no hope, but even worse, offered a treatment unknown to me that he called "Last Rites." They hastily declined and went home to prepare for the inevitable.

Jane was a woman who was deeply loved by her church community. She was known for her glorious lark-like singing voice that rang out as if angels were in the room during hymns. Her church community had been praying for her day and night. In her pained anguish, the pastor had been asking everyone she knew to pray for Jane who "sung in the angels" for the congregation every Sunday. Moved by the pastor's words, an unknown benefactor acting on sudden inspiration pre-paid $10,000 to the Hippocrates Health Institute in Florida so that Jane could get a comprehensive month-long regimen of holistic care. In wonderment and gratitude, Jane accepted and went. She ate a raw foods diet, detoxified her body, and had daily massage and bodywork. At the end of a month, she was well. Cynics may snicker and wonder, "A $10,000 benefactor? That would never happen for me." But the truth is, when we focus our attention on "singing in the angels" instead of hearkening unto our worries, anything is possible.

Amputate Phantom Limbs

We are what we think. All that we are arises with our thoughts. With our thoughts we make the world.
Buddha

My friend Judy told me a story about her mother whom she described as a "chronic hoarder." Her mom had no money to do the things she wanted to do, yet paid a monthly fee on a storage unit filled with old magazines she hadn't had a chance to read. She had even paid movers once to move an irreparably broken washing machine across the country when she relocated. She just could not let the broken down old machine go.

Hoarding broken down machines is one way of cluttering the present. When thoughts, behaviors and feelings clutter or compromise current quality of life, and parking the mind is not enough, sometimes a more radical action is called for.

Amputate phantom limbs, moods, and thoughts

In the world of chronic pain, there are patients who suffer from something called "phantom limb" pain. A person with phantom limb pain is both missing a limb, and experiencing agonizing pain where the limb once was. This condition is considered one of the most difficult chronic pain syndromes to treat. How can a person feel pain in a limb that isn't even there? Because you know something about neural wiring, you can probably quickly guess the answer to this. Plain and simple, the brain has formed a neural pain superhighway and keeps replaying the pain loop, trigger no longer necessary.

Dr. Vilayanur S. Ramachandran is a leading researcher on the phantom limb pain phenomenon. He developed a novel approach for treatment of this otherwise difficult to treat condition. He developed what he called a "mirror box" which consists of a small box in which a patient can "insert" their phantom limb. On the side of the box closest to their unaffected (healthy) limb is a mirror. By moving the unaffected limb up close to the mirror and then tapping patterns or making intricate finger movements so that a reflection appears where the other hand "should" be, the brain is tricked into thinking it is seeing two healthy hands. With just a few minutes of practice a day, subjects almost universally experience lasting relief from pain within a month. The brain literally rewires in response to the new input, and the treatment can be discontinued once this occurs. The brain, thinking it now has two well-functioning hands, ceases to fire the panicked pain loop. Subjects, in effect, "amputate" their phantom limb.

Our brains get stuck in loops of all kinds and pain is only one of them. Sometimes we have to amputate a phantom limb, and sometimes, we have to amputate a phantom mood or thought. Is your brain stuck in a loop or hoarding a thought, mood, or feeling you'd be better off without?

Amputate reflexive feelings before they fire

My brain has been stuck in many loops in my lifetime. But what do you do if your brain is stuck in a loop and you are *asleep*? It can require some creative mental Jiu Jitsu to figure out how to rewire a brain that isn't even awake.

From the time I was six years old until 28 years of age, my sleep was marked by nightmares that produced a terror so intense that it took hours before I could shake the fear enough to fall back asleep. This happened night after night. I would have some stretches of a few weeks or months at a time without any nightmares, but ultimately they would appear again, wreaking havoc with my sleep. Over the years I tried anti-anxiety pills, sleeping pills, benzodiazepines, herbs, Chinese constitutional herbs, acupuncture, homeopathic remedies, massage, vigorous exercise, and many types of therapy to find relief. The nightmares persisted.

One day an acupuncturist said something to me that would spell the end of decades of recurrent terrors at night. What he told me I later found out was practically a cliché from the realm of psychology and dream study, yet it worked. He explained to me that the terrorizer in the dream was symbolically *me,* and that I should pay close attention to who in my life I was treating in the way I was being treated in the dreams.

That night, I was awakened with the usual forceful fear and terrorizing images but immediately turned my attention to the detail of the dream. As I wracked my brain trying to identify the exact nature of the distress and to whom I might possibly be causing a similar distress, I attained a weirdly detached vantage point on the dream world. Though frustrated that I couldn't identify a similarity, I easily fell back to sleep within a few minutes. It happened the same way the next night, only this time I decided there was no one I was metaphorically chasing or intimidating or frightening. By thinking about my dream in that detached way, my thinking mind had kicked in before the reflexive anxiety pathway fired off, and so had aborted the adrenaline surge. I had effectively interrupted the biochemical cascade from its wired habit. Though I have since had a few instances of strange or intense dreams, I never had recurrent nightmares again.

When our brain has gotten stuck in a rut and is firing the same old overwhelm, anxiety, anger, or depression signals over and over again, an amputation is in order. Here is yet another way to refocus attention on a different thought leading to a different feeling, whereby we can eventually rewire the brain to habitually fire a different signal. The next time you are caught in a reflexive mood or habitual non-optimal feeling state, engage your best creativity and find a way to amputate it.

Find the Inner Jewel of Joy

Lean toward joy.
In every moment in which you have a choice, which is most moments, lean
toward the movement, the land, the people, the sound, the work, the gesture
that will most fill you with that sense of joy rushing through you.
Maria Sirois

I want a life that sizzles and pops and makes me laugh out loud. And I don't
want to get to the end, or to tomorrow, even, and realize that my life is a
collection of meetings and pop cans and errands and receipts and dirty
dishes. I want to eat cold tangerines and sing out loud in the car with the
windows open and wear pink shoes and stay up all night laughing and paint
my walls the exact color of the sky right now. I want to sleep hard on clean
white sheets and throw parties and eat ripe tomatoes and read books so good
they make me jump up and down, and I want my everyday to make God belly
laugh, glad that he gave life to someone who loves the gift.
Shauna Niequest
Cold Tangerines: Celebrating the Extraordinary Nature of Everyday Life[93]

Blissful joy is an inner jewel that is our birthright. Yet amidst the challenges of modern life, it is rarely sustained unless cultivated. It can't be faked, and when it is present, it sparkles more brightly than any earthmade jewel. It is a manmade jewel, and is made through the focused inner alchemy of transforming all of the troubles inherent to the human drama into a powerfully one-pointed Open Heart Consciousness. Life serves as the guru, and when marked by stress, relationship breakdowns, fluctuating moods and a pressing sense of inner discontent, this is feedback that our inner practice is insufficient to nourish joyous bliss. Though we may continually attempt to distract ourselves with outer pursuits, the discontent is never relieved until this inner jewel of joy is recovered. As long as we continue with the delusion that our inner state is dependent upon outer variables, we will change jobs, marriages, houses, hobbies, and our looks in attempts to relieve inner discomfort.

Improving outer variables as a path to inner joy never works. In fact, the better one is at playing the outer game, sometimes the harder it is to cultivate the inner jewel. Two people I know who set out on contrasting paths illuminate this fact well.

"The Everything Man" and "The No-thing Woman" are the stories of two people who awakened me keenly to the importance of never postponing the cultivation of the inner jewel of joy. The Everything Man's story illuminates some of the ways we may get captured in habits of thinking, living, and being that move us farther and farther from true joy. The narrative of the No-thing Woman calls us back to the true meaning of fulfillment and success.

I nicknamed these two "Everything" and "No-thing" both to summarize their economic reality, and to ultimately demonstrate that what we think of as everything, and nothing, may be quite opposite from what we expect. As Meister Eckhart advises, "To be full of things is to be empty of God. To be empty of things is to be full of God." Freeing oneself from unnecessary accumulation and commitments clears more space in our hearts and our consciousness to be filled with the inner jewel of joy.

My HeartMindBody and peak performance consulting work puts me in touch with interesting people from all over the country, and I was contacted by the Everything Man at the suggestion of a former client of mine. My client felt that our work around meditation and opening his heart had made a marked difference in his stressful and high-paced business life, and that both his work and home life creativity and problem solving were enhanced. He wanted such an opening for his friend. My client advised me that his friend had *everything* we commonly strive for in this culture. He explained that this friend was handsome, wealthy, intelligent, charismatic and in excellent health. He had done what any of us who is good at everything might do, and had married a gorgeous, kind woman, started a delightful family and become ultra-successful in his business. He had become a philanthropic pillar of his community, receiving many awards and accolades in domains both business and personal.

The Everything Man, as I came to think of him, played prominent roles on multiple boards of businesses and was active in fund-raising in his church. By every measure of success in our society, he had reached the top. How irresistible would it be to check off absolute success in every domain valued by most people? By such measures, he had it made. Yet my client had made the referral because he knew his friend was in deep trouble.

On the advice of his respected colleague, The Everything Man reluctantly contacted me. In our one consult, he confessed to me that he was miserable. He told me that he had been striving for satisfaction for decades, thinking that it was just around the next corner. Because he was looking for inner satisfaction through the pursuit of external milestones, satisfaction had been maddeningly elusive. He awoke one morning feeling trapped by his life and all of the obligations and expectations he felt saddled with. He could not conceive of a way to find joy and peace in the context of a life that he now perceived as unbearably stressful.

I worked with him to explore new ways of thinking, feeling, and being, ways that would feed his heart, not his ambition. We looked to find the treasures and beauty hidden under the "trappings" of his success. But The Everything Man felt so trapped in upholding his image as a successful man that he considered any changes impossible. He had used everything he had to "get to the top" and was now facing the realization that his efforts had left him frazzled and empty. He felt he had no energy or inspiration left with which to change, and no hope for ever finding the elusive feeling of satisfaction he thought success would bring.

In stark contrast, The No-thing Woman falls far short of the great American expectation of success. She has chosen to live in a small condo and drives an old car that is missing two hubcaps. Her husband is in prison serving a life sentence. She lives with very few material possessions. Though she is self-employed with a clientele that hungers for her services, she works only enough to cover her few material needs, reserving the rest of her time for volunteering helping others. The No-thing Woman battled obesity her whole life until cancer treatment reduced her ability to swallow, making eating difficult for her. She had overcome uterine cancer years before. Then, Stage IV throat cancer and the side effects of her treatment had prompted her to seek acupuncture treatment with me. As if all this were not hardship enough, she lives with both a Thoracic aortic aneurysm that could cause her to rapidly bleed to death, and a brain aneurysm that might leak or rupture at any moment, causing a stroke or debilitating mental or physical injury.

The No-thing Woman has served on several boards, one a University and another a non-profit for the homeless, and with her keen intellect and infectiously warm personality has had every opportunity to be very materially successful. Instead, she made a choice at a certain point in her life to leave striving and accolades behind in favor of what she described as "a simpler life that left room to be connected to God." With her high energy and easy mastery of technology, she could have collected many accomplishments and accolades. Yet instead she has chosen to use her time and passion to impact those less fortunate: the homeless, low income seniors, and the underprivileged children she works with on a one-to-one basis. I tell all of this not to glorify her selfless service, but to glorify something of how The No-thing Woman relates to her hardships, which we could call exceedingly difficult or unfortunate.

At any point along the way, if the No-thing Woman were to be consumed with worry, bitterness, depression, or any of the host of emotions we associate with misfortune, we would have excused her. Many people would expect this, given her health circumstances. Instead, this woman has an absolutely profound sense of abundance and blessings, of being taken care of and of being delightfully in the flow of the mysterious unfolding of life. She is connected to God and radiates joy, humor and good will to all she touches. She is like a light that the fireflies, including me, cannot resist. We are nourished in her presence. People speak her name with a reverence, in awe of her ability to tap into the Divine and share love as she does. The No-thing Woman requires nothing of her external circumstances to sustain her inner joy and peace.

In our time together, I would observe that the No-thing Woman could always find something meaningful, interesting or joyous about circumstances over which the average person would despair. She would exclaim, "The Universe is plotting in my favor!" When things got particularly hard, she'd say, "Hmm, That's an interesting way for God to send a blessing." Instead of despairing over the hardships, she would spend time looking for that hidden blessing.

Her doctor had recommended long-term disability insurance to her, knowing that her brain aneurism was likely not to kill her but to do just enough damage to eventually, as he described, land her in a nursing facility requiring around-the-clock care. Knowing she couldn't afford this insurance, she declared to me that she was choosing her own insurance: "The choice to be happy in a nursing facility. The choice to find one person there who is nice and choose to be happy about that one person. In turn, maybe it will brighten up the whole place!" She then remarked, "You don't need to be clean or well-fed to be happy. Rather, I can choose joy no matter what."

The No-thing Woman finds riches in circumstances where joy is easily overlooked and in response to which many of us might permit ourselves a permanent state of misery and self-pity. She intentionally lives a life of abundant peace and contentment. The Everything Man, who found riches in health, wealth and notoriety, and who had every marker of a "happy" successful life, could ultimately never reach a place of internal satisfaction and peace. A year after our one fruitless consult, he committed suicide.

The moment we think we need the external conditions of our life to be a certain way to find the inner jewel of joy, is the moment we step onto the gerbil wheel on which the Everything Man exhausted himself and then perished. How long will we delay our ability to declare life beautiful, abundant and fulfilling just as it is? How long will we hold out on our connection with love and all that is sacred, awaiting the attainment of some future goal or the improvement of the conditions of our life? How long will we rush and strive and tighten our muscles against the flow of life, in search of something that truly comes from slowing down, surrendering to the mystery, and softening into it? As Tracy Goss offers in *The Last Word on Power*, "No matter how much you strive, you never connect all the dots of fulfillment."[94] Fulfillment comes from within, and is a choice. Start cultivating an inner fulfillment that is not hooked to circumstances right now, if you haven't already. Find the inner jewel of joy.

Break up With Normal

The day I broke up with Normal was the first day of my magical life.
Unknown

An absolutely startling number of cancer patients seeking acupuncture come to me in their 20s. One such young woman named Cara came to me in remission from a brain cancer that had been deemed incurable. She had accepted emergency surgery as the only conventional treatment despite the recommendation that she undergo chemotherapy and radiation. She had been following The Gerson Therapy in all its details, including daily coffee enemas and a largely organic vegetarian diet consumed in juiced portions every hour. Cara was one of the most motivated and diligent people I have ever met. Her continued remission is considered impossible by the medical profession, and yet she has defied the odds. Despite her unbelievable experience of spontaneous healing, Cara couldn't stop worrying whether the cancer would return.

The brain surgery had left Cara with seizures that required her to use an anti-seizure medication despite attempts to manage them naturally. The medication worked beautifully and without side effects: an incredible second miracle. She had come to peace with using the drug, but was frightened that it might stop working after her doctor suggested the medicine may lessen the possibility of seizures but was no guarantee. What would it be like to never know when or if you might have a seizure; with no warning to suddenly experience total instant loss of control? Once touched by cancer, seizures, or any unusual functioning of our body, how do we go on with living fully, free from fear, and with joy?

In hopes of helping, I told Cara the story of the No-thing Woman, who had not only had a cancer that could recur, but also an unpredictable and potentially fatal aneurism in her brain. The No-thing Woman manages to live not in the grips of worry, fear, or distress, but rather dances through life with an openhearted abundant glee. The expression "don't die with the music still in you" reminds me of how she lives each moment. Her music rings out to the benefit of everyone who comes in contact with her. I wished for Cara this same freedom, and this same relief. To hear and be moved by the No-thing Woman's story and her attitude toward hardship is one thing, but the ability of any of us to figure out how to make it our own is quite another.

How could I help Cara find the freedom the No-thing Woman had found? How could I help her heart leap with hope rather than anxiety, and help her thoughts dwell on all the ways her life was still rich with possibility? How could I help her to dance free, while knowing it

100

may all end in an instant, as it may for any of us? Grappling spiritually, mentally, and emotionally with a serious medical illness is one of the most challenging things that any of us may ever do.

The No-thing Woman, whose real name is Normale (pronounced Norma Lee) gave me permission to share her name, both with Cara, and here. In the course of conversation one day, I said to Cara, "Anyone would understand what you are going through and would consider it perfectly normal to feel intense worry and fear. "But," I practically shouted, "Do you want Normal, or do you want NORMALE?!" We laughed so hard the tears streamed down our faces. Through laughter, we purged the spell-like grip of fear and worry, blasting open the gateway to Open Heart Consciousness. As the Hawaiian Kahuna shaman had foretold, "the 'laughter of God' shatters the ridiculousness of hopelessness."

Several days later, I sent Cara an email, telling her that the Great Divine Intelligence must be determined that she permanently trade Normal for Normale. In my inbox that morning had arrived a photograph that was one of those images that speaks a thousand words. The woman pictured had a look shining from her that no "pose" could have imparted. From her inner state arose an expression of face that was at once wise, sexy in a tastefully shocking way, and free. This was a purposeful, meaningfully engaged woman who knew her own sacred beauty and the beauty of life in an earthy, real way. I found the image riveting. The caption read, "The day I broke up with Normal was the first day of my magical life."

We all must break up with Normal. Breaking up with Normal takes practice, commitment, and diligence. It is the decision to pass on the temptations of worry, fear, and upset even when they are so familiar, so justified, and so reflexive. It is opening to life even when it is all too inviting to shut down and contract. It is finding laughter, lightness of being, playfulness, and joy even when life is impossibly hard. It is consciously living in the space of magic and laughter, even when it seems that all is lost.

Never Stare at a Bad Guy's Back

Reality is not a given; it is a possibility that we shape and control.
Deepak Chopra
Creating Health[95]

My friend Ann once told me that she believed the biggest secret to a happy marriage is the cultivation of the ability to adore your spouse no matter what. She told me that for more than 50 years of marriage, every day when he woke up, her husband would enthusiastically and genuinely say to her with a twinkle in his eye, "I am so glad to see you this morning."

When we take the time to create a blanket of good feelings around our family and our community, every person can thrive in ways that may be impossible otherwise. The invisible blanket of love acts as a silent fertilizer, enriching each person's good heart. People literally burst into bloom when fertilized with unconditional love; it's amazing to behold. Because of my friend Ann, in our house we now greet each other in the morning with the same twinkling salutation, "I am so very happy to see you this morning, my love!"

One day I was discussing this topic with my friend who is a retired Navy SEAL. I was describing to him my belief that our thoughts and feelings literally change matter. I mentioned to him that I believe both positive and critical thoughts have an energy to them and influence the ability of others to reach their personal best. To my amazement, he nodded. Though I had thought he might find the topic a little "woo woo," I couldn't have been more wrong.

My friend's response was most unexpected. He told me that any good SEAL knows that you should "Never stare at a bad guy's back." As he explained, when tensions are high and you are training the sight of your gun on a sniper who has just killed 30 people, and you've got only one chance to make sure his career in killing is over for good, you have to "look softly" through the sight. Otherwise, if you stare too hard, they "feel it" and move.

Every thought we think and feeling we feel carries an energy that shapes and influences our experience and the experience of those around us. Even if we are acting politely, if we are thinking thoughts of annoyance, dislike, disgust, or frustration, it subtly affects those around us. Often, our recriminatory thoughts and feelings are moods we harbor when people habitually don't do things the way we would like. Expectations like "he always..." or "she always..." cause us to brace for the predictable worst that we are sure is coming. Yet those expectations can be felt. Like my SEAL friend described, and as Peter Ragnar alludes to in *The*

Awesome Science of Luck, "Your consciousness is a subtle form of matter that allows your physical sight to be a subtle form of touch." [96]

J. Allen Boone wrote in *Kinship With All Life,* describing his time as a companion to the show dog Strongheart, "No matter where I happen to be or what I am doing, my mind is always much more on display than my physical body and the clothes I happen to be wearing. Neither my inner life nor his inner life nor the inner life of any other living thing is private or concealable. We are all mental nudists, always on public display for all to freely observe and evaluate." [97] When we interact with others with a motive to fix or change them, or with dislike or criticism as our fundamental orientation, it is felt as well as a gunman's stare. Boone went on to say, "(O)ne's thinking, in all its nakedness, always precedes him and accurately proclaims his real nature and intention." [98]

If a child, a spouse, or a co-worker is acting in a way that is disappointing or frustrating to you, don't "stare" at it with a triumphant, "There it is!" Take inspiration from my friend Ann's husband and find an authentic feeling of gladness that you can share with that person. Remember that most people want to bring their best game to the challenges of life, and most people flourish in a climate of love. Let your consciousness be their silent fertilizer.

Avoid Voodoo Death: Ignore the Bone or See a Shaman

While most of us are aware of the healing influences of the placebo effect, few are aware of its evil twin, the nocebo effect. Just as surely as positive thoughts can heal, negative ones—including the belief we are susceptible to an illness or have been exposed to a toxic condition—can actually manifest the undesired realities of those thoughts.
Bruce H. Lipton Ph.D., and Steve Bhaerman
Spontaneous Evolution[99]

Voodoo Death, a term coined by Walter Cannon M.D. in 1942, describes a phenomena from aboriginal societies known as "death by cursing." If a witch doctor operating in a culture that believes in such things points a "cursing" bone at someone, it is societally accepted that the person will soon die. The "victim" usually complies with expectations within 24 hours to a week! This is the HeartMindBody connection and the internal apothecary at its deadliest.

Our culture has its own versions of the cursing bone. I once had a patient who's aggressive, advanced lymphoma completely disappeared. She had come to me as a last resort after undergoing chemotherapy, four lengthy hospitalizations for more extensive infusions, and a bone marrow transplant, all of which had failed. When she later excitedly told her doctor that she attributed the disappearance of her cancer to our meditation, acupuncture, and hands-on energy healing, she told me he shouted at her, "If you believe that, you are crazy! What you had is a spontaneous remission, and the thing about spontaneous remissions is, the disease always recurs!" We had some serious counter-witch doctoring to do to free her from that voodoo curse. Five years later under the surveillance of a new, optimistic, miracle-receptive oncologist, her scans still show no trace of cancer.

Another patient of mine went to a chiropractor who told her that her spine had been through so much trauma that she was very vulnerable and should be careful all the time. She told me that she realized she was acting like a cripple after that proclamation, so she fired him. She didn't need anyone to free her of the cursing bone, she freed herself. In honor of her chutzpah, I gave her a nickname she loved: The Sassy Lassy!

A student of mine told me that when her doctor told his European grandmother she had three months to live (20 years before she died) she brassily shouted at him what translates to,

"Go shit in the sea!" Sometimes we have to "think outside the hex" and fire people, shout heartily, and throw the cursing bone far out to sea. If your health care provider doubts the possibility of making Inner Molecules of Medicine through Feeling Mantra as a significant factor in your healing, gently suggest they seek treatment for their Divine Deficit Disorder. Be a statistical oddity demonstrating a different outcome by embracing an inner state as one of the most critical aspects of your treatment.

Many drugs may prolong life or manage symptoms, but by and large do not promote healing. Anyone authentically in search of healing is not going to be satisfied with disease management, but rather is going to seek out true means of healing. Don't let your faith in things that heal be minimized by the loud voice of an industry that wants your monthly co-pay.

Not everyone is as fierce as the Sassy Lassy or the Brassy Grandma, and sometimes words like those of a careless chiropractor or an ominous oncologist sink deeply into our psyche and are difficult to shake. If upon surveying your life you notice there is a bone, real or metaphorical, pointing at you and you can't ignore it, do what any savvy tribal person knows to do. Bring in a shaman! Whether it's a cultural assumption defining your health or the careless yet powerful words of a doctor, don't hesitate to call in a second opinion. If you are dissatisfied with a diagnosis or prognosis and believe there may be a better way, find someone of equal or greater wisdom authority who believes something different is possible for you. This may be another doctor, a mental health practitioner, a neighbor, or a stranger on the bus. It doesn't matter who the "shaman" is, it matters that they believe powerfully in a different outcome for you. Work with them until you deeply believe in a new future reality for yourself. Do not complacently accept the curses of the careless people around you. Practitioners "bone" their patients every day, including holistic practitioners like the acupuncturist who wanted to do "Last Rites" for the woman who ultimately healed from cytomegalovirus.

Excise a psychic hex with psychic surgery

When a sweet couple came to me for help with fertility, I spent an hour doing a very thorough intake and assessment. This woman had given birth before, but seven long years had passed and the infertility center she consulted could find no reason for such a prolonged spell of infertility. After my assessment, I told her I could find no reason from my holistic lens to explain her infertility either, and so based on past cases I had treated like hers, I suspected she may in fact become pregnant very quickly. She looked at me directly and confidently stated, "Oh, I know I'll be pregnant soon, my psychic told me I would. But, she told me I'd need to have a surgery first, and I can't imagine what surgery that might be."

I stared at her a long moment, considering my options. Though ultimately optimistic, this psychic had planted what I considered in that moment to be a voodoo hex of a sort. I was concerned that my patient so believed in the necessity of this mysterious unidentified surgery, that potentially extensive unseen processes were likely at work in her body assuring that her biochemistry would comply with the powerful proclamation. If I ignored the "hex" and treated her with acupuncture, it could take months or years to override those potent words. I suddenly saw how I might use this voodoo hex to my advantage.

Though this couple was demure and quiet and what I intended to do was a little wild and outside the lines of conventionality, I overrode all hesitancy and explained to them in a tone half joking that they were in luck as I had "recently attained some expertise as a *psychic surgeon.*" The couple chuckled, said that a psychic surgery sounded perfect, and asked if we could do it straightaway. Figuring a psychic surgery for an infertile woman would be best done over the abdomen, I hovered my hands there, hoping the required action or intervention would make itself known.

Suddenly as if seized by an invisible force, I grabbed at something dark and cold near the region of her belly button, and borrowing poetic inspiration from Walt Whitman, I belted out my *most barbaric YAWP* as a I flung whatever the thing was, away. In a matter of seconds, it was over. Though none of us were really even sure what constituted a psychic surgery, we enthusiastically agreed an effective one had clearly been done—we had literally perceived something come out of her belly. The couple left in good spirits, but they never called for a return visit. I figured I'd scared the hell out of them.

Twelve weeks later I got an ecstatic email. My patient was 11 weeks pregnant. She had waited that long to tell me because it took a sonogram to confirm the baby; her body had not shown the usual first trimester increase in human chorionic gonadotrophin associated with pregnancy. Perhaps babies conceived by "psychic surgery" need not comply with our biological rules. Seven months later, I cradled that tiny miracle baby in my arms. Though he was only a few weeks old when I first held him, a time when many babies have a glazed look in their eyes, a photograph captures him peering up at me with a look of complete recognition. In some strange way, I felt like I knew him too.

While we can never be totally certain what reversed my patient's long stretch of infertility, conventional intervention had not been successful. Voodoo death, cursing by bone, and hexing of patients, while often unintentional, are powerful and real phenomena. Sometimes we need to take powerful action to undo their impact. May we all become better practitioners of the art of spreading helpful healing hexes for one another.

Remember, if you have been accidentally hexed, cursed, or boned you may be surprised by who may be able to help you. The most unexpected people can become momentary shamans or psychic surgeons. Clearly, neither training, practice, nor experience are prerequisites for effective curse lifting.

Find No Mind

Any movement we make in skiing—or in anything else, for that matter—requires literally hundreds of instantaneous instructions from the nervous system to different muscle groups in our bodies. Who is doing all this? Whoever, it is certainly a lot more sophisticated and competent than a nagging Self 1 who, thinking it is in control, keeps yelling, "Bend your knees, stupid!"

Timothy Gallwey and Bob Kriegel
Inner Skiing [100]

The aim of this exercise (the Taoist method of The Secret of the Golden Flower for clarifying the mind) is to free the mind from arbitrary and unnecessary limitations imposed upon it by habitual fixation on its own contents. With this liberation, Taoists say, the conscious individual becomes a "partner of creation" rather than a prisoner of creation.

Thomas Cleary
The Secret of the Golden Flower: The Classic Chinese Book of Life [101]

When you are in this "no thought" state, you become very relaxed, and can even relax deep down into your internal organs. When your body is this relaxed, your Qi will flow smoothly and strongly. This kind of still meditation was very common in ancient Chinese scholar society.

Dr. Yang Jwing-Ming
Qigong Meditation: Embryonic Breathing [102]

Tennis coach Timothy W. Gallwey says to his students, "(I)f your body knows how to hit a forehand, then just *let it happen;* if it doesn't, then *let it learn.*" [103] He goes on to describe, "When a player experiences what it means to 'let go' and allows Self 2 [No Mind] to play the game, not only do his shots tend to gain accuracy and power, but he feels an exhilarating sense of relaxation even during rapid movements." [104] What Gallwey calls "Self 2" is a state I call No Mind where our body figures out how to do things that our brain simply can't effectively instruct it to do.

My earliest experience in understanding the HeartMindBody connection occurred when I was 10 years old. Because of the paralysis I had on the right side of my body, I was particularly clumsy and lacking in athleticism. Over the years I had broken fingers several times due to my inability to correctly determine where in time and space my contracted fingers were when balls came toward me. A large helping of anxiety combined with clumsiness resulted in consistently unspectacular sports performance.

One day my inspired dad set out to help me. We began a practice of catch with a lacrosse stick and ball. Dad wisely discerned that a large part of the problem at that point was my mind: I didn't *think* I'd be able to catch a ball. He instructed me to "think" the ball into the net. As he put it, "forget about trying to catch the ball. Just see it landing in there!" He instructed me to leave it to my reflexes (cellular intelligence) to figure out the coordinated series of movements. Without calling it such, he was pointing to No Mind. What I had to do was identify my intention, relax, and *let it happen*.

The result was nothing short of miraculous. After just a moment of practice "thinking the ball into the net" I could consistently catch most of the balls my dad threw. Even better, I never broke a finger trying to catch a ball again.

In what ways in life are we "trying" to do and be things that are best left to our cellular intelligence? In what ways are we failing to guide that cellular intelligence through the power of our thoughts and intentions and then relaxing with the trust that our body can do it? In what ways are we forgetting to relax and "think the ball of our health" into the net?

Remember, we know from race car drivers that if you don't want to hit the wall you only look where you are going. We know from Olympic athletics that you envision perfect performance. And we know from tightrope walking that you never look at the ground. Why do we forget these things with our health? Instead we indulge speculations on how awful a lifetime of dealing with our symptoms will be. We tend to think about every possible thing that might next go wrong, or ponder the ways we are likely to deteriorate. We endlessly search on the Internet purportedly seeking to "understand" a diagnosis but instead of sorting for the hopeful we fixate on the awful and finish with a mind and heart filled with dread. Were we a race car driver irresistibly compelled to glance at the wall, we'd be toast.

While working more recently to rehabilitate the tightness in my right hand and arm with my friend who is a personal trainer, we realized that my hand and arm are the best meditation and biofeedback monitors available. The moment I drop into the space of deep, trancelike meditation, or No Mind, my hand and arm then drop all trace of tension. But when I think, even a whisper of a thought, I involuntarily tense. In some traditions, a meditation master walked around with a bamboo rod to whip students back to No Mind. With so much "arm jerk" reactivity to even the faintest, most pleasant thoughts, there was no chance I could delude myself that I was maintaining No Mind when I'd lost it. I learned more about meditation in an hour working with my tense hand as my teaching advisor than I had in years of workshops, trainings, research, and practice of meditation.

My aim was to rewire my brain to relax into a state of No Mind where I could carry on with the thinking and acting of life *without* tensing the hand. This is the Taoist way of "doing without doing." Ironic as it is that the space of No Mind I was after is a non-striving inner state, my busy mind needed something to do. The moment I began focusing on my breath and lengthening and deepening my breathing pattern, listening to the ocean-like sounds instead of my thoughts, suddenly I could sustain No Mind for longer and longer.

My son had recently had a roller skating birthday party and some of the moms who were skaters in their childhood talked me into skating with them. I had not been a childhood skater and had no muscle memory for the movements. I noticed immediately that every time I thought about how my weight should be balanced, how my feet should move, and whether my posture was upright, I looked like some cartoon character waving my arms around wildly to keep my balance. But if I forgot about skating and talked to my friends, No Mind coordinated a rather decent skate. I even came in 2nd place of the adults daring to limbo. My body didn't know how to skate, but I had *let it learn*. When I was tempted to think, I simply breathed deeply and brought myself back to No Mind. It was impossible not to notice when I subtly transitioned from No Mind to thinking; the flailing, thrashing limbs were a dead giveaway. Turns out roller skating is great meditation practice. My husband who grew up surfing in Virginia Beach tells me this is the same reason people are irresistibly drawn to get up before dawn every morning to surf before work.

Where have you found No Mind? Art, music, breathing, meditation and athletics are only a few of the ways people commonly touch into this space. Yet it is easy to let life crowd out the activities that foster No Mind. As Eckhart Tolle said, "All true artists, whether they know it or not, create from a place of no-mind, from inner stillness...Even the great scientists have reported that their creative breakthroughs came at a time of mental quietude." [105] But No Mind doesn't find us, we have to find it.

As my dad knew, "Think the ball into the net. See it going right where you want it!" With a simultaneous intention paired with relaxation into No Mind, I got the ball-catching outcome I was after. Tense and without intention, the results were landing far and wide—everywhere but where I wanted. What intention must you relax into in order to land better health? What inner processes can you trust your body to coordinate if you relax into No Mind and let your body do the healing? As Dawson Church wrote in *The Genie in Your Genes: Epigenetic Medicine and the New Biology of Intention,* "Your intention in this dimension, acting in the quantum field, may collapse the swarm of probabilities in such a way as to influence health. Such ideas stretch the boundaries of our imagination, yet they hark back to shamanic journeys, or aboriginal walkabouts in the dreamtime, into which our ancestors traveled to find cures."[106] Like a dreamtime walkabout, No Mind gives us access to a new field of probabilities.

In *Inner Skiing*, Timothy Gallwey and Bob Kriegel have this to say, "We can, through growth, guidance and experience, achieve a lasting state of consciousness that none of us would want to trade for a lifetime of skiing breakthroughs. The breakthroughs on the slopes are only intermittent indications of far greater experiences attainable by skiing the 'inner slopes.'"[107] Adopt a practice that helps you touch the space of No Mind and start to experience breakthroughs on your inner slopes of consciousness. And don't forget the power of the breath to get you there. Surrendering into the great ocean wave of the breath frees us of many subtle things from which we otherwise cannot be free.

Key #4   Nourish Your Body

Roll Like a Drunk

Tension is who you think you should be. Relaxation is who you are.
Chinese Proverb

Ellen was a woman in her 70s who had just completed a series of acupuncture treatments for spasms in her back. She had been pain-free for several weeks and I was confident that she was practicing enough deep relaxation and stretching to maintain her pain-free state. She left the last appointment of her acupuncture series feeling so good that she drove to a nearby lake for a walk. As she crossed the road at a pedestrian crosswalk, though the light was red to traffic, a distracted driver failed to brake and drove straight into Ellen.

What happened next was most astonishing. Though Ellen had been thrown into the air and landed on the pavement with a sickening thud, she methodically tested each limb and each joint, and realized she was uninjured. The horrified onlookers refused to believe that a hit that hard would not produce injuries and an ambulance was called. They literally forced her to go to the emergency room. As Ellen later retold this to me, she laughed, saying, "No one could believe an old lady could survive such a hit." Not only did she survive, the hospital could not find anything wrong. As she described, "It's like when a drunk falls out of a wagon. They hit the ground so relaxed that nothing breaks. I was so relaxed after acupuncture that I fell with no tension in my body, so nothing was hurt."

I tell kids who are learning to meditate, "Let your body be like jello, and your arms and legs like noodles." When we can change our orientation to life from one of bracing for the worst to relaxing into whatever shows up, we come out far ahead. I watch many people squander their resources of energy and creativity by being constantly tied up and tensed up in upset, worry, and resistance against life. To learn to be free: free in mind, free in heart, and free in body, frees up huge resources of energy and creativity.

Holding tension in the body can also inhibit immunity. I never thought of it this way until studying the anatomy drawings of my friend, a renowned artist and human body illustrator, Vincent Perez. Though I'd studied anatomy in college, I had it in my head that we had a few lymph nodes scattered here and there in the neck, armpit and groin. But after looking with amazement at Vince's drawings, I realized there is lymphoid tissue *everywhere*. The lymph, unlike the blood, is a passive system and requires not only our participation by regular movement to keep things flowing, but requires the *free space* to move. The more tight and tense we become, the more this clamps down on and inhibits the proper movement of lymph through our system. (I suspect this has something to do too with why we "catch colds."

112

Being cold constricts the muscles which slows down the proper movement of lymph.) Love your lymph and cultivate a warm, relaxed body.

Peace is the way

My friend I'll call Ben is truly extraordinary. He is accomplished, wise, compassionate and kind. I have known him for almost 30 years. He amazes me as much now as he did when I was 12 years old. Ben has two full time jobs—one as a prominent doctor, where he is recognized for his incredible creativity and compassion with patients, and the other as a professor at a prestigious college where he is so loved and admired that a nearly steady stream of students stops by his house on any given evening or weekend to visit. In the decades I have known him, I have never seen Ben rushed, stressed, or upset. He cheerfully goes about doing what needs to be done, and is never too busy for someone who needs him. Over the years I too have dropped in unexpectedly many times to visit him and his family at their home. Often I'll find him playing the piano, making handmade sourdough bread from an ancient starter he keeps going, or tending his vegetable garden. He is one of the most loving, peaceful, and productive people I know.

One day I asked his wife how he does it; how is it possible to be so busy, and yet so at peace? She cited two very valuable habits that he has. The first, she told me, is that he stays absolutely relaxed. She says he has an uncanny ability to put aside worry and stay simply present in the moment enjoying whatever there is to do. As she described, if he is swimming, he is swimming. When he is with patients, they are his sole focus. When it is time to sleep, he sleeps.

The second habit his wife related to me is what she calls "the weird thing he does with naps." The moment he feels tired, he simply stops what he is doing and falls asleep. She said he goes into a sleep so deep that he snores in less than 60 seconds. He then sleeps for approximately 17 minutes, and awakens completely refreshed. She noted that recently they were on a long drive when suddenly he pulled off at a rest station for a "quick rest." He fell asleep sitting in the driver's seat and was snoring almost instantly while she sat quietly, waiting. As suddenly as he had fallen asleep, he awoke, precisely 17 minutes later, and resumed driving with full energy and vigor for the rest of the day. He has the energy of a teenager yet is almost 70 years old.

When we live life strung too taught like the bow string that has been tight so long it eventually looses its proper tension and becomes slack, we forfeit a continual supply of vigor and vitality that is available to us otherwise. Learn to be present to the task at hand without worry. Learn to be loose, and roll like a drunk when the challenges of life rock your wagon. Learn to nap when your body says so even if you think you can't or shouldn't–work places that have implemented napping have high productivity and morale! Learn to breathe deeply. Allow yourself to be moved in your heart and enjoy all that you do each day whether it is "work" or "play." This is Open Heart Consciousness, and it will set you free.

Use the Breath of Power

"Tsk, tsk...terrible. You cheat yourself, little friend. The air is free. Look, like this." Volanko sucked in air through his nose while bringing his hands together over his head. Then he exhaled through his mouth and pumped his arms, working his lungs like a bellows. "Breathing is life, Yosselle. Without air, the fire dies. Now try it again."..."How long do I have to do this?" the boy asked gasping. "For the rest of your life," Volanko replied.

Ed Spielman
The Mighty Atom[108]

Though it is not well known, our Native Americans strapped their babies to boards with their chin angled toward the chest so that as the baby slept it was impossible to breathe through their mouth. Even without the benefit of modern technology, early people knew that for the most vital health, it is essential that we breathe through the nose. The Mexican Native American Tarahumara barefoot runners who are known to run up to 200 miles in one session and 80 miles in a day for fun, run with a pebble in their mouth so as not to be tempted to mouth breathe. For a vital breath, use your nose. Even more important, use your heart. As Rumi observed, "There is one way of breathing that is shameful and constricted. Then there's another way; a breath of love that takes you all the way to infinity." It is a gift to every cell in our bodies to breathe that breath of love, and to let our hearts touch the infinite.

When my son was five, he was very strong but lacked stamina. We were running every day with our dogs, but he would peter out quickly and want to walk. I noted him panting, open mouthed, to catch his breath. Reminders to keep his mouth shut went unheeded. He declined my offer of a pebble. Thus was born what we call the Breath of Power. As I explained it to him, the Breath of Power would unlock a powerful gate within him that would allow him to go long distances without fatiguing. The anticipated thrill of gaining an athletic superiority over his mouth-gasping contemporaries achieved my end.

Now my son conspiratorially whispers to me, "Mommy, let's use the Breath of Power so we can run faster and further than anyone else!" After he mastered the simple mechanics of breathing powerfully through his nose while keeping his mouth shut, I added one last detail: breathing in a feeling state (Feeling Mantra) that moved his heart to joy: Rumi's breath of love. He nodded knowingly, no further direction or explanation needed. I'm often amazed at how quickly many children learn and grasp new things, things that might be called "hard" by

115

adults. Children are brimming with enthusiasm for growth and change, and less invested in proving why something won't work for them. They just *do* the thing instead of trying so hard to figure it all out.

If you want to increase your energy, mental clarity, and better oxygenate your body, breathe both in and out powerfully through the nose. For added intensity, pull the breath in so that it not only vibrates your nostrils, but makes a fierce sound. Imagine that an elixir of love is coming in on that air and permeating all your cells from the inside. Envision the magical hand-off where your blood grabs the oxygen rich air molecules and pulses those molecules through every crevice of the body. To avoid hyperventilating, keep the breath long and slow.

In *Perfect Health for Kids*, Dr. John Douillard describes a study he did with patients whom he simply taught to switch from mouth breathing to nose breathing (known also to increase relaxation) while exercising on a bicycle. As he commented in summary, "Imagine accomplishing the same amount of work and handling the same amount of stress in your life, but instead of feeling maxed-out at a perceived exertion level of ten, you are handling your work effortlessly with a perceived exertion level of four? This is analogous to how the nasal breathing students felt in the exercise study." [109] As Dr. Douillard also notes, "A screaming, mouth-breathing child is instantly calmed when nursing. This is illustrated in **stillen,** the German word for breast-feeding, meaning to still or quiet the child. When babies nurse, they are forced to breathe through their noses. The turbinates allow air to be directed deeper into the lungs, soothing the child by activating the parasympathetic nervous system." [110]

Authors Al Lee and Don Campbell share a Native American proverb in *Perfect Breathing*, "Every breath, every step, is a prayer." [111] Breath the Breath of Power as a prayer, infuse it with love, and let it take you to infinity.

Run Like a Lung-gom-pa Runner Monk

Flowing water never stagnates, active hinges never rust.
Dr. Sun Ssu-mo
Chinese Physician and Tao Master who lived to 101, 1,300 years ago

*Imagine yourself next to a powerful waterfall that has tremendous force and movement. How does it feel? You most likely feel energized, vibrant, and relaxed all at the same time. Now imagine yourself next to a stagnant pond. Do you experience the same feeling? Probably not. **Movement creates energy.** The movement of the waterfall can produce electricity and power. A stagnant pond invites pests and potential malignant growths. The same analogy applies to exercising your mind and body.*
Ross Pelton
Mind Food & Smart Pills[112]

In a comic strip by Randy Glasbergen, he jokes, "What fits your busy schedule better, exercising one hour a day or being dead 24 hours a day?" Between illness and the fact that my weight rocketed to an excess over 90 pounds, my journey with exercise was a challenge. One of the hallmarks of Chronic Fatigue Immune Deficiency Syndrome (CFIDS) is something called post-exertional malaise. That means you feel as if you've been flattened by a bus for days after exercise. For me with that diagnosis, it was downright dangerous to exercise. CFIDS patients have been shown to have highly abnormal responses to exercise; instead of the benefits most people receive, they are at risk for further damaging already compromised mitochondria. Distinct blood abnormalities that appear after people with CFIDS exercise have been associated with DNA damage.

A doctor who knew little of this disease once suggested that I needed to try harder and help myself. He gave the recommendation that I use "graded exercise" which meant gradually increasing exercise until I recovered. For many people attempting to address physical and stamina issues this might work. I was frustrated to no end that I had lost my ability to exercise, but knew this was wrong for me. I later learned, had I followed that advice without correcting the immune deficiency part of the syndrome first, I could have exponentially worsened my condition.

Once my immune system healed, exercise resulted in feelings of increased clarity, energy, and euphoria. Exercise is a significant component to optimal health. Do what you can to correct hormone imbalances, nutrient deficiencies, inflammatory cascades, and immune weaknesses that may hinder your ability to feel energized and rejuvenated by exercise. There is a great feeling of strength, accomplishment, and exhilaration that comes with fitness. Exercise is an excellent vehicle to unlock the heart of healing!

Fall in love with vegetables

Initially, with 90 pounds to lose, running was not high on my list of activities that might expedite transport into Open Heart Consciousness. In fact, pain in my joints and my lumbering size made it impossible to do more than laboriously walk a few blocks. First I had to fall in love with eating voluminous amounts of vegetables each day, which I did by reading and studying everything I could about the nutrient content of vegetables and what they could do for my health. I took inspiration from Dr. Terry Wahls and her TEDx talk detailing her story of how she got herself out of a wheelchair and reversed multiple sclerosis by eating nine cups of vegetables a day. [113] With my own multiple sclerosis diagnosis too, I considered Wahls' idea more than just a "nice idea" and I grabbed onto it like gospel. Though a stool test just a few months before had tipped off my doctor that I ate practically zero vegetables, (I "hated" them, I told her) I started practicing Open Heart Consciousness while eating salads. By gratefully appreciating nature's foods while focusing on my genuine awe at the medicines they are, I not only enjoyed the vegetables but watched the weight melt away.

Eating nine cups of vegetables a day meant to me a "moving toward" orientation rather than the deprivation associated with dieting. I mostly ate what I wanted as long as I got in those vegetables. Though Wahls ate both cooked and raw vegetables, I observed in my own body that cooked vegetables digested like carbs, while raw vegetables digested like fiber. Because carbs seemed to stick to my hips like glue but fiber passed out in a satisfyingly voluminous mass, I focused my appreciation most zealously on vegetables in their raw natural state. Pretty soon, to my shock, my tastebuds changed and rewired and I actually started to love and crave raw vegetables which I now eat with most meals. Soon, I was thin enough to run (well, trot).

Interestingly, in morning seminars I often show slides of my salads while talking about falling in love with vegetables. I'll ask if anyone's mouth is watering over the pictures. Every hand goes up! If you think you can't eat salad for breakfast, is it your mind telling you that, or your body? When a plate heaped with crisp greens adorned with nature's vibrant reds, oranges, and purples, topped with a glistening piece of glazed salmon and dressed with a swirl of olive oil with garlic and lemon juice is available, this is no hardship.

Run as if your feet are rapturously kissing the Earth

In *Go Wild*, authors John J. Ratey, MD and Richard Manning make the case that we are born to run. Citing research from *Nature* magazine, they point out that unlike apes, we have 26 adaptations of our skeleton specific to running, not walking. These include a springy arched foot, our elongated Achilles tendons, long legs relative to the rest of the body, and counter-rotational pivoting hips.[114] Vigorous exercise excites many biochemical changes that support our health, and running has long been recognized by many as the exercise most likely to facilitate an ecstatic or transcendent state. Many people report mystical experiences while running. In *Meditation: The First and Last Freedom,* spiritual teacher Osho remarked, "...my own observation is that a runner can come close to meditation more easily than anybody else." [115]

Thich Nhat Hanh once said, "Walk as if you are kissing the Earth with your feet." When I took up barefoot running to heal a herniated disc in my back, I learned something about how feet can kiss the Earth. The moment I removed my shoes one early fall afternoon and went trotting down a county trail feeling the explosions of springy moist grass, hot dry pine needles, crinkling leaves, and damp, cool earth in the shade of the trees, my feet woke up in a way they never had before.

I'm sure my feet awakening was much like the eating experience my patient had once her throat healed after being on a feeding tube for five years. The awakening of a sense that has long slumbered can truly touch the ecstatic. Now the repetitive feeling of hard jarring pavement against heavy rigid shoes is intolerable to me. It would be like making my feet live on a meal replacement shake when a smorgasbord of gustatory delights is available. Running, even through snowbanks in the winter in slipper socks with only a hint of a flimsy sole to break the cold, is truly a rapturous kiss with the Earth. For those who have never run without shoes, worries like stepping on glass, bees, and dog poop predominate. And yes, those things occasionally happen. But as Richard Manning describes of his experience in *Go Wild*, "(R)unning with unrestricted feet is more fun. No other way to put it. More giggles and smiles in it." [116] He even goes so far as to call shoes "foot coffins."

I had read accounts of the Tibetan Lung-gom-pa runner monks who practice running as an intensive meditation and become so quick and light on their feet they appeared to hover in the air. In Tibetan, "Lung" means air and chi (vital energy) while "Gom" means focused concentration through meditation. Tibetan Lung-gom-pa monks dedicate their lives to spiritual practice and rigorous physical training. They harness a spiritual energy that allows them to transcend the physical limits of the body. I also was aware that the Mexican native American Tarahumara people ran incredible distances on rugged, mountainous terrain, in a "shoe" akin to a flip flop, laughing all the while as they too transcended physical limits as we know them. I used the Runner Monks and Runner Indians as inspiration for my barefoot running path to Open Heart Consciousness.

The gap between misery and bliss can be vast for the sedentary person becoming active. I can't say euphoria was available to me in those first weeks of jogging. But I had a plan, and I was determined. Though I slowed to a walk if joint or muscle pain proffered a serious warning, at all other times I trained my mind steadfastly on a Feeling Mantra. I chose a powerful memory from my past associated with a peak state. I remembered all the familiar smells, sights, and sounds associated with that memory. I remembered my body posture and facial expression and remembered just how I felt in that past moment. I listened to the music that best helped me "move into state." Any time I felt about ready to keel over from weariness, breathlessness and fatigue, I just kept running and returning to my Feeling Mantra. Within a month, I no longer needed to try to induce a peak state while running. My brain and body had so hard-wired the experience, it arose spontaneously just moments into the run.

In *How and Why We Age,* Leonard Hayflick humorously reports the following on research subjects devoted to a lifetime of vigorous exercise, "...one commentator reasoned that, although 80-year-old exercising alumni gain up to 2.15 additional years...the total time required to expend 2000 kilocalories per week in the 60 years between graduation and age 80 would range from 1.18 to 2.37 years. The years they gained were thus spent jogging!"[117] If you run to extend life, whip your body into shape, or burn calories, you are going to have a starkly different outcome than if you run to kiss the Earth with your feet, expand your heart with love and wonderment, and open your bodily channel to something bigger than you. I highly recommend the latter.

I watch grim, tight-lipped women jog by my office every day in a fierce battle against aging and weight gain. Exercise executed grimly does not help us become more free, more joyous, more filled with holiness, nor more energized to address the challenges in our life. I once asked a patient of mine who men consider "hot" but who to me looks stressed and strained, how much she ran every day to keep such a great figure. "Oh, about three miles a day," she grimaced. "I make myself do it first thing in the morning before I can think about what I'm doing" she confessed. Personally, I couldn't imagine the willpower it must take to sustain such a joyless grueling practice. "How fast do you get your runner's high going?" I queried hopefully. "Runners high?" she looked at me blankly. "I've never had a runner's high."

There is no doubt that any commitment to exercise has benefits. But exercise delivers exponentially when practiced in an uplifted state of heart and mind. Please, commit to exercise in a way such that it liberates deeply locked stores of playfulness, vital energy, and joy. Your time is too precious to spend it wearily executing "should" tasks that qualify as drudgery rather than dancing in a state of Open Heart Consciousness. If such a notion seems strange and unfamiliar to you, take a cue from the Lung-gom-pa Runner Monks and use the vehicle of exercise to cultivate a holy ecstatic meditative practice.

Correct Nutrient Deficiencies: Wisdom From Ducks

The proper functioning of the brain is known to require the presence in the brain of molecules of many different substances. Mental disease, usually associated with physical disease, results from a low concentration in the brain of any one of a number of vitamins: thiamine (Vitamin B-1), nicotinic acid or nicotinamide (B-3), pyridoxine (B-6), cobalamin (B-12), biotin, ascorbic acid (vitamin C), and folic acid.

Linus Pauling, Two-time Nobel Prize Winner
Forward, Brain Allergies, by William H. Philpott, M.D., and Dwight K. Kalita, Ph.D[118]

The brain is the most sensitive organ in your body. The biochemistry of intelligence depends on and is very sensitive to what you eat. Your moods and even your memory can change dramatically in response to what is eaten in a single meal. The chemical substances involved in thought processes, learning and memory processes, and other aspects of mental performance come either from your diet or are made from nutrients in your diet.

Ross Pelton
Mind Food & Smart Pills[119]

It is said that the Buddha once remarked, "Without a perfectly healthy body, one cannot know bliss." Patanjali, too, in ancient writings on yoga–a practice originally intended to open the body further to the Divine–cited bodily illness as the first of the nine obstacles to the yogic path. While changing our inner feeling states may change the biology of our body, sometimes we can work the equation from a different angle. By changing the health of our body, we can change our capacity to know and experience Open Heart Consciousness.

Referring to the ways imbalances in our biochemistry may impact our brain health, neurophysiologist Ralph Gerard once said, "There is no twisted thought without a twisted molecule." By understanding root causes, it becomes possible to "straighten" things out. One infrequently considered process that may be at play twisting our heart and mind away from Open Heart Consciousness is nutrient deficiencies.

Right dose

Our first two adorable little ducklings came in the mail at just two days old. We had researched the care of ducklings extensively, and were prepared with everything a baby duck would need to thrive in the absence of a momma. By the end of our first day together, both ducklings had nuzzled into my hair atop each of my shoulders and fallen asleep. I fell quickly in love with these tiny cheeping creatures.

Just about the time we were first researching the care of ducklings, I had also been reading some fascinating accounts of the use of orthomolecular medicine in the treatment of mental illness. Orthomolecular medicine, a term coined by two-time Nobel Prize winner Linus Pauling, means "the right molecules in the right amount." Pauling was most famous for his usage of large doses of Vitamin C in treating and reversing a wide spectrum of illnesses. Combining large doses of ascorbate (Vitamin C) with the B-vitamin niacin seemed to do for mental illness, he had observed, what high doses of ascorbate alone did for the common cold.

What was most unique and original about Pauling's work, but what also to this day fuels its opponents, is the fact that in some cases, "right molecule in the right amount" may appear to be a "mega-dose." People are inherently afraid (as they should be) to use a "mega-dose" of anything. But Pauling showed that what we think of as a mega-dose may be nothing of the kind. It may in fact be the appropriate dose.

To understand this better, consider the fact that the Dietary Reference Intake (DRI) recommended by our U.S. National Academy of Sciences for vitamin C is 45 mg. This was the amount determined long ago by researchers intent on warding off scurvy. Pauling uncovered research which shows that most mammals manufacture their own Vitamin C, and humans used to be one of them. It is thought that somewhere in our evolutionary development, we lost the fourth of four enzymatic steps (the L-gulonolactone oxidase enzyme) that is necessary to complete the last step in the manufacture of vitamin C. Our bodies complete steps one through three, and then at the fourth phase, because of a universal human mutation in the enzyme, we are not able to complete the process, and so disassemble it and start over. Therefore, we must take all of our vitamin C requirement in through our diet.

This sparked Pauling and others to wonder what amount of Vitamin C we would likely have circulating in our bloodstream had we not lost the ability to synthesize it. If we consider a goat that can complete all four steps and can manufacture vitamin C internally, we find that the average daily amount produced is around 13,000 mg under normal conditions. During times of stress this amount increases. This truly looks "mega" next to our 45 mg DRI. Assuming the goat wouldn't make an excess of what it needs, it is an interesting number to consider. Pauling promoted the idea that doses right in this range of around 13,000 mg of Vitamin C have the ability to correct many human diseases and imbalances, because ingestion or administration of this amount is, in light of his interpretation of this information, the right amount of the right molecule to account for the human genetic mutation. Pauling himself reported taking upwards of 18,000 mg of vitamin C a day. Dr. Michael Colgan of the Colgan Institute found oranges in supermarkets with *zero vitamin C* due to the ubiquitous commercial practice of picking fruit before maturity to survive long shipping. This highlights another reason why good diet alone may no longer be enough.

Abram Hoffer, M.D., Ph.D. attests that we are currently in the middle of the same sort of population-wide genetic mutation occurring in relation to the B vitamins. Some people are able to utilize small quantities of B vitamins easily, while others are not. Years ago I had some medical testing done and realized that I had a SNP (pronounced "snip" and standing for "single-nucleotide polymorphism") for folic acid. This is a genetic variation that requires an individual to take in a much larger quantity of folic acid in order to properly utilize it sufficiently. One reason all pregnant women in the United States are advised to take 800 mcg of folic acid for the duration of their pregnancy to prevent spina bifida is that it is far cheaper to have all women take the vitamin than it is to test all women to see which ones have the SNP and actually require that amount.

In Hoffer's book *Vitamin B-3 & Schizophrenia: Discovery, Recovery, Controversy* I was interested to find descriptions of the usage of high doses of niacin in the treatment of mental illnesses including schizophrenia and bipolar disorder. The results were what anybody would consider extraordinary—long-term mentally ill patients were suddenly meeting what Hoffer described as the three criteria for wellness: "no signs or symptoms, getting on well with family and the community, and working full-time (paying taxes)."[120] Mental illness is considered intractable in many circles, and yet here were cases where a simple vitamin intervention was reversing the most extreme of symptoms—patients who had been hallucinating just days before were interacting peacefully with family and hospital staff.

These findings were of particular interest to me as two of my ancestors had been hospitalized with mental illness years ago, and two decades ago I personally had experienced hallucinations after a stressful period in college that prompted a well-meaning psychologist to attempt to "help" me by diagnosing schizophrenia. The hallucinations lasted only briefly, but it would be years before I realized that symptoms like I had can be related to many environmental challenges to the brain. Because celiac disease causes malabsorption of vitamins, here possibly was one of those challenges.

Literally within a day of learning about this nutrient-brain connection, I was making a final review of the care of our soon-to-arrive baby ducks. I knew that niacin was a critical nutrient for ducks—in fact every resource we had consulted had stressed the importance of adding niacin to the water of domestically raised ducks in their first weeks of life because deficiency would stunt their growth and cause their legs to bow. Apparently, this humble B vitamin to which I'd never given much thought had a role of great importance for humans and ducks. The particular resource I consulted that day mentioned an interesting distinction. A baby duck with a niacin deficiency may develop a black tongue. I froze as I read this. Both of my ancestors with mental illness had, at the time of hospitalization, a black tongue.

An Internet search revealed that indeed a black tongue in a human may also be indicative of a niacin deficiency. It was disturbing to think that my "mentally ill" ancestors, both still symptomatic though treated with the anti-psychotic drug thorazine at the time, may have been textbook cases of the extreme manifestations of a niacin deficiency. We will never know, as both had died with active mental illness before I came across this information. Such information was available, but not well known at the time of their hospital admittance. Research by both Pauling and Hoffer had been published in peer-reviewed journals in the early 1970s.

Many natural avenues for supporting brain health have slipped into the annals of history. My friend who trained as a psychiatrist in the 1950s tells me that back then, talk therapy, and interestingly, Benadryl, were the only known interventions. As more drug therapies crept onto the scene, he tells me that psychiatrists were mandated by insurance companies to bill only for drug-based interventions. In his psychiatry practice, he was no longer reimbursed to practice the therapy he had trained for. In this type of climate, it is easy to understand how natural interventions were neglected. They simply weren't a service for which a psychiatrist would be reimbursed. Because therapies such as niacin were never popularized in a scene dominated by drug therapy, and because the orthomolecular medicine approach and large doses of any vitamins are generally regarded with too much suspicion to become mainstream or standard of care, a common duck breeder generally uses niacin more adeptly than the psychiatric wing of a hospital.

As Dr. Herb Slavin said to Suzanne Somers in an interview for her book *Ageless*, "Sometimes I ask people, 'What is the most important nutrient?' Answer: The one you're lacking. The most important component of a healthy lifestyle is the one you're not including." [121] Schizophrenia secondary to vitamin deficiency is only one example of a possible biological contributor to mental or spiritual illness. There are many great books on the subject. One is *Nutrient Power: Heal Your Biochemistry and Heal Your Brain* [122] by William Walsh. Did you know that one cause of postpartum depression is hypercupremia? That means copper overload. William Walsh knew. He describes what to do about it in his book. I wish I'd known in the year after I gave birth. I had postpartum depression, and it would be three years before a doctor thought to test my blood to find I had a significant copper/zinc imbalance. Several months of supplementing with zinc drove down the too-high copper and fixed the imbalance. Walsh covers nutrient strategies for ADHD, Autism, and Alzheimer's, too. Ultimately, I'm a fan of deriving nutrition from healthful foods wherever possible. However, if your brain is starved of the amount of nutrition adequate for its unique needs, it is not going to work correctly. While improved nutrition may not provide a tidy solution for everyone struggling with brain health, it is worth checking into in case it applies to you.

Consider Cerebral Allergies

Ecologic mental illness is an important facet of man's total reaction to his natural and synthetic environment. This form of mental illness is often associated with many other types of often unrecognized hypersensitivity disorders as well as common allergies. **The human brain may be viewed as a complex allergic shock tissue which is easily reached by inhaled and ingested excitants from the environment via its rich blood supply.** *No physician can render adequate care to any sick individual unless he acquires a thorough knowledge of ecologic disease.*

Marshall Mandell, M.D.
Cerebral Reactions in Allergic Patients
Illustrative Case Histories and Comments
A Physician's Handbook on Orthomolecular Medicine[123]

People used to be as intelligent as lower animals who will avoid, **for the rest of their lives,** *any food that adversely affects them. Now people have been brainwashed to believe chronic or episodic complaints are due to drug deficiencies or couch lying deficiencies.*

Steven Rochlitz
Allergies and Candida: With the Physicist's Rapid Solution[124]

The term "allergy" was first coined by Clemons von Pirquet, M.D. in 1906, to describe an "altered reactivity" to some environmental substance. Our current concept of allergies tends to be limited to sneezing and hives generated from pollens and molds, or anaphylaxis from peanuts or other food allergens. We have forgotten that the original term was much broader in both *cause* and *effect*. By the meaning of the original term, allergens can include any kind of fume, chemical, food, or airborne particulate. Effects can impact every system of the body. For our purposes here, we will consider the impact of allergens on moods, feeling states, and Open Heart Consciousness.

Most people have never even heard the terms *cerebral allergies* or *brain allergies,* yet clinical work by Doris Rapp, M.D. and others support that sometimes what people are allergic to affects their brains. As Dr. Marshall Mandell described in the quote above, the brain may be viewed as a *complex allergic shock tissue.* Such allergies can cause symptoms of schizophrenia, depression, bipolar disorder, ADD, ADHD, and more, and can make kids and adults act like angry and defiant jerks. Cerebral allergies can make it hard for kids to learn, and can deteriorate their fine motor control, resulting in terrible handwriting, and scribbles instead of "art." I love Doris Rapp, M.D.'s book *Is This Your Child?*[125] This book is instructive for the parent interested in pursuing an understanding of how cerebral allergies may affect their child.

If researchers Marshall Mandell, M.D. and William Philpott, M.D. suspected a patient was experiencing symptoms of mental illness because of cerebral allergies, they would put them in an environment free of fumes or cleaning products of any kind, away from gas stoves and gas heat, and have them fast for four days. If in four days the mental illness resolved, they knew they had a cerebral allergy on their hands. Altered reactivities to our environment can profoundly affect us.

One day I briefly made mention of this research on cerebral allergies in a class I was teaching, and I mentioned that gluten has been identified as a cerebral allergen for some people. The association between gluten and schizophrenia was fascinating to me, given my own temporary diagnosis and my familial history. Remember Tina who had successfully learned to "ignore" the schizophrenic voices in her head? Unbeknownst to me, Tina was in the audience listening in amazement, shocked to hear that there was any approach to schizophrenia outside of the conventional medication-based approach. After the talk, she immediately went home and put herself on a gluten-free diet. The next time I saw her, she was absolutely radiant. Her hair was brushed smoothly, her cheeks glowed pink, and her eyes had a new shine. "What happened to you?!" I exclaimed. "You know what happened to me," she replied. "No, I don't," I remarked, puzzled. I stood there just gawking at her, not sure what could possibly be responsible for such a transformation.

Tina told me that within three days of starting a gluten-free diet, the voices in her head had completely ceased for the first time she could remember. She was so shocked at the change that she had reported it immediately to her doctor in hopes that what she learned could help others. She was experiencing absolutely no schizophrenic symptoms—no voices, no paranoia, and no depression. Her doctor told her it was impossible, that diet could never cause such a change, and that she was absolutely not to change her medication. Yet oddly, the tardive dyskinesia symptoms caused by her medication had disappeared too, so as she told me, she was not in a hurry to change anything, other than her doctor. Her experience convinced her she wanted a health care provider with an open mind and a greater belief in the ability of the body to heal.

For some people, the experiences of anxiety, depression, hopelessness, irritability, anger, insomnia, forgetfulness, difficulty concentrating, and more may be triggered or worsened by commonplace foods or drinks we consume. Though I'm a huge proponent of following the communications of the body toward health, because chemical compounds in certain foods (like the gluteomorphins in gluten and the caseomorphins in milk products) bind with the morphine receptors in our brain, we might ravenously crave the foods to which we are most reactive.

People assume that when I was 90 pounds overweight I was eating fast food and junk. Actually, I was on an organic Weston A. Price diet eating whole and fermented foods. But because I had severe, though difficult to ascertain, reactions to wheat and dairy products, including the cravings triggered by their "morphins" at the morphine receptors, my weight careened out of control despite what could be called "healthy" eating. Healthy eating is what is healthy for an individual. When a food reaction is present, it doesn't matter if you grew the food in your back yard in perfect organic conditions.

If it seems harder than it should to find Open Heart Consciousness, consider cerebral allergies. A book I love is *Brain Allergies* by Philpott, Kalita, and Pauling.[126] Any of a number of books or Internet instructions on "elimination diets" or "clean diets" may also provide a good starting place. As Hippocrates said, "Let food be thy medicine, and medicine be thy food." What we eat truly harms or heals. And the food that heals *is the food that is uniquely healing for each of us*. Renowned physician Dr. Charles Mayo, founder of the Mayo Clinic, remarked, "Here let me repeat one solemn truth which should be repeated over and over each day until everybody comprehends its meaning and acts upon it. Normal resistance to disease is directly dependent on adequate food. Normal resistance to disease never comes out of pill boxes. Adequate food is the cradle of normal resistance, the playground of normal immunity, the workshop of good health, and the laboratory of long life." Find the foods that are a cradle of resistance, playground of immunity, workshop of good health, laboratory of long life, and *at the heart of healing physically, spiritually, and cerebrally for you.*

Use the Mood as the Clue

We need to move from herbalism as a kind of "let's-eat-organic-today" choice (unless we're really sick; then we'll go to the emergency room) to a "we-can-depend-on-this-for-our-life" form of healing.Stephen Harrod Buhner
Herbal Antibiotics: Natural Alternatives for Treating Drug-Resistant Bacteria[127]

You know how when you're sick, you just feel blah, not particularly upbeat or playful, and don't feel like doing much? Sometimes people become chronically mildly sick, don't realize it, and wonder why it is hard to feel a deep love, an ecstatic awe, and a profound sense of the Divine. I have come to appreciate that plant medicines hold a centuries-old place in maintaining physical, mental, and spiritual health. To determine when they are needed, sometimes, the mood is the clue.

Certain plants–usually hallucinogens–are categorized as "entheogens," defined as "generating the Divine within." As you will soon understand why, I would petition that certain plant medicines with antiviral or antibacterial effects be reclassified as entheogens as well. Through their antimicrobial effects that in turn influence how we think and feel, these plants may indeed enhance our ability to generate the Divine within.

While taking a break from reading an excellent resource book, Stephen Harrod Buhner's *Herbal Antibiotics*,[128] I learned that my friend's niece had just died from meningitis. The section by Buhner I had been reading only moments before had discussed at length the fact that meningitis is one of 21 diseases for which there are serious antibiotic resistant strains. My friend's niece is one of a growing number of people who die from these antibiotic resistant diseases.

Buhner had laid out specific protocols for each of several different resistant strains of meningitis using plant medicines that have been demonstrated in clinical trials to effectively fight resistant meningitis. Since the hospital where my friend's niece was treated had to do a spinal tap to determine what strain of meningitis they were trying to treat, odds were they knew it was a resistant strain. Until the end, they provided treatment that is accepted as standard of care, but is known not to work.

The more people become educated about the benefits of plant medicine, the more we will all have access to potentially lifesaving treatments that are not yet standard of care. A life-threatening infection like meningitis that takes the life of someone we know is a dramatic example. But what if a stealthy pathogen is at work more subtly to undermine moods or health?

Suicidal rats

Some researchers became interested in the strange behavior of rats that got infected with the parasite toxoplasma gondii. T. gondii is the parasite that causes toxoplasmosis in cats, and is responsible for the general recommendation that pregnant women avoid changing cat litter boxes that could put a fetus at risk of acquiring this infection. Rats happen to be the most common vector animal that pass the t. gondii parasite between cats.

These researchers were alarmed to find that rats infected with t. gondii would literally fling themselves in the path of oncoming cats, as if they wanted to be eaten, and thereby complete the lifecycle of the t. gondii–which needed to get out of the vector rat and into its final host.

This is stunning. T. gondii in essence hijacks the brains of the rats, causing them to act in ways completely counter to normal behavior or their best interest. If you think a parasite could never cause you to fall into a funk or experience strange moods, you may be suffering from excessive positive thinking (just kidding).

As it turns out, anti-psychotics commonly used with schizophrenic patients also happen to suppress T. gondii. The researchers published a paper titled *Parasites as causative agents of human affective disorders? The impact of anti-psychotic, mood-stabilizer and anti-parasite medication on Toxoplasma gondii's ability to alter host behaviour.*[129] The scientists describe the fact that the mood stabilizing and anti-psychotic effects of some medications may be due to their ability to inhibit T. gondii in the brains of humans. Some cases of schizophrenia were directly attributed to the presence of a T. gondii infection in the brain. Just like humans who improve on anti-psychotic medications, T. gondii-infected rats that were treated with the schizophrenia drug haloperidol *stopped throwing themselves suicidally in front of cats.* Here was an example where non-life-affirming behavior was directly linked to a parasite.

The microbiome that constitutes you is genetically only between 1% and 10% composed of "you" and "your" DNA. The rest of the stuff floating around inside your skin, between 90% and 99% of the 50 trillion or so bits of stuff, is genetically distinct. These genetically distinct organisms (including bacteria, viruses, and fungi) operate for better or worse as "you." Microbes are essential for our survival. But if you wonder why you keep doing something weird and non-life-affirming over and over, look to pathogens as a clue.

In *Meditation as Medicine*, Dharma Singh Khalsa, M.D. and Cameron Stauth say, "The same receptor that attaches to the happiness neurotransmitter norepinephrine also attaches to viruses. Therefore, if a virus gets attached first, there may be no more room on the receptor for norepinephrine. But if norepinephrine gets there first, there may be no way for a virus to become attached to the receptor."[130] It behooves us to practice Open Heart Consciousness to fill our receptor sites with happiness neurotransmitters so mood altering viruses and pathogens have less places to park.

Change the frequency

Just as living in Open Heart Consciousness strikes a vibrational note within the body, which then changes the frequencies in and around every particle that comprises us, plant foods and food medicines similarly utilize a vibrational note to change the inner microbiome. When the microbiome has been bathed for years in soda, sweets, chips, and nutrient poor foods, a climate arises in which pathogens can persist. When the microbiome is bathed in green leafy vegetables, or plant food medicines used in the kitchen such as lavender or thyme, or when garlic, spices, turmeric, and the like are used, a new note sounds to which the system can tune. Thereby, errant or damaged cells have a chance to heal, or "raise their frequency."

In the search for my own health, I thought early on of trying to "kill candida and parasites," "decimate worms and stealth pathogens," and generally adopted a warlike orientation toward things that could harm my health. Inherent to this approach is bombing the system with chemotherapeutic agents like antibiotics, anti-fungals, de-wormers and other anti-life agents. This leaves a scarred and injured battlefield. Now I think in terms of improving vibrational frequencies through thoughts, feelings, and plant food medicines so that stealth pathogens won't be able to stand it inside me, and will be encouraged to make a beeline for the nearest exit.

The mood is the clue

My friend Kim actually knew a "pathogen" was adversely impacting her brain and used this knowing to direct her cancer treatment and improve her health. Kim has lived for over 10 years with Multiple Myeloma, a cancer she was told she would likely die from within one to three years. Her key to success is fascinating. She can *feel* when her cancer counts increase because as she describes, she is "come over by a strange feeling of deep depression and hopelessness."

My normally cheerful friend did not accept her doctors' opinion that "living with a terminal illness is depressing and that is why you feel depressed." Rather, Kim convinced her oncologist that the symptom was a valid cancer indicator. They would simply initiate a round of chemo whenever the odd depression showed up. This has allowed for a much more finely matched timing of chemo with actual increased cancer activity. As they were not drawing her blood every day, the inevitable consequence, were they dependent solely on blood tests, would have been a time lag between increased cancer activity and treatment. Because Kim knows her mood every day and can get in to her oncologist within a few days, there has been no such lag. Both Kim and her doctor believe this is why the normally aggressive cancer has not yet been able to gain a toehold in her the way it typically would.

Dose matters

Consider making it a hobby to understand your health and how to preserve it. If every person traded one hour of television a week for reading, learning about, and practicing aspects of health that are enjoyable and interesting to them, it would transform the health of the planet. When I was ill with many disease processes, I visited herbalists, naturopaths, functional medicine doctors, homeopaths, osteopaths and more, and still was not able to gain an adequate amount of help or education to keep my health functioning at peak. Making understanding plant medicines a hobby turned out to be a critical part of my recovery.

Consider these plant medicine examples. I take as a general health supplement 400 mg of resveratrol a day. This is considered a large dose. The "serving size" on the bottle of the resveratrol is 200 mg. However for a viral process like West Nile Virus, herbalist Stephen Harrod Buhner recommends *4,000 mg a day!*[131] As 16 cases of West Nile virus were reported in Maryland where I live last year, and as the Maryland Department of Health and Hygiene issued a West Nile virus warning this year, this is handy information.

For an active virus such as Dengue encephalitis, which two of my patients have contracted during foreign travel, Buhner recommends *1,200 mg of Cat's Claw a day*. I keep Cat's Claw on hand for its anti-viral effects; the serving size on my bottle of Cat's Claw says 500 mg, and I bought the most potent one I could find.

Dose matters. As two-time Nobel Prize winner Linus Pauling suggested, citing a 1981 report by Dr. Robert F. Cathcart, "You cannot cure a '100-gram cold' by taking a few grams of vitamin C."[132] Most people consider 500 mg of vitamin C an appropriate dose. Note that Pauling mentioned *100 grams*. That would be 200 over-the-counter 500 mg pills. Sometimes people think vitamins and plant medicines "don't work," but the problem may be in the dose.

To become plant medicine savvy, my favorite books are *Herbal Antivirals*[133] and *Herbal Antibiotics*[134] both by Stephen Harrod Buhner. I also like *The Most Effective Natural Cures on Earth* by Johnny Bowden, Ph.D., CNS.[135] I very much like *Prescription for Nutritional Healing* by Phyllis A. Balch CNC. I like *The Healing Power of Herbs: The Enlightened Person's Guide to the Wonders of Medicinal Plants*[136] by Michael T. Murray, and I like *Adaptogens in Medical Herbalism: Elite Herbs and Natural Compounds for Mastering Stress, Aging, and Chronic Disease* by Donnie Yance, MH, CN.[137]

These books illuminate just how potent and powerful plant medicines can be to combat the serious symptoms and disease processes we grapple with in modern life. Yance's book alone has over 4,000 references and citations to scientific studies and published research substantiating the powerful place of plants in medicine.

Use external tonics to cultivate the inner elixir

My friend who is an oncologist tells me that when drug companies hope to increase sales of a particular drug, they will visit various practices and target the doctor within a practice who is prescribing that drug the *least*. They will then hire that doctor to present a seminar on the drug. The "seminar" is usually a dinner with five or six guests in attendance. The drug company representatives aren't really interested in whether or not the presenter convinces any of the handful of guests of the efficacy of the drug. They know that in preparing to present, the doctor will become an expert on that drug, and thereby convince themselves. My friend has observed that these doctors then end up prescribing the drug far more than they would have otherwise or possibly even than is necessary.

I know that because of how much plant medicines have helped me, and because of how much I have studied and presented information on them, it is possible that I see their importance as greater than it may be. For a time, I had to be particularly mindful that I not engage too deeply in "parasite consciousness" where I overly perceived people's bodies as swimming pools filled with quality-of-life-dampening, brain-hijacking parasites needing intensive interventions to be eradicated, rather than as holy holding tanks brimming with the shining light of the Divine and flourishing whether parasites are there or not. Fill your consciousness with the thoughts, feelings, and paradigms that heal. Use plant medicines to support the health of your body if necessary, and let them go when you need them no more. Explore the ways plant medicines may work as "entheogens" to generate the Divine within. A transformative inner state heals, so utilize what help you can to get there.

Every civilization that has existed has used plants as food and medicine, and we can recover this wisdom to promote radical health, to sometimes reverse illness, and to facilitate Open Heart Consciousness. As Master Hui Ssu stated in the sixth century AD, "With the aid of external tonics, we are better able to cultivate the internal elixir within."

Protect the Elegance of the DNA

We are all so contaminated that if we were cannibals our meat would be banned from human consumption.
Paula Baillie-Hamilton, M.D.

And we have made of ourselves living cesspools, and driven doctors to invent names for our diseases.
Plato

Only when the last tree has died and the last river been poisoned and the last fish been caught will we realize we cannot eat money.
Cree Indian Proverb

When autistic author, speaker, and feedlot cow advocate Temple Grandin swam in a dip vat as a publicity stunt, it aided her goal to help better the lives of cows. But the price was steep. As Grandin describes in *Thinking in Pictures*, "(C)oming in contact with the chemical organophosphates had a devastating effect. The feeling of awe that I had when I thought about my beliefs just disappeared. Organophosphates are known to alter levels of the neurotransmitter acetylcholine in the brain...but why they affected my feelings of religious awe is still a mystery to me." [138] We come into contact with chemicals and poisons every day that may suppress or disrupt our feelings of awe or connection with the Divine.

As Brian Swimme powerfully describes in *Canticle to the Cosmos*, "The DNA is loaded with intelligence and information. It is a numinous word—at the root of being. Unfurling from that is the organism. We create chemicals that go right into the center of the cell to the DNA and disrupt its elegance. There are 70,000 chemicals commercially marketed (in 1990). Every year we add 1,000 new ones. Very, very few are actually tested...Without the DNA there is no spirituality whatsoever. If the world's scriptures stay around and the DNA is lost, none of their insights will matter anymore. The sanctity and holiness of the scriptures cannot be awakened in genetically defective humans." [139]

When I think of Temple Grandin's story, my first heartache is for the cows, dipped in organophosphate vats multiple times in their lives. How does this impact their sense of love or awe, however short-lived and different from our experience that may be? Having lived closely with and observed the miraculous pair-bonding of ducks, when I watch a momma cow gently and tenderly nuzzle her baby, I don't think such a question is overly anthropomorphic. Many adherents of the great spiritual traditions of India have gazed upon those same beatific cow faces and vowed to never eat meat again. In cultures living close to the land and interacting daily with the source of their food, the cow that gives generously of her milk, while only taking water and grass and renewing the soil with her wastes, is easily related to as valuable and holy, a *sacred cow*.

In cultures distanced from nature and not in contact with the food we eat, the loss of a sense of sacredness is only the first blunder. That the animals must then be raised in ways severely out of tune with nature, requiring poisonous chemicals to even remain alive because of dirty, crowded living conditions is the beginning of the next phase of blunders. That the final "edible" product gets to us blighted with growth hormones, antibiotics, and dipped in bleach before final packaging is all just par for the course. For consumers already accepting these blunders to then wonder, *"Might this disrupt the elegance of the DNA of our children?"* seems almost too much to hope for. It's simply not on our radar screens. As we recklessly continue ingesting chemicalized foods, the evidence of DNA being disrupted abounds.

When I look around, I see the evidence of disrupted DNA elegance. I see children suffering with autism, allergies, ADHD, having trouble learning, trouble listening, developing childhood leukemia and other cancers, brain tumors, bone cancer, and obesity. I see their young mothers diagnosed with breast cancer or uterine cancer before age thirty, sometimes even before age twenty, their fathers with colon cancer and even breast cancer while the kids are still in elementary school. When I see a severely uncoordinated child fail to learn a simple Tae Kwon Do pattern modeled patiently again and again by the teacher, I can't help but lean toward my husband and whisper forlornly, "disrupted DNA." It is painful to watch, and my heart hurts for the child, a victim of our mass ignorance. We are walking around in trances hoping that such consequences are just incidental to life, bad luck, and in no way associated with anything we have or have not done. We ignore or deny the obvious.

As Brian Swimme pronounced, *"The sanctity and holiness of the scriptures cannot be awakened in genetically defective humans."* What is lost if we allow humanity to become increasingly more genetically defective?

Take it on as a holy duty to love the body of our Mother Earth the way we would love a tiny baby. Feed and bathe the planet with things only gentle enough for a baby. Everything we do eventually ends up in the babies anyway. All of humanity pays the price of damaged DNA. For every child who cannot learn, that is one fewer capable mind grappling with the significant issues of our day. For every heart occluded by organophosphates and other poisons, that is one fewer potential lover of life deeply concerned with the struggles of humanity and inspired to do something about it. Poisoning is one of the greatest unobserved expenses that humanity pays the price for every single day.

Harlow Shapley scientifically calculated that because our air contains argon, which is a heavy gas that hovers close to the Earth, every human breath taken contains some of the same argon atoms breathed by Jesus, Mother Theresa, and Buddha. We are breathing each other's expired breaths all the time. In a year, fifteen of those same argon atoms from your exhaled breath will have circulated around the Earth, breathed and exhaled by lions, bears, and other breathing creatures of the Earth, to be re-inhaled deep into our own body again. Every day I am reminded of how little we bother to concern ourselves with our shared air; one doesn't have to look far to see the signs.

The state of our water is alarming as well. The beach where my family swims is frequently in the news, with warnings that bacterial counts are too high for safe swimming. Long before those reports hit the news, mass fish kills, likely one cause of the high bacterial counts, occur frequently. This is caused from run-off from lawn chemicals and fertilizers. What causes a lawn to grow unnaturally fast causes algae to grow unnaturally fast as well. The resulting "red tide" (algae bloom) means that so little oxygen is available in the water that the fish suffocate en masse. Many times each summer I observe this marine sepulcher, a vast expanse of ugly reddish water bobbing with a dense blanket of belly-up bodies.

Any small efforts made to protect our environment and to nourish our DNA add up over time. A child exposed to fewer toxins now may be the child whose illuminating intelligence and inspired heart later conceives of a novel treatment for a disease or problem affecting your family. Give that child a fighting chance. None of us can live as fully in a body that is always bogged down dealing with toxins. Caringly tend to our water, air, and food supply. *Protect the elegance of our global family's DNA.*

Key #5   Take on Healing

Get Conditions Right for the Body to Heal

I wish for a complete healing—not through the suppression of symptoms by drugs, but through the removal of cause. I hope you will be inspired to put yourself on a really excellent health diet. I hope you will be inspired to search for and remove all negative thoughts and feelings. I hope you will be inspired to fill your life with beautiful things-the beauty of nature, uplifting music, beautiful words and meaningful activities.

Peace Pilgrim
Peace Pilgrim: Her Life and Work in Her Own Words[140]

I shall recognize all disease as the result of my transgressions against health laws and I shall try to undo the evil by right eating, by less eating, by fasting, by more exercise, and by right thinking.

Paramahansa Yogananda
Spiritual Diary: An Inspirational Thought for Each Day of the Year[141]

Years ago my family and I were on a camping trip in a remote area, enthusiastically mountain biking through some rugged terrain, when I crashed off my bike and ended up with a scraped knee full of rocky debris. Without a first aid kit or running water available, there was no opportunity for cleaning and bandaging the wound. Rather, we biked sweatily in the heat the rest of the day, with flies continually landing on the open wound. When I arrived home two days later, the wound had become a suppurating infected mess that kept worsening rather than healing. I clenched my teeth through the pain and scoured it back to ground zero with a green scrubbie pad so that I could then clean it, apply ointment, and a Band-aid. After that, it healed beautifully in only a few days.

That the body quickly healed the knee once the dirt and fly larvae were out of its way does not inspire disbelief, unlike the remission of my patient with the aggressive lymphoma that suddenly disappeared from her body never to appear since. As you recall, that incident incited her doctor to bark at her that she was in denial and that even a spontaneous remission would inevitably recur. In another vein, when the two ER doctors removed the five shards of 400-degree glass that had melted the aqueous humor and fused to my eye, they were stunned when the eye healed almost simultaneously with the extraction of the shards. Though medical professionals may be stymied, all of these examples share something important. When the conditions are right, the body heals, and can do it fast.

Attend to the minute particulars

A friend of ours who has a whole flock of ducks was wondering why he only got a few eggs a week in warm weather, and almost none in cold weather, while our ducks lay abundantly even through a bitter winter.

When we started comparing notes, we realized that while we were both allowing our ducks free range, beyond that practice there were many differences. Our ducks ate the most expensive (and nourishing) supplemental feed available, while our friend used a cheaper grade. We gave our ducks access to unlimited supplemental feed, while he rationed the amount. Additionally, we were asking the local supermarket for its wilted greens each week, and feeding our little greens lovers vast quantities of kale, chard, and lettuce. We occasionally take a minnow trap to a nearby creek and provide our ducks a lively chase for their all-time favorite, and most natural food—minnows. We dig worms for our ducks, and turn over downspout trays to reveal the beetles and bugs our ducks love and hungrily gobble up.

Our friend provides his ducks only a place to swim in warm weather, while we run a pond heater in an oversized kiddie pool so they can swim year round. Our friend wondered about the cost of all these things we were doing. After calculating the pricey chow, the electricity, the purchase price for the heater, and the cost of frequently changing the pond water, we came to a total that still amounted to less than we would pay to buy that many eggs each week. These are our beloved pets, so beyond the "cost of the eggs," they provide us great joy and tons of personality, beauty, and, of course, fertilizer for the yard. He was spending less, but he was essentially just *sustaining life* rather than providing them the optimal conditions to flourish. If you want your ducks to lay or your body to heal, you must provide the absolute best conditions you can. Though it can be an art to determine whether what we are doing is too little, too much, or just enough, when the body has what it needs, nature often takes care of the rest.

In a selection called *The Holiness of Minute Particulars*, the poet and Christian mystic William Blake wrote, "He who would do good for another must do it in the Minute Particulars." [142] Whether it be through diet, exercise, discerning cerebral allergies, lessening toxicity, or the feeling tone we hold in our hearts, we would do well to tend to our own deep health by a holy attending to Minute Particulars.

Learn the Language of Healing

The body is a multilingual being. It speaks through its color and its temperature, the flush of recognition, the glow of love, the ash of pain, the heat of arousal, the coldness of nonconviction. . . . It speaks through the leaping of the heart, the falling of the spirits, the pit at the center, and rising hope.
Clarissa Pinkola Estés

It is amazing how many hints and guides and intuitions for living come to the sensitive person who has ears to hear what his body is saying.
Rollo May
Man's Search for Himself[143]

Pain insists upon being attended to. God whispers to us in our pleasures, speaks in our consciences, but shouts in our pains. It is his megaphone to rouse a deaf world.
C.S. Lewis
The Problem of Pain[144]

At a certain point in my experience of healing from a multitude of medical illnesses, I realized my body was speaking a language as foreign to me as Danish was while I resided for a time in Denmark. If the Danes hadn't been by-and-large amazing speakers of English, I would have bumbled around that country, disoriented and lost. Because Danes know English and are also kind and generous with their time, it was no trouble to have signs, labels, transportation maps, and newspaper headings translated for me on the spot. When it comes to our health, we would do well to become interpreters of our own body's language of distress and health.

Before I knew I had celiac disease, I did not understand why I experienced what I jokingly called a "food coma" (extreme fatigue after eating), hypoglycemia, and felt weak and listless much of the time. I had been going to doctors for years, but no one thought to run that simple blood test. Instead, my doctors repeatedly diagnosed "depression." I thought my body was flawed, and a real curse to live in. What I didn't realize was that my body was speaking to me as plainly as I'm speaking to you now, but because I didn't understand the language, I did not know what it was saying. Once I knew that my body was frantically screaming "No Gluten!" and I willingly complied with the request, I never experienced those symptoms again.

Each language has idioms and expressions, and learning to decipher these is as necessary for navigating the terrain of health as it is for navigation in a foreign country. Just as a nonnative speaker settling in a new country must learn the subtleties and nuances of the local language and customs to flourish, we must do the same to live in a flourishing state in the territory of our body. The language of health is the most valuable language you can learn, but you must learn the particular dialect of your own terrain. If you haven't already, begin a dialogue right now. Listen with a keenness of attention to the whispers and shouts from your own body. Know that just as any unknown language sounds like gibberish at first, you will begin to discriminate clear and unmistakable communication, beginning the moment you assume that every symptom signal your body gives is valid and important.

Just as a person who does not speak the same language as you knows perfectly well what is going on when you avert your eyes and ignore them or shake your fist and shout obscenities in their direction, your body interprets your moods and attitudes, too. Similarly, I've had my heart moved and tears in my eyes simply by the hand gestures and eye contact of a person in a foreign country with whom I couldn't share a single spoken word. Live in your body lovingly, and honor the two-way communication. All too often when the message is not understood, people curse their bodies. This does not foster good relations nor vital, vibrant dispute resolutions.

Some people have communications that come as whispers. I personally am glad mine arrived as banshee screams. Screams give no option for ignoring. I can't tell you how many times a patient comes to me after a cancer diagnosis or heart attack and tells me the only warnings they had were occasional tiredness here and there, and a transient feeling of being a bit stressed and frazzled. There is nothing that inspires loving habits like the banshee scream of a cancer diagnosis or terminal illness. Suddenly, getting enough rest, eating plenty of greens, savoring the joys in life, and increasing time spent in spiritual practice or meditation become paramount. We often don't recognize or we ignore the small signals of our body when it whispers. If so, what begins as a whisper will eventually mount to a banshee scream.

Modern life tends to crowd out simple healing acts of love towards ourselves. When, for example, was the last time you allowed yourself to sleep as much as your body wants? When did you last gaze up at the treetops, swaying in different rhythms as a breeze moved through, and deeply inhale the fragrance? When did you last allow the songs of birds or the crashing of waves to delight your ears with their music? Are you eating whole foods as drenched with the vibrant red, purple, and deep green colors of nature as they are bursting with flavor? When we live in these ways, we reawaken our connection to the deep pulse of nature and the currents of wisdom and intuition and energy within ourselves.

143

Leading world sleep researcher Robert Stickgold says, "The difference between smart and wise is two hours more sleep a night."[145] Sleep allows us to assimilate what we have learned during the day. In *Lights Out: Sleep, Sugar, and Survival*, T.S. Wiley humorously suggests, "Get as many hours (of sleep) as you can without getting fired or divorced."[146] I recommend getting not only as much sleep as you can, but as many moments of ecstatic delight, enjoying the richness of life as you can, as well. If this puts you in danger of losing your boss or your spouse, let them in on the secret, too. Whether it is a mounting need for sleep or some other unmet need, do yourself a favor and heed the small communications your body makes, to tend yourself more lovingly *right now*.

In order to get in a friendly communication with your body, stop looking at your symptoms as annoyances to silence. Stop ignoring the messages your body is attempting to communicate. Stop muttering disparaging remarks about your body's attempts to provide you life and health. And stop feeling hopeless if your body seems out of control. Start assuming the wisdom of the elegant arrangement of cells that constitutes you. Your body has incredible cellular wisdom, and may know something brilliant about your health that you don't unless you listen. This amazing wisdom isn't being received when your body's symptoms, the primary means of communication, are dismissed as meaningless gibberish dealt with by therapies aimed at masking or silencing it. If the only thing you do when you have a symptom is use a medication to silence it, you are effectively telling your body that its needs are annoying, inconvenient, and of no interest to you. You might as well give it the finger while you're at it. Your body may, via banshee scream, already be giving you the finger. Use a drug prescription if need be, but start to listen now, so your body doesn't have to flag you down with louder cries for help or other, more plaintive pleas. Trust your body, it knows what it is saying.

When the body "gives you the toe"

One of my patients was so attuned to her body and so responsive to its minute subtle signals (blood spotting at the "wrong" time of the month), that she got to a doctor who caught her cervical cancer so fast that the diagnostic biopsy was sufficient to remove it, and she required no additional treatment. Would if we all minded our body signals so well.

Most people have seen a Chinese Yin/Yang symbol, but many have not given much thought to what it means. In sum, those balanced and intertwined black and white swirls are to remind us that for as much generative, creative, upward moving energy as we experience, it must be replenished and balanced by an equal amount of regenerative, recuperative, restorative, restful energy. You can't cheat that basic economic reality of the body. Yet we try to cheat this principle all the time.

I was surprised to learn that in nature, a sick or wounded animal will often seek deep rest as a means to heal. In *Wild Health*, author Cindy Engel describes a wolf that lay unmoving in a snowdrift for 17 days while healing from a gunshot wound. When he was flushed out, the wounds were entirely healed. This wolf hadn't moved to eat or drink; he had used deep rest as his primary strategy for healing.[147] Unlike this wise animal, we so often do whatever we can to get back on our feet as quickly as possible, even when it means taking medicines to silence our symptoms so that we can defer or ignore the need for deep rest. However, our body's economy does not support endless withdrawals.

Jonathan Swift said, "The best doctors in the world are Doctor Diet, Doctor Quiet, and Doctor Merryman." My friend (who is a doctor!) has a long-standing habit of ignoring these doctors and violating their principles. She regularly acts invincible by not sleeping, overworking, eating poor food choices, and endlessly checking items off an ever-growing to-do list. She rationalizes her behavior as acceptable because most of the things she does help her patients. Her body has been offering warnings for years, but she has continued to neglect the message.

In Chinese medicine, each of the major organs of the body is associated with a meridian running along a specific finger or toe. What we do to violate the natural order always expresses in ways we can eventually feel or see on the body. My friend was violating the laws of nature in a particular way that would over-tax her gall bladder. So when she came in one day joking about her toe that was suddenly twisting oddly and rather forcefully up and to the side at about a 70 degree angle, looking, as she described, like "an old lady toe," I was not surprised that it was the toe associated in Chinese medicine with the gall bladder. "Wow," I told her, hoping to make a sensational enough impression that she would finally change her body-abusing ways, "your body is past the point of giving you the finger. It has to give you the toe!"

Appreciate the local dialect

Likes and dislikes can be clues with meaning as we learn to decipher the language of the body. In *Revelation: The Divine Fire*, author Brad Steiger describes research showing that listening to classical music lowers stomach acid.[148] I failed miserably in my attempts to benefit my brain and nervous system by becoming a classical music appreciator. Upon later reflection, I realized my body was likely communicating through this dislike all along. I have long suffered from *low stomach acid*. Perhaps in time researchers will find that the nightclub dance music I love that drives my dear husband nuts *increases stomach acid*. Then I can tell him it is a medical necessity, and that I must listen to it blasting at the loudest volume setting.

Fluctuations in stomach acid are only one expression of the body's unique dialect. My patient Pete's body was communicating in a dialect nobody had made sense of for over 50 years. When Pete came to me in hopes of relief from the neck pain he had experienced for decades, he was over 80 years old. He attributed his issue to the "bad posture" his wife had been nagging him about since he was 30 years old. Despite following her admonitions to "Straighten up!" and "Stand tall!" for over 50 years, Pete was so humped over he couldn't straighten his head enough to look me in the eye. He was practically in tears describing to me all the efforts he'd made over the years to correct his declining posture, and his complete frustration that still, as he described it, he'd ended up a "hunchback."

While mulling over Pete's predicament, I came across the following passage written by Mary Pullig Schatz, M.D. about our spinal vertebrae: "With no blood supply of its own, the disc is dependent on sponge action for attracting and absorbing nutrients from adjacent tissues. During nonweight-bearing rest, the discs expand as they soak up fluid, increasing the length of the spine by as much as one inch overnight. In weight-bearing activity, this fluid is squeezed back into the adjacent soft tissues and vertebrae, to be replaced by fresh fluid during the next rest period. If these normal healing mechanisms are inhibited by poor posture and loss of flexibility, the discs become thin, brittle, and easily injured. This condition, called *degenerative disc disease*, can lead to bulging or herniated discs. The movement principles of therapeutic yoga— 'spreading' (creating space in an area), 'soaking' (allowing blood and fluids to bathe and cleanse an area), and 'squeezing' (compressing fluids out of an area)-use the physiology of the disc to help in healing." [149] A spine degenerated and deteriorated, without a fresh supply of nutrients and fluids moving in and out of the vertebrae each day, eventually and gradually collapses forward, as tiny fractures inevitably form and compound over time. Yet Schatz, a medical doctor and yoga teacher, had found that yoga could reverse the degeneration.

In essence, while Pete and his observant wife had noticed something going awry five decades prior, because their strategy had primarily addressed the superficial symptom of the problem–the fact that poor posture "looks" bad and so should be pulled up–they never got to the root of the problem to heal the increasingly brittle discs. Had Pete known that his spine was starved of nutrients and fresh fluids and was rapidly becoming increasingly brittle and dessicated, he would have likely turned his fierce determination toward the problem and at least halted, if not reversed, it. Knowing Pete, had he known about yoga for the spine, and eating foods thought to ward off microscopic fractures by remineralizing bones (like bone broth and kale), he would have embraced those things heartily. Annemarie Colbin wrote an entire book including recipes that would have helped, called *Food and Our Bones: The Natural Way to Prevent Osteoporosis*.[150] Instead, though I well know that anything is possible, by the time Pete got to me, even I suspected we were squarely in the realm of pain management.

I include Pete's story not to be depressing, or to suggest that Pete is suffering now because he should have done something different 50 years ago. I've never met a person who averted all of the hardships of life through diligent research. In fact, if you are going to do only one thing diligently, you are far better off working on the tone in your heart than looking for cures. I know the scary feeling associated with a runaway disease process that has no apparent resolution. Yet like my inner transformation after watching the movie *The Secret,* when we get the tone in our heart right, sometimes information that helps can get to us more easily. Even if no help ever presents itself, an Open Heart Consciousness is always available.

When it comes to the Language of Healing, something most of us would brush off as a normal part of aging: degenerative disc disease, likely has as profound a message for us to learn and heal from as any other symptom. My work with Pete *did* yield some relief. Pete's interest was piqued and he learned new ways to care for his neck for the decades ahead. Most important of all, Pete can look back over his life with compassion toward himself and value his new sense of peace and Open Heart Consciousness, with his neck exactly as it is right now. In fact, had the neck issue not sent him to my office, Open Heart Consciousness would likely not be something that was ever on his radar screen. Just as my health hardships were some of my greatest blessings to stir within me a different inner consciousness, Pete gained the opportunity to harvest similar blessings from his "pain in the neck."

Many patients arrive at my office puzzled by signs and symptoms that seem to make no sense. A surprising amount of the time, we can do the detective work that yields a detail which turns or improves the course of that disease process. If your body has a symptom that is not responding to your efforts over time, please, *try something different.* Be an impassioned detective on the hunt for a clue. Keep learning and experimenting to identify what helps your body.

It can take years or even decades to decipher messages from our body, and sometimes people die without ever discerning the whispers. There are whispers my body makes that I still do not understand, but I am open and ever-curious. Ultimately, please never give up hope. There may be symptoms, illnesses, discomforts, and even agonies you must live with. Find an Open Heart Consciousness even as you live with these mysteries. And, as you learn to live gracefully with that which you must, vow always to further your understanding and appreciation of the local dialect.

Find What Fits—Healing is Not One-Size-Fits-All

I desire now to repeat and emphasize that maxim: We can't reach old age by another man's road. My habits protect my life, but they would assassinate you.
Mark Twain

Health is the fastest growing failing business in western civilization.
Emanuel Cheraskin, M.D.

What is medicine to one person may be poison to another. Though people may hope for checklists of foolproof techniques for healing, we are far better served to become a detective willing to uncover the techniques that are foolproof uniquely to us. What is good for me is not necessarily at all good for you. Use others' stories as inspiration, not as gospel.

In much of medicine, the line between what is "good for you" and what is not, is much hazier than most people believe. People are too individual and unique for a one-size-fits-all approach. An example that comes to mind has to do with orange juice. I have a friend whose daughter was sick from September through March every year from the time she was a small child. When she moved to live with her dad full-time, he began to give her one glass of orange juice a day with breakfast, and she immediately stopped getting sick. It was like a miracle cure for her lifelong propensity for illness. On the other hand, I have a friend who manages his diabetes through diet. He wouldn't dream of drinking a glass of orange juice and describes it as "crazy high" in sugars. He is cautious even eating an actual orange and never has more than half of one at a time. So is orange juice a miracle cure or a harmful sugar bomb? It depends on the unique individual. Our exquisite bodies are so varied, so diverse. Learn yours, listen to yours, love yours.

Identify your own body language, locks, and keys

My friend hosts a local radio show and she was excited one night to feature two prominent oncologists from an internationally acclaimed hospital who would address topics of holistic healing in a research-based, methodical way. Only seconds before going on air, my friend the host mentioned in an offhand way that she would try to steer the questions away from some of the more controversial topics like taking herbs or mega-doses of vitamins during cancer treatment. "Good!" asserted one of the oncologists, "I don't even let my patients take a multivitamin," she said. "Are you kidding?" shouted the other oncologist, "The first thing I do is put all my patients on a multivitamin!" My friend was in panic as the seconds ticked down to airtime and these two renowned colleagues argued back and forth. In the end, they avoided all questions relating to vitamins on that show. Even those "in the know" do not always agree or "know."

Another example that comes to mind involves a preteen who sought me out for acupuncture during her recovery from a serious concussion and whiplash. Shockingly, the treatment regimen she had been prescribed by her neurologist involved a neck collar, heavy-duty drug therapy, a pessimistic projection for the future, and a dismissive attitude toward acupuncture. Her family wisely sought a second opinion. Neurologist #2 vetoed the neck collar, nixed the drugs, wholeheartedly endorsed acupuncture, recommended a vitamin regimen emphasizing nutrients to help her brain heal, and was optimistic that the girl would be fully recovered quickly. She followed this advice and recovered completely in a month. Experts may vary that dramatically in their approach.

We all would do best to take into account our unique body and how our unique body responds as we try different things. If you are going for fast healing (like fast food) it might be quick and easy, but it might not deeply nourish and sustain over the long term. There is truly no one-size-fits-all approach to healing. To unlock a new possibility of healing, you will need to take your time and identify your own body language, locks and keys.

Hunt for the Miraculous

There are two ways to live your life.
One is though nothing is a miracle.
The other is though everything is a miracle.
Albert Einstein

Never lose a holy curiosity.
Albert Einstein

My neighbor Eric called me, a bit frantic that his brother had just been diagnosed with Stage IV cancer. Eric was researching day and night to learn everything he could about people who had survived with the generally fatal type of cancer his brother had. Though Eric is not a doctor, he has a Master's degree and can efficiently sift through hundreds of medical references and discern useful possible courses of action, including approaches that were not yet conventional standard of care. Eric called me a second time, sputtering with frustration that he had told his brother some holistic and controversial things people had done along with their surgery, chemo, and radiation to increase their odds of survival. His brother had replied, "No, I'm not really interested in all that." As Eric confessed to me, he wanted to shake him and tell him, "Dude, do you realize that if you only do what your doctors tell you to do, you have a 100% fatal disease? You have to do something different if you want to live!" Not wanting to add stress to his brother's already stressful situation, he kept his mouth shut.

It takes a special mindset to maintain Einstein's "holy curiosity" about the possibilities that lie within our bodies. It takes an even more special mindset to overcome premature cognitive commitments about what is or is not possible, and then hunt for the miraculous. It takes an incredibly special mindset to do the things that encourage the miraculous. Mostly, fear and constricted views abound. Patients are often discouraged from hoping or hunting or doing anything different. To entertain the possibility of an unusual or miraculous or spontaneous healing or remission may require the inner ability to swim counter current. "Worldwide, an estimated 169.3 million years of healthy life were lost because of cancer in 2008," said the International Agency for Research on Cancer.[151] I think it is a swim worth taking.

In the medical world, "spontaneous healing" and "spontaneous remission" are terms that tend to produce reactions. People sometimes take downright offense at the topic. At the hospital campus where our healing arts center is located, I'm not allowed to use the term "healing" in the names of any of my talks. In a hospital setting, no one is supposed to use the word "healing" on anything. A hospital may "debride" or "excise" something, or "scan" or x-ray something, or "radiate or apply chemotherapy" to something, plus a whole bunch of other somethings ending in -centesis, -ectomy, -opsy, -oscopy, -otomy, -plexy, or -plasty, but no one must express intentions to "heal" something. There would surely be a lawsuit if that procedure failed! Forget about spontaneous healing. No question, such a thing is regarded as a quaint superstitious belief of the ignorant, perpetuated by false hope!

Don't mistake what I am saying. I love working in the science-driven climate of a medical pavilion. Despite the boycott on "healing," our campus is filled with closet "healers," as evidenced by the fact that an extraordinary number of patients seen by doctors there get well and are exceptionally happy with their care (they tell me this). Very many of the varied and diverse medical practices refer to, and work in partnership with, our healing arts center, which is distinctly progressive in the medical milieu of this age.

Most doctors operate in a model that confines them. They are limited in the time they have to hear anything outside of a report of progress on the current course of treatment for the body region in which they specialize in. Therefore, many doctors operating in this model have an artificially reduced incidence of hearing about the many miracles that patients experience. The miraculous happens every day, it's just not the first thing most patients are calling their doctor to report. They simply cancel their next appointment. To compound this problem of unawareness, unusual incidents of the miraculous and spontaneous remissions are not often well studied or written up in double-blind, placebo controlled, scholarly articles for publication and peer review.

To make sure I am not unduly influenced by the pervasive viewpoint that bodies require drugs and painful expensive procedures to heal, I keep by my bedside a massive tome called *Spontaneous Remission, An Annotated Bibliography* by Brendan O'Regan and Caryle Hirshberg[152]. This is no light reading, but I find if I'm beginning to feel hopeless about a health issue I or one of my patients is facing, odds are somebody spontaneously healed from it and it is documented in this book. The 1,574 citations cannot help but stimulate a sense of wonder and hope at our capacity for healing. Miracles and spontaneous healing are more common than we tend to think and if you learn the art of unlocking a healing state and then pass it on, we'll see a downright revival. I have been on the lookout for reports of spontaneous healing for over 20 years now, and am bowled over by the frequency of their incidence.

Hunt Miracles

In his book *Flourish,* Martin E. P. Seligman describes the positive psychology work that he pioneered with the military. His program includes resiliency training, and one of the categories of his training is called "Hunt the Good Stuff." Sergeants are taught to keep a gratitude journal detailing the blessings in their life.[153] "Hunt" is an excellent word choice because it insinuates that we must go out looking for those blessings, and then must do something like write it down to "bag the kill," lest it get away from us. My 86-year-old patient knows a lot about this; when I once remarked, "Lola, you look for the good in everything, don't you?" She quipped back, "I hope so, I don't want to find the bad!"

My neighbor Eric kept hunting for solutions for his brother with Stage IV cancer, and patiently explained to him that he needed to stack his odds in favor of a miracle. I happened to know about a holistic doctor in Baltimore collaborating with Johns Hopkins oncology doctors in a quietly conducted study using homeopathic mistletoe in conjunction with conventional oncology treatment. Because of connections Eric has, he got his brother in with the holistic physician and the collaborating Hopkins oncologist within two days. So far, with this collaborative approach, Eric's brother is beating the statistics for his disease.

I want to make mention here that people often assume that miracles and spontaneous healing denotes either spiritual intervention or alternative treatment. I think these assumptions are too limited. Miracles and spontaneous healing arise from the *right* treatment, which may be conventional or not. Healing may arise with *no* treatment, reflecting that in some cases a change of the state of heart can be the healing agent. My healing from the glass shards in my eye included the very practical treatment of having an ER doctor *remove the shards*. There are no rules for miracles, and I personally like to use any and all available resources to stack the odds in my favor.

One of my patients had made the decision to use only holistic modalities to heal from cancer. Though she came for only a few acupuncture treatments, she was soon sleeping better, feeling more vitality, and noticed she was no longer constipated. In the meantime, she met an energy healer who assured her he could heal her cancer using hands-on healing. But he insisted she stop everything else she was doing. He so powerfully convinced her that other modalities would interfere with his work that she wistfully informed me she was discontinuing acupuncture. It doesn't take medical training or a healer's credentials to know that sleeping better, having more energy, and eliminating more easily are basic building blocks of healing. What "healer" would deny a critically ill patient access to resources and set stringent conditions by which someone can or cannot heal? To me, this amounted to holistic malpractice. If you find a practitioner like this, run.

Cultivate a holy curiosity. Hunt for miracles. Look for evidence of such things. You will be amazed by what you find.

Work Ecologically With the Native Terrain

The new "miracle" drugs are the worst of all. The premise of drug intervention is this: If A is healthy and B is sick and C is drug therapy, C will somehow return you to A. On no planet can C ever be A. C is always even farther from A than even B was.

T.S. Wiley with Bent Formby, Ph.D
Lights Out: Sleep, Sugar, and Survival[154]

It is no measure of health to be well adjusted to a profoundly sick society.
Jiddu Krishnamurti

One of the first duties of the physician is to educate the masses not to take medicine.
Sir William Osler, M.D.
(one of the four founding professors of Johns Hopkins Hospital)

In *Lights on Life: The Yoga Journey to Wholeness, Inner Peace, and Ultimate Freedom*, B.K.S. Iyengar refers to the human body as "mortal clay."[155] We are truly clay, shaped by our thoughts, feelings, and lifestyle habits. Iyengar also says too, "Technically speaking, true meditation in the yogic sense cannot be done by a person who is under stress or who has a weak body, weak lungs, hard muscles, collapsed spine, fluctuating mind, mental agitation, or timidity."[156] To the busy person immersed in work and family life, covering all of the self-care bases Iyengar mentions may seem somewhere on the spectrum between daunting and impossible. However, prevention always works better than clean-up.

When the Dalai Lama was asked, "What thing about humanity surprises you the most?" His answer was, "Man, because he sacrifices his health in order to make money. Then he sacrifices his money to recuperate his health. Then he is so anxious about the future that he doesn't enjoy the present. As a result, he doesn't live in the present or the future. He lives as if he's never going to die. Then he dies having never really lived." These things surprise me, too. What surprises me about humanity even more is that while man is sacrificing his money to recuperate his health, he fires off like a madman, shooting drugs and procedures at his problems with no regard to the ecological concerns inherent to the care-taking of his native terrain.

Don't kill the terrain

I'll never forget my surprise and horror to find that something safely sold as a plant fertilizer could act as a toxic killer. When I was 20 years old, I decided to turn my one- room apartment into a jungle sanctuary. I covered every surface with plants. I hung them from the ceiling, crowded them onto the windowsill, and left only a small open space on my desk. One day my mom came to visit and admire my plants. Hoping to be helpful, she asked what I was feeding them. *"Feeding them?"* I asked. It hadn't occurred to me to feed the plants. She assured me they needed feeding (they do!) but from her viewpoint at the time this did not include things we would both later come to prefer, like fish emulsion and homemade compost tea. Rather, she considered the best food to be a well-known commercial product that, once mixed, turns a cheery fluorescent blue. I wasn't much of an independent thinker back then, so I did not mull over the fact that feeding anything fluorescent blue to a living entity seems generally like a bad idea. Instead, I dutifully doused my plants.

Within an hour, a worm emerged on the surface of one of my plants, writhing furiously. As I watched, it desperately hurled itself over the edge of the pot and landed on the floor where it continued to thrash around. As I watched in astonishment, it occurred to me that the worm was moving *as if it had been burned*. Though I rinsed it off and gave it some fresh dirt unsullied by blue potions, this worm that had been living in my potted plant for months was, by morning, shriveled and dead. I was just a beginning gardener, but I knew that worms are essential for optimal living soil. Something that killed the worms was clearly not ecologically sound, and did not respect and honor the whole of the terrain.

I slowly began to transform my approach to gardening, to an organic and "wholistic" approach. Now I think about how to *encourage* my worms, how to *encourage* beneficial bacteria and fungi in the soil, and how to turn out a final product that, if eaten, won't pollute the body eating it. I even think about whether what I am releasing into the toilet each day has a downstream destructive effect, or whether my humanure will healthfully compost back to something enriching to the environment.

Given that our groundwater, streams, and coastal water creatures test exceedingly high in prescription drugs from our wastes, this is no joke. There is a downstream effect to our actions. One of my patients was instructed to use a bathroom separate from the rest of her family for *six months* while her chemo passed out of her. Her children were at risk of absorbing the chemicals coming off of her through her sweat, pores, and bathroom excretions. What happens to the rest that is flushed is not something we take much time to ponder.

Whether it later shows up in the food we eat and water we drink is a serious consideration not to "flush" out of our consciousness. Do your best to embrace early preventive care that spares you such decisions. Do your best to learn how to support health through means that won't come back to hurt you or your descendants later. Support and encourage research using new, more life engendering approaches to the illnesses and ailments of our time. There are increasingly more researchers at the cutting-edge of science developing approaches to cancer and infectious diseases that support the immune system rather than bombing the terrain.

Heal green

Help to unlock the healing efforts of as many people as you can by keeping your personal environment, living habits and your approach to illness as "green" as possible. Set an example through thoughtful enlightened action. My friend tells me his lawn treated only with cornmeal grows more lushly and stays green longer than that of his neighbor, who hires a service that uses heavy chemicals. The neighbor has a very sick child and an even sicker dog who both play on the chemically treated lawn, but he sees no connection. It takes gentle education to change the tide; cornmeal is not backed by a massive advertising budget, so we must give the gift of our time to be the educators.

Doctors have done a great job of ceasing to prescribe antibiotics for viral illnesses, but then send the virally sick patient home with no treatment. I have patients in bed with viral illnesses for weeks or even months because the doctor told them there is "nothing they can do." Yet we *can* "do something." There are vitamins and plant medicines that science shows are effective at treating viruses that can help us in an ecologically sound way. In *Herbal Antibiotics* and *Herbal Antivirals*, Stephen Harrod Buhner highlights many plants we consider weeds that grow in the United States, and that can be found within miles of most people's homes. These have the power to treat not only colds and flu, but also illnesses that are completely resistant to prescription medications. Perhaps most importantly of all, if gathered in nature as Buhner suggests, they are free.[157]

The same could be said for many simple food and plant remedies that may work in ways similar to prescription drugs. Though I am glad prescriptions such as antibiotics exist and are available for life-threatening infections, personally I am unlikely to take an antibiotic without first trying Vitamin C dosed on the hour until bowel tolerance (loose stool) is reached as I learned from the work of two-time Nobel Prize winner Linus Pauling. If that fails, there are garlic, andrographis, and many, many other plant and food medicines that can be used after learning about and understanding their effects.

One of my students tells me her relative survived months as a "dead body cleanup crew" worker after the outbreak of the Spanish flu pandemic that killed between 50 and a 100 *million* people. His secret? Eating a clove of raw garlic every hour washed down with a generous swig of whiskey. In *Eating on the Wild Side,* Jo Robinson points out that garlic has been called "Russian Penicillin" and that 1 mg of allicin equals 15 international units of penicillin. One mg is found in approximately three cloves, and Robinson recommends mincing the garlic and letting it sit for ten minutes to develop the highest allicin content. Robinson points out that bacteria are 1,000 times more likely to become resistant to modern antibiotics than to garlic.[158] Not only that, garlic nourishes rather than harms the native terrain.

I'm not too big on tossing garlic back raw, particularly with anything resembling whiskey, but freshly minced garlic is delicious floating in hot broth, mixed with melted butter as a dip or topping for toast, whisked with lemon juice, olive oil and salt as a dressing, or even, as a local pediatrician recommends for children with sore throats, mixed with honey and licked from a spoon.

As I became increasingly interested in learning about powerful foods with medicinal properties, I also learned that garlic, for example, is one of nature's "anti-quorum sensing compounds." This means it interrupts the chemical signals that bacteria use to coordinate among themselves to know when to become virulent and make us sick. Researchers such as Princeton University Molecular Biologist Bonnie Bassler are looking at ways to develop drugs to interrupt the chemical language that allows bacteria to coordinate defense and mount attacks. Her team is developing anti-quorum sensing molecules to be used as a new approach to replace current antibiotics that kill bacteria but foster drug resistance.

Bassler's approach is an example of the cutting edge science that will help healing become more "green" as long as we can culturally move past the health paradigm of bombing things with toxic chemicals. Quorum sensing inhibitors would be the new generation of broad-spectrum antibiotics that work by interrupting the ability of bacteria to come to a quorum–the agreement–to "attack" us. Bassler's TED Talk on "How bacteria 'talk'" describes her work based on the unusual methods bacteria use to coordinate the efforts that make us sick. [159] In the meantime, while teams such as Bassler's continue to research, nature's quorum sensing compound garlic is available to us at every meal.

I share these interesting facts about garlic because most people have no idea how much food medicine they already have sitting on their kitchen table, nor how enjoyable it can be to learn about the medicinal properties of food. I do not intend to suggest that a reader delay appropriate medical care, but don't pass on the fun of understanding nature's medicine as well.

It takes time to learn and understand the use of such things as garlic, and patience to dose so frequently as the Spanish-flu averting corpse-handler did. There have been instances in which plant antimicrobials like garlic have worked for me after antibiotics had failed, though the plants require that I rest, too–not just swallow a few pills then pop back into action.

Most importantly for me, every time I have taken a prescription antibiotic, the paralysis in my right hand worsens exponentially for sometimes as long as a month—twitching and spasming and clenching tightly. My neurologist tells me this may be because there are cells in my brain in the damaged area that are not destroyed, but that are more vulnerable than normal cells. Whatever the reason, the motivation to replace an agent that is harming my brain with friendlier antimicrobials overcomes any reluctance I had to learn.

In the age of the artificially enriched green lawn as a status symbol and quick-fix symptom relieving drugs, educating ourselves and others can take commitment, creativity, patience and chutzpah.

Look for solutions that enrich rather than harm the whole

My husband and I have long loved organic gardening. We first decided to bring in ducks in response to the aphids on the roses, the slugs on the lettuce, and the caterpillars on the kale. Ducks have added so much joy to our lives. Not only do they spend the entire day foraging for bugs and thus eliminating our pest problem, they also add valuable fertilizer to the soil via their abundant poop, and they provide many eggs each week. If we had used chemical pest control, we would have robbed the soil of valuable microorganisms and killed our valuable worms. By using a thought-out, ecologically sound plan, we could maximize our particular situation with its unique variables.

If we had not been blessed with the "problem" of outdoor pests decimating our crops, we would never have bothered to consider creative solutions and we would never have experienced the joy of pet ducks. Sometimes the challenges of illness and "indoor" disease-causing pests in our body may awaken our creativity in new ways. To unlock the heart of healing, look for creative ways to maximize and protect the inner ecology.

Let Healing Burst Into Bloom

Illnesses do not come upon us out of the blue. They are developed from small daily sins against nature. When enough sins have accumulated, illnesses will suddenly appear.

Hippocrates

Doctors pour drugs of which they know little, to cure diseases of which they know less, into people of whom they know nothing.

Voltaire

One of my patients works as a caretaker for injured or elderly people requiring assistance. She was absolutely beside herself with upset over a man under her care who was in his 60s and had suffered a stroke but who was unwilling to make the effort to participate in his own recovery. She was so upset, she offered him an ultimatum. Either make the effort to rehabilitate the paralyzed side of his body, or find a new caretaker. He loved her as a caretaker, but told her firmly that the effort to recover was too great and he preferred to spend his days reading. She was devastated and left the job.

Is there anything wrong with this man's decision? NO! Each of us is the artist of our own life, and we get to decide for ourselves how to glorify the terrain. This man was thrilled to finally have the opportunity to catch up on all the books he had wanted to read over the years, but had never allowed himself the time for. Making peace with our situation is no less valuable an orientation to healing as rehabilitating.

My patient, who is wired a little more like me, will probably be trying to outsmart illness and death when she's 103. For us, we don't often shy away from the efforts, even when healing asks much of us. She soon found a new client who *wanted* a cheerleader and a taskmaster, and delightedly took her on. For those who enjoy the challenge of tending the health of your body, I urge you to *Take on Healing*. For those like the man relieved to finally relax and read, rest assured that your artistic decision also glorifies the terrain. Even motivated-me has made decisions to relax and accept certain aspects of my health that could be improved. Remember the mirror box used for phantom limb pain? That same box has been used to rehabilitate people with the exact kind of paralysis I have. I've got a mirror box, yet I have used it only once. Though I worked with a trainer to rehabilitate my hand and arm and found No Mind, inspiration to use that mirror box never grabbed me. I know that the science suggests a positive outcome with only ten minutes of practice per day for a month, but even so, I'd rather be doing a number of things other than tapping my fingers against that mirrored box.

My son, who is only seven as I write this, has an incredible inner sense of when to take on healing, and when to leave things alone. When he reports a symptom or ailment to me, I've learned to listen quietly. I'll ask him, "Would you like some help with that or not?" He confidently informs me what help he might like, or just as often states, "Mommy, my body can handle this one. I'm just going to leave it alone." For the times you know some efforts may be in order, I offer you the following stories about taking on healing.

Help Yourself Using the Opportunities at Hand

I have been asked why, if I know how to make medicine in my body, did I also take handfuls of vitamins and plant extracts over a number of years? This question reminds me a little of the Parable of the Flood in which a drowning man prayed to God to save him. Three times offers of help came his way, but he declined with the explanation that he was waiting for God, whom he was certain would save him. Finally, the man drowned and when he got to heaven he demanded of God, "Why didn't you save me?" God replied, "I sent you a pick-up truck, a boat and a helicopter and you refused all of them. What else could I possibly do for you?" Sometimes we have to do things to help ourselves using the opportunities at hand.

For me, having lived with celiac disease that went undiagnosed for 35 years, and a parasitic worm infestation from Indonesia that carried on for 13 years, eluding the vigilant testing of multiple doctors, my body had become severely malnourished and weakened. Despite eating the best foods, I had spent decades absorbing much less nutrition than is necessary for vibrant health. The celiac disease expert who finally confirmed my diagnosis advised me that it would take a full five years of high-level supplemental vitamins to recover a normal nutrient status. She was adamant that leaving my nutrient recovery to nature by eating good organic whole foods as my sole strategy was not an option; I was too far depleted. My intuition told me she was correct. For me, rebuilding my weakened body and battered immune system became a top priority. I knew full well that our inner diet of thoughts and feelings nourishes as much as what we eat. I partook of a careful selection of nourishing foods, nourishing vitamins and plant medicines, and a heaping serving of nourishing thoughts and feelings each day.

Sometimes healing is a full-time job

Sometimes the efforts people make toward helping their body are puny in relation to the insults their body has endured. If your body is very ill, like mine was, you may need to take radical action, as I did. My patient Clare did much, much more.

Clare came to me literally covered in eczema. She was not only humiliated to go in public with her swollen and inflamed skin, she could barely stand the unremitting itching. Of course she had seen doctors—lots of them. She'd seen dermatologists, allergists, endocrinologists, gynecologists, and many other -gists. Despite their titled designations, no one could get the "gist" of what was going on with her. She'd taken every prescription they'd been able to come up with, and still had no improvement in her condition.

Though Clare had seen acupuncturists before, she dialed me from the parking lot of a department store after a patient of mine sympathized with her in the checkout line and told her I was known for a creative approach. We got right to work and laid out a plan for her recovery. Clare was amazing. She was willing to not only do anything, but *everything* she could to get well.

Following the guess that food reactions were involved, and going on her suspicions as to which foods were worsening her condition while also following research suggesting possible eczema-related food culprits, Claire made radical changes to her diet. She cut many foods out, especially potentially inflammation generating foods like gluten, dairy products, soy, and eggs. She added new foods in, including detoxifying foods such as kale, asparagus, and Brussels sprouts. She began taking supplements known to detoxify the body and heal the skin. She took up a Feeling Mantra meditation. She began exercising and lost a substantial amount of weight. She came for acupuncture every week for months—and through all her extreme and diligent efforts, she got better–about 50% better.

Most patients would have quit right there, saying, "enough is enough." Clare, however, was not willing to live with a simmering case of eczema for the rest of her life, so she did what anyone who takes on healing would do—she kept searching, and kept experimenting. She eventually found a holistic doctor who had some new ideas. He agreed with every strategy Clare had adopted. He believed that the deep cellular dysfunction Clare was experiencing required a *more extreme* regimen. He radically increased her supplements. He restricted her diet even further-to an unrefined, completely grain-free "Paleolithic" diet. He instructed her to do daily coffee enemas and a weekly colonic. (Detoxing through the colon is not a "new" fad. Chinese physician Chai Yu-hua wrote over 300 years ago, "Purging the bowels eliminates the source of poisons, thereby permitting blood [essence] and energy to regenerate naturally." [160]) He had her purchase a home infrared sauna to use for detoxification three times a week. She complained to me, exhausted, that she had never realized healing could be a full-time job.

At one point, Clare asked her doctor, "Why do I need to do all of these things and other people don't?" He said to her, "Because the eczema is just the outward sign to us that your liver has lost its ability to detoxify your body. If we don't do the detoxifying work for it until it recovers the ability to do it on its own, you'll end up with breast cancer." "Oh," Clare replied, shocked that her skin could have any relationship to her risk for cancer, "my mom just died from breast cancer."

Though Clare's mom didn't have the opportunity to explore other pathways to health, Clare followed this doctor's advice to the dot. Within two months, her skin was completely healed. It now shimmers, like gorgeous luminous porcelain. That such beautiful delicate skin lay hidden under the disfiguring eczema, and that the eczema was nothing more than a desperate banshee scream for help, still shocks even me. Sometimes healing is easy and happens fast. Sometimes, we choose peace with our health circumstances exactly as they are. Sometimes, the best thing we can do is take on our healing as a full-time job.

Grow health like a plant that needs enough time with ideal conditions to burst into bloom

I don't mean to suggest that healing must be a long, weary climb up a mountain. Every day I am amazed by the human capacity to heal, and how fast people can recover from symptoms. In my acupuncture treatment room, it is not unusual for a patient to lament, "Why didn't I come here *first*? I can't believe I spent the last two years managing my symptoms and now they are just gone." Healing can definitely happen fast, sometimes like a light switch flicking on or off. Sometimes getting the conditions right for that switch to flick happens *really* slowly.

My patient Louise healed fast, but getting the necessary factors right took so long I didn't think it would ever happen. When Louise came to me, she was often sick, depressed, and lethargic. Her mind generated an impressive array of anxious and defeated thoughts. The moment I could help her stretch into some new possibility and indulge a glimmer of hope that she might change, she would snap right back to her old familiar ways. She would lament that she was working very hard to get well, but never seemed to really get anywhere. Louise had taken on healing as a full-time job, but was getting nowhere fast. She came for acupuncture every week for a year. I was Louise's greatest cheerleader, but I began to wonder whether continuing on was a colossal waste of my time and her money.

One day Louise showed up for her appointment with a gleam in her eye. She proudly told me that it had finally clicked for her what it meant to live in Open Heart Consciousness, irrespective of circumstances. The moment the click happened, she explained, she went out and made a business decision that was so enormous and fraught with risk it made me shiver. I didn't think *I* could have handled what she had chomped off, and for months, I held my breath

161

wondering whether she could. I silently wondered whether she had temporarily gone insane, or whether she had truly changed. I fretted whether my advice to live in Open Heart Consciousness had rendered her overly elevated with excitement, and temporarily out of her mind, with disaster soon to follow. But Louise had been diligently working to heal herself for a year, so while the external evidence of it was slow to appear, when it finally happened she was rock solid. Her business decision and her new powerful, joyous way of pursuing it resulted in a success so personally and financially stunning, I still marvel that such a thing could happen.

If your own personal transformation seems like it requires a lot of work but is getting nowhere fast, stick with it. Growth and change often build a quiet momentum, just waiting for the right conditions to burst into bloom.

Observe the Laws of Nature

You cannot escape the immutable biological laws of cause and effect through ingesting medicinal substances.

Joel Fuhrman, M.D.

Eat to Live [161]

*Tame people, to me, are people who live by man-made laws. In America, particularly, we have a government that tries to control our morals. Wild people are controlled only by the laws of nature. There are lots of things you can't do, but you can't do them because **nature** tells you so.*

Robert Wolff interviewed by Thom Hartmann

The Edison Gene: ADHD and the Gift of the Hunter Child [162]

My patient Leah came to me because of infertility, yet I learned at the intake that she was sleeping only 3.5 hours a night. Between working full-time, raising her son, and trying to be a supermom, Leah told me the only time she had to fold laundry was at 3:00 in the morning. She was looking to acupuncture as a way to persist in her insane lifestyle, hoping to overcome the laws of nature and get pregnant. Such a thing is not possible. Though I pressed this point with her and asserted I wouldn't treat her if she didn't also make efforts to sleep, Leah furtively continued with her sleepless lifestyle. Soon after, she enthusiastically reported to me that she was pregnant. Yet a month later, she learned she had a blighted ovum, which means her body had made a sac, but there was no baby in it. Her body bank account had simply *not had enough reserve to fill that sac*. Happily, Leah heeded that painful message and began to sleep properly. The baby she is pregnant with now reaps the rewards. Gregory Bateson said, "The major problems in the world are the result of the difference between how nature works and the way people think." Not everyone heeds nature's messages as well as Leah eventually did. We persist in the delusion that we can get away with violating the laws of nature.

Many people act as if the only laws by which we must abide are those that man creates. I see it in my practice every day—people living as if natural law, the laws of nature, don't even exist. The violation of natural law extracts a heavy price. We're not accustomed to thinking of our body as a reflection of our harmony (or lack thereof) with nature, so when our body provides us with symptoms in response to, for example, our lack of sleep, lack of fresh air and sunlight, absence of exercise, and paucity of nutrient dense foods, we don't really think of it in terms of breaking a law. Rebels break laws, not us good people. However, the laws of nature are the truest laws, are not arbitrary, and cannot be skirted or outsmarted.

One law of nature we are *not* to break is the law that says sun burns baby's skin. We just would not consider laying a newborn out on the patio in the blazing sun with no protection from dawn until dusk. That baby would burn badly, and the parent would be arrested for child abuse.

Who will arrest you or remind you if you are breaking a bodily law of nature? What if the law you are breaking is hard to discern, like something as seemingly innocuous as eating a food that is making you subtly sick every day? What if it is a food which you crave, and can't imagine giving up? Sometimes people unknowingly react to the foods that they crave. If you break such a law, you may not be arrested, but you still will pay the fine. It is human nature to try to "get away with" whatever we can. In one case I observed, the consequence of breaking just such a law of nature almost resulted in the penalty of death.

This story, also from the journey of Clare who had the eczema, illustrates what can happen when we violate natural law. In nature, we know not to make a meal of Hemlock or the Deadly Nightshade plant. As we learn the laws that govern our own unique bodies, we may find there are other things that are just not okay to eat.

Don't fall victim to concept lousing up percept

At one point along the way of understanding the mystery of her extreme eczema, Clare decided to see an allergist. I happen to know this allergist, and she is not only quite brilliant, but has a huge heart and is totally dedicated to helping her patients. Clare went to this allergist seeking testing to pinpoint which foods she might be reacting to, as she experimented with a restricted diet to clear her skin. The allergist told her she was making a grave mistake, that she should absolutely not restrict her diet, and that there was no scientific evidence that foods could cause eczema. She advised Clare it would be a wasted effort and an unnecessary hardship to change her diet. Though Clare had just finished doing her own research that showed there *was* a food/eczema connection, her trusted doctor's dismissive attitude caused her to second guess this information. She would later laughingly joke that the doctor must have been reading stone-age medical journals.

The allergist ran the standardized allergy testing and determined that the only food to which Clare was confirmed allergic, and thus should avoid, was peanuts. Clare mentioned that she had been avoiding eggs for many years, as she had observed it worsened her skin. Absolutely not, the allergist rejoined, she could eat all the eggs she wanted—*the tests said so*.

Now anyone can understand human nature in this situation. Despite the fact that I urged Clare to heed her own body wisdom and stay off the eggs, which *she knew* worsened her skin, Clare felt like she got a home free pass from a medical authority.

As the fates would have it, it only took one egg to demonstrate that human faculties and feedback systems are far superior at detecting what our body does and does not like than the allergy test could be. Not only did her skin react to that egg, she went into full anaphylaxis with airway obstruction, requiring an ambulance ride to the ER complete with massive IV's full of steroids, an oxygen tube, and a serious scare for her life.

I wish I could tell you the story ended there. The hospital told Clare that this was a serious anaphylactic allergy, to diligently avoid eggs and to follow up with her allergist for an EpiPen®. Clare went back to the allergist, who truly is very caring and smart. It would be easy to conclude this doctor is not very good, and that is incorrect. The attitude of complete loyalty to testing over all faculties of observation is prevalent, and Clare's experience in that regard is not unusual. Such doctors are victims of "Houston's Law," named after Dr. Jean Houston, which states, "Concept louses up percept." The allergists' attachment to allergy concepts prevented proper perception of reality. The allergist told Clare it was a fluke, that she was not allergic to eggs, and sent her away **without** an EpiPen® with the encouragement to eat eggs as much as she wanted, because THE TESTS SAID SO.

The next time it happened, Claire didn't even eat a visible egg. She ate one bite of a cupcake that had been made with an egg, and she was in full blown anaphylaxis with almost complete airway obstruction within minutes. By a true miracle an ambulance got to her while there was still time. The ER doctor who remembered Clare was outraged and declared the allergist "an idiot." Needless to say, Clare no longer eats eggs. Unfortunately, the allergist, who was humiliated by what happened but staunch in her reliance on tests, sent a letter to both me and the ER doctor stating that the anaphylaxis was not caused by anything containing egg, that Clare WAS NOT allergic to egg, and that she had a psychosomatic illness in which her emotions were causing these life threatening allergic-like reactions.

Diagnostic testing is a necessary and valuable part of modern day life. However, please, let's not forget the value of good old fashioned observation using our sensory faculties. These faculties are so complex and sophisticated that no test yet developed rivals them in their ability to detect subtlety and nuance when it comes to our own health. Do not become beholden to any authority or diagnostic procedure when it contradicts your own deep wisdom. Always observe the laws of nature as they apply to you. As T.S. Wiley summarizes in *Lights Out: Sleep, Sugar, and Survival*, "The very word 'influenza' referred to the 'influence' the sun, the moon, the planets, and the stars had on our health. We always knew that there were certain rules for staying alive in harmony with all other living things—how much you could eat, how long you could stay awake, and how much stress you could endure. In our hubris, we've flaunted the rules. We used to *know* better."[163]

Empower an Inner Authority

A teacher who likes to demonstrate how much more he knows than his student often reinforces the pupil's self-doubt. If the implication is that you cannot learn without the teacher's instructions, the student loses any reliance on his own natural learning process because he will be dependent on an outside authority for approval and guidance. Learning happens best when both instructor and student recognize that experience is the teacher.

Timothy Gallwey and Bob Kriegel
Inner Skiing [164]

Healing is a matter of time, but it is also sometimes a matter of opportunity.
Hippocrates

When our boat wouldn't start, my husband Brandon started calling marine engine repair shops to get it serviced. The only problem was it was February, near Annapolis, and every place was booked three months out in preparation for the impending boating season. In despair, we called my dad who was an old boater and savvy with engines. After running some basic diagnostic tests and finding no clue, he gave us the phone number of a friend of his whom I dubbed "Mr. Marine." My dad described him as "the best engine guy in Annapolis." Mr. Marine was booked for three months as well, but as a favor to my dad, he came out sooner for a consult. After running several more diagnostic tests, he turned to my husband and said, "There is no way to figure out what is wrong with this engine without tearing it apart. It will take you months to get on anyone's calendar including mine to do that, and it will cost you thousands of dollars. The problem is probably a simple one, but there is no way to tell until you get the thing apart. You're a smart guy; go download the engine schematic off the Internet and tear the thing apart yourself. It will be one of four problems; two of which you can fix easily by cleaning, the other two which can be fixed with cheap parts. That would be my recommendation." He nodded reassuringly to my uneasy husband, then turned and left.

Taking responsibility for something as complex and potentially intimidating as a four-stroke engine can be as disturbing as the thought of taking responsibility for our own health. But my husband knew Mr. Marine was right, and besides, if we didn't take matters into our own hands, we would be without a boat for some time. Mr. Marine was confident Brandon could do it, and so with that encouragement spurring him on, he did. Several weeks later, our boat engine was humming beautifully.

Over-booked marine doctors are not the only technicians who may empower our inner authority rather than insisting on being the authority. Great practitioners from any field often practice in a style that emphasizes teaching rather than fixing.

Imparting self-sufficiency

Some years ago, while living in one of the tougher neighborhoods in Baltimore, I cut my finger badly on a piece of glass. I had been snapping stained glass pieces for a project when the glass slipped and sheared a deep slit in my finger that went all the way to the bone.

The local ER was a practical place, with an amazing can-do attitude. To rectify the true problem the hospital had: far too many gruesome issues without nearly enough staff to meet the overwhelming need, they employed an enlightened style of medicine: imparting self-sufficiency. There I was with my little cut, sandwiched in between the victims of gunshot wounds, stabbings, rapes, and drug overdoses. This hospital addressed my situation in a way that caught me by surprise. "If you'd like I can put in a few stitches" said the doctor, after cleaning the wound. "Or, I can show you how to apply a butterfly bandage and it will heal better and leave less of a scar."

After staring at him silently for a moment as I wrapped my head around what he was suggesting, I stammered something like, "Are you sure I don't need the stitches?" He explained again, "It will heal more cleanly with a butterfly dressing, but you'll need to watch me do it so you can do it again when you change the bandage." He then showed me how to neatly line the skin up just how we wanted it to heal, and then to affix a bandage in such a way as to apply tension so the skin would stay exactly as we intended until it could knit together on its own. That deep, gaping wound would heal with barely a trace of an imperceptible scar. I've seen people with far lesser wounds than mine leave hospitals with three, four and five stitches that left raised, rumpled wavy lines of scarring.

I received a dual blessing from this enlightened overburdened doctor, and the cosmetic appearance of my finger was the far lesser of them. When it came to the "littler things" he aimed to teach rather than fix, and to empower an inner authority rather than to be the authority. The instruction and education by my doctor that day to trust my inner authority has blossomed into a calm sense of stewardship of my body that I had never permitted myself prior to receiving that wise doctor's gift. Albert Schweitzer, M.D. once said, "It's supposed to be a secret, but I'll tell you anyway. We doctors do nothing. We only help and encourage the doctor within."

Engage your capacity for surprising insight

I am a big fan of John Taylor Gatto, proponent of open source education, a 30-year teacher in the public school system and former New York State Teacher of the Year. In all five of his brilliant books, he chillingly illustrates that every person who is a product of the compulsory schooling system (most of us) has been trained for a minimum of 12 years to by and large suspend critical judgment and accept and memorize information presented to us by authorities. In *Weapons of Mass Instruction*, Gatto contends, "The ideal hireling is reflexively obedient, cheerfully enthusiastic about following orders, ever eager to please. Training for this position begins in the first grade with the word, 'don't.'"[165] Gatto also remarks, "We could encourage the best qualities of youthfulness—curiosity, adventure, resilience, the capacity for surprising insight...by giving each student the autonomy he or she needs in order to take a risk every now and then."[166]

When it comes to our health, we need to awaken those same qualities: *curiosity, adventure, resilience, and the capacity for surprising insight*. It is simply not enough to suspend critical judgment and accept the diagnosis, prognosis, and insights of outside health authorities unquestioningly. When it comes to our health, to "pass the test with flying colors" means to steward our body to the most flourishing state we can. To do that with excellence is to be a curious and engaged learner.

There is a great post called *Who lived longer? The Emperors, the Chinese Medicine Doctors or the Monk?* written by pharmacist and Chinese medicine practitioner Wilson Ngai in the *Healthreason.com* blog. Ngai describes that upon examining the age of death for 240 emperors through 24 dynasties, it was found that the mean age of death for emperors was only 41 years, vs. 67 years for monks, and 75 years for traditional Chinese doctors. It is not much surprise to me that the emperors died early; they were known to live an overindulgent lifestyle. But of great interest to me was the difference in mean age of death between the monk and the traditional Chinese doctor. I pondered this for a long time. Monks are known for their simple lifestyle, peaceful inner state, and higher likeliness of being steeped in a sense of the holy divine. These are all practices I associate with longevity. But the traditional Chinese doctors may have had one thing over the monks: a greater knowledge of how to keep the body in peak health. I suspect that knowledge bought them that average of eight extra years of life.

Be a world class specialist on you

It is possible to use the Internet to increase your health knowledge by finding the useful information that is relevant to you. My friend, a veterinarian, asked me, "Are you sure you want to recommend that? I spend half my time talking my clients out of the strange diagnoses they come up with for their dogs. They come in so convinced that their pet has some rare disease requiring complex treatment that they aren't satisfied when I tell them something more simple. We end up running tests that really aren't necessary so that they can stop worrying."

Researching information on the Internet is potentially fraught with problems. People can post anything they want, unsubstantiated by research and potentially dangerous. Many forums are heavily slanted towards negative experiences, and may "bash" doctors or medical treatments. Anomalous experiences can be grossly overrepresented, building on fears that every little symptom is indicative of something catastrophic. The power of suggestion can influence our experience, increasing our likeliness of experiencing every little symptom associated with a disease. That said, I have seen many patients learn something indispensable to their recovery after becoming meaningfully engaged in learning about and understanding their condition.

While having a team of health care practitioners you trust is important, becoming well-informed on your own condition is the best insurance of excellent care. People want to turn things over to "the experts," but doctors, even specialists, because of having to effectively treat more than one person, are generalists. You want to become the most educated expert on what you've got, and on how the various treatments work or don't work for you. The only person who can truly be a world class specialist on you is *you*.

Specialized forums dedicated to your symptom or diagnosis (I use mostly Yahoo groups), are a place to share intelligent conversation with people who have symptoms or diagnoses like yours. It can be instructive to follow a forum conversation over time. For any symptom or condition I am dealing with, I also do an Internet search for "treat xxx naturally." Just about any "xxx" you can think of will have natural treatments. You may have to check several pages deep into the search results to get past the conventional sites posing as holistic resources.

The websites that interest me always cite published research and footnote liberally. Even so, such sites may not be representative of "standard of care" in medicine; often the featured information may be used by some doctors but has not become standard practice. Such sites are potentially filled with hope and possibility for the person at an otherwise dead end. I often order many books on a health topic from the library and skim them for unique or interesting information, bypassing the droll and uninteresting parts of the texts. One patient of mine learned something unique that turned the course of her illness after reading the Medical Mysteries column in the Washington Post. Resources are everywhere. Sometimes you will discover cutting edge therapies that work, are supported by valid science, but which may not have made it yet into standard of care practice. My patient Susan found a study by a major medical center investigating the effects of mushroom extracts on HPV. She emailed the head researcher in hopes of learning what brand and dosage the researchers were using. The doctor emailed her back within a few hours and told her that while she wasn't yet able to disclose such details on the still-to-be-published study, she could tell her what was working in her own practice. Susan now tests negative for the HPV that troubled her for years.

Jenny came to me to manage the pain associated with her grossly swollen lymph nodes from CLL, a type of leukemia. If you have never paused to savor a moment of gratitude for your lymph nodes, which work silently on your behalf every day, do so now. When they swell to the size of softballs along your armpits and groin without allowing a moment free of agonizing pain or relief even with narcotics, it quickly becomes apparent how much they are daily taken for granted. Jenny did not have the luxury of taking hers for granted.

Jenny's cancer was so advanced that she no longer qualified for conventional or experimental treatment. Her sole treatment when I met her was "palliative care," but her lymph nodes were so painful that the heavy doses of narcotics she took every few hours could hardly be considered palliative. The first thing we did when Jenny reached my office was do an Internet search for "alternative treatment for CLL." I was stunned to find that the first few hits were scholarly research articles published on *PUBMED.gov*, our U.S. National Library of Medicine/National Institute of Health research citation search engine. This was solid, peer-reviewed, cutting-edge science.

One of the studies by researchers at M.D. Anderson Cancer Center cited curcumin and epigallocatechin-3-gallate (green tea extract) as plant agents with "marked effect" combatting CLL. We found that not only were they cited as safe to use during chemo, but in very elaborate ways, these plant medicines had been found to augment and enhance chemotherapy, the exact drugs that Jenny had been taking.[167]

Because the plant medicines are not yet standard of care, it was not in the oncologist's scope of practice to recommend them to Jenny, and Jenny had never thought to go looking. By the time we found the information, the cancer had already developed resistance to the particular drugs with which those plant medicines synergized. Jenny had also surpassed the safe lifetime limit and so could no longer use those particular chemotherapeutic agents. The plant medicines alone were not enough to treat her end-stage CLL, so it was in essence too late for any of this potentially life-saving information to be of use for Jenny.

We need not be attached to heroically preserving life at all costs, but the information was *right there*. My sadness at this inspired me to write this section though I risk raising the ire of people who think researching on the Internet is a dangerous and slippery slope. Jenny knew she was close to the end and so did not waste time lamenting what could have been. She found the practice of Open Heart Consciousness to be a breakthrough for her mentally, spiritually, and physically when her pain grew particularly intense.

My friend who is head of an oncology department told me about the work of Dr. Jeanne Wallace in bridging the gap between conventional oncology and plant-based medicine.

My friend was so excited that she purchased copies of Dr. Wallace's DVD *Become an Epigenetic Engineer: Evidence Based Nutrition*[168] for many of the oncologists in her department. Wallace proposes novel testing and natural treatments to augment conventional therapy. Because of one doctor's passion in championing Wallace's work, many doctors will have access to new ideas that are not yet standard of care and will help patients like Jenny. My doctor friend is identifying the health care practitioners who can partner with her team in a collaborative and integrative approach. Meditation and training in Open Heart Consciousness will be a part of that program. Because of my friend's vision, new relief, greater respite, and help of many varieties is available to patients with potentially terminal disease.

Live in continuous creative response

Don't forfeit the wisdom of your inner authority. Be willing to think and evaluate using your own genius faculties. Increase your understanding of, and currency on, the issues you face. Seek information from abundant resources. Take interest in people who have healed themselves of what you have. Know that every moment new discoveries are made, and our understanding of diseases and their treatment increases every day. Remember, there is no way you could have foretold when you were ten years old that a person could be healed by robotic surgery performed over the Internet by a doctor working remotely. Miracles abound, both natural and technological. Set out to find the ones that may help you. Meanwhile, live as fully and richly as possible, even while answers may not be obvious, and even if it takes decades for an answer to emerge

Excellence is not perfection, and you don't have to frantically go searching the Internet fueled by fear seeking the perfect solutions for your health. But do bring your best excellence to bear. Our culture supports turning to others for the care of our health. We have to recondition ourselves to take at least part of that responsibility back.

Remember this life orientation recommended by yogis: "I live in continuous creative response to whatever is present." In *This Thing Called You*, Ernest Holmes said, "Create or perish is the eternal mandate of nature. Be constructive or become frustrated."[169] Choose creativity and constructivity, and leave frustration behind as you learn what it means to live in continuous creative response to your challenges, both health and otherwise. Many times over the years I've witnessed inspired patients come upon jewels of information and helpful finds. The continuous and creative response to health challenges need not be tense and nervously pursued. It is best pursued in a spirit of hope, joy, and fun. Find an inner feeling tone of wonder and awe in your heart, live in a state of Open Heart Consciousness, and enjoy unearthing mysteries that may help you heal in ways that may seem beyond possibility.

Key #6   Love

Fall in Love With Your Miraculous Body

Men travel to gaze upon mountain heights and the waves of the sea, broad-flowing rivers, and the expanse of the ocean and the courses of the stars, and pass by themselves, the crowning wonder.

Saint Augustine
The Confessions of St. Augustine[170]

Here in this body are the sacred rivers: here are the sun and moon, as well as all the pilgrimage places. I have not encountered another temple as blissful as my own body.

Saraha
Tantric Song

I have often pondered the fact that we can make a wax replica of a human so lifelike as to be eerie, and yet we could never make one that "works." The intelligence that innervates and informs all living things is a creative force beyond what we are able to imitate or fully conceptualize.

In his book *The Wine of Life and Other Essays on Societies, Energy & Living Things*, Harold J. Morowitz opens with a delightful chapter titled "The Six Million Dollar Man." In 1979, the year the book was published, Morowitz humorously and rather astoundingly described the cost if you were to attempt to acquire each of the biochemical components of a human: Hemoglobin at $2.95 a gram, purified trypsin at $36 a gram, bilirubin at $12 a gram, human DNA at $768 a gram, follicle-stimulating hormone at $4,800,000 a gram, and so on. The raw materials alone, after adjusting for the fact that we are 68% water, would come to a total of approximately $6,000,015.44, making us a Six Million Dollar collection of raw materials. [171] To then assemble them into a functional human is of course another order of business entirely.

When we take for granted the miracle that is our body, or grow disenchanted when our body evidences aging and illness, it would serve us to remember that we are operating a piece of machinery worth a minimum of 6 mil in parts alone. We are more likely to let something we don't value very much fall into disrepair. If this is true for you, find a new inspiration for stewardship of your body. It is immeasurably more valuable than anything else you'll ever own. Take the time to readjust your valuation vantage point if you experience anything less than sheer awe and wonderment at the conglomeration of cells that is you.

If you interfere with this natural awe by habitually fixating on what you consider reasonable justifications for contempt, such as not liking how you look, being disgusted by out of control habits, hating your weight, or feeling that you are driving a "defective model" that is always breaking down, notice that this is not unlike the parent who thinks a useful way to interact with their child is to constantly tell them they are stupid, ugly, or a failure. No one flourishes under that kind of abuse.

One day I was doing an ancient Chinese therapeutic technique called Gua Sha on the upper thigh of my patient, a woman in her late sixties. As I applied the Gua Sha tool over the site of her sciatic pain, I couldn't help but exclaim, "Mary, your legs are gorgeous!" She mumbled something about cellulite and flab, truly unaware that her legs were exquisite. "I did have nice legs when I was young," she said, "but I didn't really realize it then and only saw the flaws. Now that they are covered with loose skin and cellulite, I wish I had appreciated them more in my youth." I remarked, "You are doing the same thing now that you were doing then. Yes, your legs are appropriate for an adult woman, and beautiful. Don't miss their beauty now, love your glorious legs!"

When we hyper-fixate on what we don't like, we can't sufficiently savor all that is right. Mary's error in perception was not unique to her. It is like a defective program that likes to run in the human mind. We do this to our own bodies, to our spouses, to our children, to our jobs, and to many other aspects of life if we are not vigilantly aware and awake.

Never lose sight of the miraculous and extraordinary truth: that for every single human alive, millions of dollars buys only our parts.

Become a Miracle

I thank God for my handicaps, for through them I have found myself, my work and my God.
Helen Keller

Friends are always sending me amazing photos of, and articles on, people who have only half a brain. Some of these people are born missing a full lobe of the brain, and some have had a hemispherectomy (removal of half a lobe) to halt seizures. Many people with only one brain lobe go on to live remarkably normal lives, some with only slightly noticeable clumsiness or other minimal challenges. People love sending me these moving accounts because they know I have only three quarters of a brain.

Luckily no one realized the size of my brain until I was 17 years old. By then I was just about to graduate from a private high school where I had taken honors classes, been the editor of the school literary magazine, acted in plays, graduated cum laude, got an award in 2-D Art, received the Senior Superlative *Most Artistic,* plus received $25,000 in scholarship offers from five different colleges and a full ride offer from another. Had those markers of reasonable mental functioning been absent, I may have never recovered from the shock that the MRI image delivered.

As it was, what I saw triggered an upset that took years to shake. Of course I had lived with a paralysis on one side of my body, but I had never given thought to what the brain behind the scenes looked like. There it was: an MRI image of my brain, with one lobe looking normal and robust, and the other looking like a shrunken walnut only half the size of the normal lobe. "Where is the rest of it?" I kept thinking over and over. It was horrifying. Though classified as cerebral palsy, the underlying neurological injury had occurred when I was six months old, close enough to receiving a vaccination bundle as to be associated with that event. There was nothing to be done. My brain had grown as much as it would, and as 17-year-old me reviewed the image of my scan in a panic, I wondered with horror how I'd ever learned to do anything at all.

It would be decades before I would retrain myself to think of what I have achieved with awe and wonder rather than worry and terror, and release the deep fear that my body and mind might quit on me at any second. A permanent state of wonderment and love is a chosen state, and we can choose that state even if we are missing part of our brain.

Like Mary with her legs, I had to learn to love my brain with any war wounds or battle scars collected along the way. That learning liberated me to drop even more deeply and more fully into Open Heart Consciousness. Truly, there is not a single reason I can think of that warrants holding back from the relief of living in a transformational state of consciousness. Freedom is available in an instant when we seek it, and surrender into it. As Nick Vujicic wrote in *Life Without Limits,* "If you can't get a miracle, become one."[172]

Harvest the Gifts of Hardship

You can't grow a lotus on marble. It has to grow in mud.
Thich Nhat Hahn

The Sufis know that precisely the right disaster comes at the right moment to break us open to the helplessness that an opening of the heart requires.
Coleman Barks
Rumi the Book of Love[173]

The pessimist sees difficulty in every opportunity. The optimist sees opportunity in every difficulty.
Winston Churchill

Hardship is the seed of happiness.
Dalai Lama

When I was 23 years old, one of my teachers taught me the wisdom tenet that within our greatest hardship often lies our greatest blessing. The adopting of that belief suddenly allowed me to see all the intricate ways life had mysteriously moved and changed me. Indeed, each hardship endured seemed meaningful and even useful in the context of the bigger picture. That learning allowed me to begin to transform from a person living with a chip on my shoulder about every little thing I thought was "wrong" in my life, to a person agape with wonder at the mystery and meaning of it all, who could take the bumps, dips, and hard times in stride.

Just as the compressive forces of the earth form the diamond, the compressive forces of life help form our inner beauty. Also, like the diamond, once formed, there is much to cut away to reveal the beauty. We have to cut away anger, resentment, and feeling sorry for ourselves. Like learning to be peaceful with the war wounds and battle scars to my brain, we have to cut away inner convictions that we have been harmed or diminished by our experience. We must look with artful eyes to see where the beauty sparkles, and choose carefully what to keep and excise, and where to cut the facets. It is not always obvious. Often our weakness, our injury, or our handicap needs no excising. Rather, we must reshape our attitudes to highlight beauty. In a moment of unexpected freedom, my friend Fran figured this out.

Fran and I take the same step aerobics class. One day right there in the middle of step class, Fran discovered that what she thought was a handicap was instead a great gift. Deep inner transformation and healing can truly take place anywhere.

Step aerobics is my "favorite exercise." That said, for much of my life I had experienced exercise as a rather grueling, sometimes excruciating, almost always agonizing effort to burn calories, unaware that there was another way. One thing I had noticed in years prior was that there were one or two students who, when present in step class, would shout out "Woohoo" excitedly, causing a strange joyous synergy to arise among the rest of us. Neither of those students had been in class for years, and the "Woohoo" infusion of energy was a distant, though longed-for, memory.

To "Woohoo" properly requires not only confidence but an intuitive sense of timing. There is a magic moment when the music and movements have built to just the proper crescendo. To unleash a wild "WOOHOO!" just at that moment stirs the class to "Woohoo" enthusiastically in response. When timed poorly, it obliterates the instructor's cue or falls flat. To my imaginative mind at the time, a weak or ill-timed "Woohoo" would be horrifyingly humiliating.

The proper "Woohoo" must have energy and excitement. It can't be a wimpy little thing. I toyed cautiously with the idea that if I wanted "Woohoos," I was going to have to bring them. I practiced them in my head. After many months of mental practice, I decided to heed the words of William James who said, "Our errors are surely not such awfully solemn things. In a world where we are so certain to incur them in spite of all our caution, a certain lightness of heart seems healthier than this excessive nervousness on their behalf." So, I mustered my best lightness of heart and decided to ignore my very, very excessive nervousness.

The first "Woohoo" I tried was nothing more than a tiny, ill-timed peep, but the instructor heard it and let out an excited "Woo!" in response. I couldn't believe it—I had help. It was an epiphany. From that moment, I grew increasingly confident, until eventually it became second nature. Others caught the excitement and "Woohoo'd" too. Our Saturday morning step aerobics class transformed into a bunch of whooping, hollering, Woohooing wild women.

Then Fran started coming to class. Fran is a very kind and very beautiful woman who happens to have Tourette's syndrome. Tourette's patients, including others I've known personally, describe their sudden outbursts as an irresistible urge that mounts until they have no choice but to express it. Fran would make random guttural growls and belabored attempts to disguise swear words (there is actually a name for this; the medical name for involuntary swearing in Tourette's patients is *coprolalia*). She would suddenly let loose a "Shhhhii-uuumph!" or "Fuuuu-ppuh!" despite an intense effort to suppress the outbursts. We felt her struggle keenly. It was an explosive force that could not be ignored.

One day Fran must have had an epiphany much like mine. Our friendly whooping and "Woohooing" may have been a liberating sort of help. Suddenly, this kind woman who had been trying for probably her entire life to suppress her raucous exclamations, embraced them instead. Instead of trying to stop her Tourette's outbursts, she started whooping, hollering, cheering, and yawping! She spurred us on to the highest heights of "Woohooing" of all time! It was incredible. I had tears of joy running down my face for most of that class. It was unrestrained enthusiasm! When we stop resisting what is and look for what we can love about what is, the result can be surprising. What some may call a handicap or hardship became to us a most precious gift, bestowed each week upon our group of grateful "Woohooing," stepping women.

Transform From Rage to Sage

Consciousness would be curing people today, I am convinced, except that we diagnose disease too late, after years of stress have hardened the physiology and made it difficult for bliss to penetrate.

Deepak Chopra

Quantum Healing[174]

A man named John came to me for treatment of pain in his neck. Most patients who come to acupuncture to relieve their pain have already tried numerous other interventions. They've tried anti-inflammatories, heat, cold, chiropractic, physical therapy, injections, and more. What I always marvel at is that many interventions are aimed at relieving the pain, but few are aimed at alleviating the *cause* of the pain. Necks don't hurt without a cause. There is usually a very good reason.

As I methodically considered John's history, the cause was easy to pinpoint. During his daily commute into Washington, D.C. at rush hour, in animated response to the horns blasting, middle fingers flying, and sudden swerving lane changes by other drivers, John experienced a daily dose of road rage. He wasn't all that concerned with the road rage; as he described to me, it was "warranted." He, like many consumers of holistic care, just wanted the neck pain fixed.

After a few weeks of acupuncture his symptoms disappeared but the road rage did not. I was not pleased. You can't fool your body and it would only be a matter of time before some new symptoms popped up, like a "check engine" light flashing wildly, trying somehow to convey to its recalcitrant driver that road rage is the wrong octane fuel.

It seemed that no matter what suggestion I made or strategy we took, this patient was attached to the idea that he was justified in his anger, "Hey, people are driving like idiots!" he proclaimed. Though my determination was great, I was not sure I could ever convince him that it *did* matter—idiots or not, the rage was optional, and the option he was choosing was potentially harmful to his health. The biochemicals of anger flooding his system in a daily dose came with consequences too expensive for him or any of us to afford.

He considered being rage free under D.C. beltway conditions an impossible request. I prayed for a miracle. Suddenly, in the uncovering of a strange bit of information, I came upon a solution.

This man had once had the incredible honor of driving Mother Theresa from a Maryland airport to her destination in Washington, D.C. As he related the experience, his countenance transformed before me. He had been profoundly moved in her presence. He described how a feeling of love seemed to emanate from Mother Theresa and filled the car and how he experienced that feeling deep in his own body while with her. He was teary-eyed as he related the story to me. In the remembering and retelling of that cherished 45-minute drive, he touched a state of peace and an awareness of the sacred and profound once again, as if he were with her even then.

Finally I could see how to help. His assignment from then on was to drive "with" Mother Theresa. He left with strict instructions that the moment he even anticipated another driver about to do something "idiotic," he was to again recall and relive his time in her presence, and rekindle that feeling in his heart. The other driver swerving, or tailgating, or cutting him off with no signal then became not a nuisance, but the monastery bell—*ringing to remind him of his practice.*

His neck pains are long gone. Nowadays, a bad driver is not experienced as an "idiot," but as a tap on the shoulder by Mother Theresa. Those taps remind him to touch into the deep pool of love that is available in each of our hearts, at any time. He has, in effect, softened his physiology enough, as Deepak Chopra has suggested, to allow "bliss to penetrate." This is a healing state available always, but forgotten frequently in all of our human racing and raging around.

Bless Everything

Jewish tradition encourages adults to say 100 blessings of gratitude a day. To fill a blessing quota this huge, you have to be vigilant about looking for things to be thankful for.
Wendy Mogel, Ph.D.
The Blessing of a Skinned Knee[175]

The rabbis knew how easily we slip from counting our blessings to coveting things, money, and neighbors' spouses. That's why they treated gratitude as a character trait that needed constant vigilance.
Wendy Mogel, Ph.D.
The Blessing of a Skinned Knee[176]

It is not joy that makes us grateful, it is gratitude that makes us joyful.
Brother David Steindl-Rast

While the milieu in the world of oncology is still one of "killing cancer cells" and "winning the war on cancer," there is another way. *Radical Remission* author Kelly A. Turner, Ph.D. tells the story of Shin Terayama's path to remission from advanced metastatic kidney cancer. In stark contrast to our generally accepted cultural hatred for all cells cancer, Shin considered the advent of cancer a most important awakening in his life, and an awakening to all of the ways he had come to mistreat his body throughout his life. Instead of hating the cells, whenever he became aware of them due to pain, he said, "'Oh, thank you very much for saying you are hurting. I love you, my child.' I touched this (points to his kidney) and said to my cancer, 'I love you, I love you, I love you.' And pain decreased! That's why I sent love to my cancer always, from morning til night...Unconditional love, that's unconditional love. I said (to it), 'Thank you very much for existing.'"[177]

Shin believes that when loved, cancer cells revert to healthy cells. There is a body of research that shows that damaged and cancerous cells can be rehabilitated into healthy cells through the epigenetic changes that occur by changing moods, feelings, diet and exercise. Some researchers and teachers engaged in these types of study are Dr. Dean Ornish and Jeanne M. Wallace Ph.D., CNC. One thing we know for sure is that when cancer cells are bathed in an elixir of Molecules of Medicine sprung from Open Heart Consciousness, miracles are possible.

Shin's case is just one example of how loving what we may otherwise reflexively hate, heals rather than harms.

Send out waves of blessings

In *The Art and Science of Raja Yoga,* Swami Kriyananda says, "When you meditate, begin by sending out waves of blessing to all men. If there is anyone, especially, with whom you have a difference, send him your love. Until you have this attitude you will never be able to meditate deeply. Subconscious antagonism will keep you tensed physically, as well as egoistically aloof from the great stream of life into which meditation should help you merge." [178] One of the all-time masters of sending out waves of blessings was concentration camp survivor Corrie ten Boom. Besides blessing humans, Corrie ten Boom also realized the wisdom in sending waves of blessings to fleas.

The blessing of fleas

At one point in Corrie ten Boom's time in a concentration camp, she was moved from solitary confinement, reunited with her sister Betsie, and moved to Ravensbruck. Betsie was very ill at the time, and the inhumane treatment in the concentration camp caused her illness to quickly worsen. She would eventually die there.

One day Betsie and Corrie ten Boom were moved to Barracks 28, sleeping quarters that were more flea- and lice-ridden than any of those where they had previously stayed. The straw that was spread on hard sleeping platforms swarmed with fleas. Corrie was horrified at the situation and what it would mean for Betsie's health. As Betsie urged Corrie, "Give thanks in *all* circumstances," she quoted. "It doesn't say, 'in pleasant circumstances.' Fleas are part of this place where God has put us." Corrie relented and stood with Betsie between the bunks to give thanks for the fleas. Corrie later wrote, "I was sure Betsie was wrong." [179]

Betsie and Corrie ten Boom had been spending their days in a workroom supervised by inhumane Nazi guards with whips, but after several weeks she and Betsie were assigned to a new workroom. This room was even more infested with fleas than their bunks. In fact, the workroom was so crawling with fleas that guards refused to enter. This meant that the women prisoners spent each day unattended and without being whipped. Because the sisters could knit rapidly and meet their quota within a few hours, they spent the rest of each day conducting a bible sermon for the other women prisoners. Though it had taken patience to understand the mystery of how it could be, there emerged a true and real blessing in fleas.

Corrie ten Boom said, "Happiness isn't something that depends on our surroundings...It's something we make inside ourselves." When ten Boom was finally released from the concentration camp due to a scribe error that mistakenly wrote her name on the "release" list rather than the "execute" list, she immediately set to work developing rehabilitation centers for concentration camp survivors. She later returned to Germany and set up rehabilitation centers in the former concentration camps *for the very guards who had sadistically mistreated so many prisoners including her sister and herself only months before.*

One day, ten Boom stood face to face with one of her former tormentors. As she stood there, without, as she described, "the slightest spark of warmth or charity," she prayed for help, for forgiveness. She then related, "As I took his hand the most incredible thing happened. From my shoulder along my arm and through my hand a current seemed to pass from me to him, while into my heart sprang a love for this stranger that almost overwhelmed me." Through a miracle arising from her sincere surrender and forgiveness, Corrie ten Boom was freed of her hurt, her hate, and her angry vengeful thoughts. Her body recovered from the illness and deprivation from her confinement and starvation. She worked passionately and energetically into her 90s delivering her message of forgiveness and peace.[180]

How can we truly bless everything? Can we declare blessedness even in the most difficult hardship? This is not something we can rely on our faculties of reason and rationality to find. Rather, this is a state that arises in the heart and heals from within, through an unseen force. It has to do with trusting in an intelligence that guides all things. We may do well to heed Corrie ten Boom's behest, "If you look at the world, you'll be distressed. If you look within, you'll be depressed. If you look at God you'll be at rest."

The holy gangster

I was talking to my friend Anna about all of the subtle ways people "armor up" and go through life hardened against potential hurts, ever wary of being harmed or "had." Such armoring acts like the valve on a faucet: clamping out access to the Divine flow by the hardened or suspicious or cynical stance toward life. I laughingly remarked that having a heart brimming with love may be more protective than all that armoring. Stories of muggers and thieves absolutely unable to carry out their intended deeds in the presence of a holy person beaming at them with unconditional love do not surprise me. Anna replied that one of the most important philosophies of her entire life was to look for the holiness in every person, even while living and working in one of the most violent areas of L.A. She told me the following story.

Anna had been a founder and principal of a school in one of the roughest areas of L.A., designed for children who were deemed "unfit" for the public school system. As she described, that meant most of her students were hardcore gangsters. If Anna had not truly understood that life is participatory and that her expectation mattered, she may have braced herself against the attitudes, violence, lying, and lack of impeccability society has grown to expect from such "types." Instead, she hugged every one of her students as they arrived off the school bus each day. She chose to see what she called their "holy light," and as a result, the gangsters loved her deeply, and applied themselves to schooling with a pride and enthusiasm they had *never* had before.

One day Anna went to the hospital for an elective surgery that went well, but when she awakened she was startled to see one of her most hard-edged students hovering over her hospital bed. "What are you doing here?" she exclaimed in surprise. "I'm gonna get you out of here!" he whispered. "I've got the car out front!" Anna looked at him quizzically, and finally asked, "WHAT car?" It turned out, this young man had stolen a car and broken into her room to see his beloved principal. Though he was a seasoned criminal, when it came to someone who loved *him*, he had, as Anna described, "a heart of gold." Most people are the type of people who "take care of their own." Sometimes, like Corrie ten Boom did with the Nazi guard, we just have to widen our definition of who it is that is "our own." The holy gangster was still not a model citizen. But because Anna had loved him unreservedly as her own, and he had loved her unreservedly as his own back, he was improving every day.

Love is in the air like dew

Ultimately, the struggles of life seem to all point one-way arrows in the same direction: toward love. In a talk he gave over a decade ago, I watched as Hans-Peter Dürr, the world-famous physicist, Heisenberg Professor of Physics, and executive Director of the Max-Planck Institute, used a ball of red yarn to teach about love. "It is the fuzz," he said, tossing that red ball of yarn into the air, "that holds the yarn together. Love is life's fuzz. It holds life together." While physics may not yet fully account for the fuzz and the love, they are forces always in action. Whether we are awake to those forces or not, or living in a way that works with them rather than at odds with them is our choice.

Marc Ian Barasch articulates the importance of such a choice in *Field Notes on the Compassionate Life* when he says, "People living in arid countries have found a simple method of collecting water. They spread out sheets of fabric at night and siphon off the dew that condenses on them each morning. Like moisture, love really *is* in the air. It will settle upon the thinnest reed, scintillate on a bare tip of grass, free for the taking. It is an elixir that can heal, drop by drop, all the sorrow and separation in the world. It changes pretty much everything."[181] The choice of love is free, abundantly available, and indeed, can change everything. It's up to us to choose it.

An inner state of love prevents communities from growing ill and diseased

Which do you think resulted in better hand hygiene among health care professionals—a sign above a sanitizing and soaping station stating: *Hand hygiene prevents you from catching diseases* or one stating *Hand hygiene prevents patients from catching diseases*? In an article titled, *It's not all about me: motivating hand hygiene among health care professionals by focusing on patients*[182] psychological scientist Adam Grant and colleague David Hofmann describe what happened when they researched that question. Turns out, health care professionals used 33% more sanitizer and soap and were 10% more likely to wash their hands when the sign indicated that it was the *patients* who would receive the benefit. The researchers attributed this both to an "illusion of invulnerability" in the face of disease held by the health professionals plus a desire in those professionals to improve the well-being of others.

In case altruistic motivation is not only inherent in health care professionals but in the population at large, and in case people will "use" more love if they know it will help others, I'll add to the conversation by posting my similarly inspired public notice:

Inner hygiene, a.k.a. living in Open Heart Consciousness, helps prevent individuals, families, and communities from becoming ill and diseased.

Practice The Art of Love

Your task is not to seek for love, but merely to seek and find all the barriers within yourself that you have built against it.

Rumi

Love all God's creation, the whole and every grain of sand in it...If you love everything, you will perceive the divine mystery in things.

Fyodor Dostoyevsky

I feel that all disease is ultimately related to a lack of love, or to love that is only conditional, for the exhaustion and depression of the immune system thus created leads to vulnerability. I also feel that all healing is related to the ability to give and accept unconditional love. I am convinced that unconditional love is the most powerful known stimulant of the immune system. If I told patients to raise their blood levels of immune globulins of killer T cells, no one would know how. But if I can teach them to love themselves and others fully, the same changes happen automatically. The truth is: love heals.

Bernie Siegel, M.D.
Love, Medicine & Miracles[183]

Once we open our body, mind and heart to love, then we have to practice it. As Ursula K. Le Guin wrote in *The Lathe of Heaven*, "Love doesn't just sit there, like a stone; it has to be made, like bread; remade all the time, made new."[184] How is it possible to remake love when life provides ample moments of stress, anger, and upset? What do we do when unjustified anger is directed at us? As I mentioned at the outset of this book, a moment such as this with my neighbor served as a great awakening.

My neighbor was angry at where my guest had parked on a busy holiday on our already crowded street, and enthusiastically shared her opinion. Other neighbors looked on with interest as she angrily vented, as if enjoying a good Jerry Springer episode. Sensing no possibility of resolution, and finding no one suffering without a parking spot, I walked away. Remembering my patient who "deletes" people from her life by de-friending them on Facebook, I realized that without meaning to, I had done something akin to that with my neighbor. Martin Luther King defined *Peaceful Protest* as "a courageous confrontation of evil by the power of love." Confronting anger by walking away, even if done in a spirit of love, clearly holds more of the flavor of a "delete."

How is it possible to practice the art of love when you've been unjustly attacked, violated, or treated poorly? How do we make room in our hearts for the "temporarily error intoxicated" to borrow a phrase from Paramahansa Yogananda? What if inside us there is an impulse to seek justice, or to hurt or attack in return? How tempting it is to delete or retaliate! We are a culture of deleters and retaliators, and this perpetuates the cycle of anger-retaliate-more anger. Someone has to model a new way. As Colman McCarthy says, "Why are we violent but not illiterate? Because we are taught to read. Unless we teach our children peace, someone else will teach them violence."

Practicing the Art of Love means practicing holding the heart vibration of Open Heart Consciousness, even when people are acting abominable, ugly, self-entitled, or trying to discharge their own stress by venting on somebody else. It doesn't mean standing meekly by and taking it, but it does mean standing for something bigger, even when temptation invites a tit for a tat. Behavior is contagious like a virus, and the viral loads of anger run unacceptably high on our planet. If we practice the Art of Love even when people are at their worst, we spark the possibility of changing the tide to a virulent epidemic of love.

We want to practice cultivating an inner state of love that is big enough so that it doesn't wobble when others are rude, mean, or trying to rile us up. It doesn't mean the bad behavior is right; The Dalai Lama refers to the invading Chinese as, "my friends, the enemy." Hector Black, in the court case against Ivan Simpson, who had raped and murdered his daughter, said to Simpson, "I don't hate you. But I hate with all my soul what you did." In *Be Love Now,* Ram Dass relates how his guru Maraj-ji said, "You can get angry at someone as long as you don't throw them out of your heart." [185] In a slightly different take on things in *Excuse Me Your Life is Waiting,* Lyn Grabhorn says, "Forgiveness is a releasing of our resistance to positive energy." [186] Positive energy is always available, but we have to make the choice to take it. Love without conditions heals the lover even more than the receiver.

Exhale love through your eyes

I've been practicing the Art of Love for many, many years, and yet there is still a justice-oriented part of my brain that immediately thinks toward my neighbor, "Really? You've got multiple cars parked on the street and you're going to pick a fight with someone you see every day, because a visitor parks near—not even in front of—your house for two hours on a holiday?" Alas, we humans are not known for the grace and glory of our interactions driven by the justice parts of our brain. This is why we keep millions of lawyers well-occupied and well-paid to sort out the heaping piles of justice messes we generate. No, the justice part of the brain is not going to guide in a way that deeply heals.

Even leading our remarks with the now culturally popular expression, "Really?" lets the listener know the speaker is amping up the drama to unleash a diatribe against somebody. We need to quit spreading the "Really?" virus and pass on the Open Heart Consciousness virus instead. The great poet Rumi advised, "Love is the cure, for your pain will keep giving birth to more pain until your eyes constantly exhale love as effortlessly as your body yields its scent." Are your eyes exhaling love right now? I know I am hugely thankful to Rumi for the reminder.

I was shocked to learn from his book *An Autobiography: The Story of My Experiments With Truth,* that as a young man, Gandhi was not what you would consider an impeccable character. He relates examples of ways he was jealous, controlling, sometimes violent when suspicious of his wife, lustful, and driven to choices of which he was ashamed by his "carnal desires." [187] Who in your life needs you to hold a vision of their "inner Gandhi" for them, allowing them the time to clean themselves up? Is it possible for you to stay peaceful in yourself even if that person acts abominably? In Gandhi's case, his wife Kasturba remained faithfully at his side through all their early challenges.

On a more personal note, one of my dearest friends describes to me events from his childhood, including making smoke bombs from the Anarchist's Cookbook using stolen saltpeter. The bomb filled two city blocks with a heavy cloud of dense smoke, brought in a fleet of fire trucks and police cars, and burned a gaping hole in the tennis court from which it was detonated. Other stories he relates include blowing up G.I. Joe figurines with gunpowder, and playing "laser" tag with his buddies using flaming Roman candles as the tagging devices. To make money to afford all this entertainment, he would steal packs of condoms and sell singles at a steep markup to middle schoolers. Today, he is one of the most spiritually generous and loving-hearted people I know. If an exquisitely thoughtful and deeply kind man can blossom from such early habits, anything is possible.

Search for the soul of kindness

We are so quick to try to correct the behavior of people in our lives, but our linear analytical efforts rarely produce the results we are after. When we take care of our own inner state, it changes the way we look at that person, changes the tone of voice we use, and increases our access to creativity. When we are different, the people around us are different. Think of someone in your life whom you don't enjoy spending time with. As you think of that person and their distasteful behavior, can you soften your eyes, and soften any furrow of your brow? Soften your heart and find an Open Heart Consciousness and allow it to melt inner edges and soften you even further. When the flame of love in my heart grew more powerful through practice, it simply burned up much of the hurt and hate I had held onto before. People who used to push my buttons with ease suddenly looked like little Buddhas, with all their error intoxicated provocative behavior provided especially for me to learn an extraordinary spiritual lesson.

Buddha said, "Holding on to negative emotions is like grasping hot coals. You are the one who gets burned." And Mark Twain said, "Anger is an acid that can do more harm to the vessel in which it is stored than to anything on which it is poured." What do we do if those acids and hot coals are burning holes in our hands and our heart and our flame of love is not yet powerful enough to burn them up? When I need to get into an authentic inner place of love and forgiveness, yet am tempted by justice oriented-ness and self-righteousness, I like to peruse websites like *www.theforgivenessproject.com* for real-life examples of love and forgiveness at work. I can't read more than a few examples from The Forgiveness Project, inspired by the peace work of Desmond Tutu, without getting tears in my eyes. In *Field Notes on the Compassionate Life*, Marc Ian Barasch stays true to his subtitle: *a search for the soul of kindness*. His real life stories of the complex challenges faced by warring people, victims of horrendous crime and other atrocities, and what happens when the response is kindness, stirred me many times to tears. [188] These are just two sources of moving stories that come to mind. There are many.

You can't stir a flower without troubling a star

One of my favorite sayings from Jesus is, "Forgive them, for they know not what they do." To me, that simple saying has multiple layers of meaning beyond the obviously intended. Truly, if a person knew what was happening on both the macroscopic and microscopic levels when they act in anger, unkindness, or hatred, they would never, ever elect to cause such widespread injury. On the macroscopic level, destructive emotions cause electromagnetic storms that ripple out, causing untold effect. If you've ever walked into a room with an angry person and felt the "bad air," you know what I mean. In the documentary *I Am*[189], Tom Shadyac, director and producer of film and television hits such as *"Evan Almighty," "8 Simple Rules," "Bruce Almighty," "Liar, Liar" and "Ace Ventura: Pet Detective,"* demonstrates the macrocosmic effects of angry thoughts in the lab of the HeartMath Institute. Electrodes hooked up to a carton of yogurt next to him registered spikes on an electric meter when he thought about his agent and his lawyer, as he was experiencing a strong negative emotion.

If you think an electrical spike in yogurt is no big deal, consider Edward Lorenz's MIT meteorological computation known as *The Butterfly Effect,* which suggests that a butterfly flapping its wings can alter weather in distant parts of the world. The tiny alteration in air currents factored into his equation utterly transformed his long-term forecast, a point Lorenz wrote about in his 1972 paper titled, "Predictability: Does the Flap of a Butterfly's Wings in Brazil Set Off a Tornado in Texas?"[190] The poet Francis Thompson once alluded to the effect of our tiniest actions when he wrote, "All things by immortal power/ Near and Far/ Hiddenly/ To each other linked are/ That thou canst not stir a flower without troubling of a star."

From a practical point of view, everyone can relate to the "kicking the cat" phenomena, in which the ripple effect of an angry neighbor causes a husband to be rude to his wife, who in turn yells at their son, who in frustration kicks the cat. Every thought we think and feeling we feel causes invisible ripples and cascades around us, influencing not only others, but in turn the environment in which we must then live. We need to generate cascades of "hugging the cat." Though getting from anger to love marks one of the great human spiritual challenges, Albert Einstein gave us a great starting motivation when he warned, "Anger dwells only in the bosom of fools."

On the microscopic level, these ripples generated by emotions spread out just as far and wide on our insides. How many microscopic changes are initiated by one bad feeling? How much less serotonin will be available for relaxation and peace that week? How much of a decrease in immune functionality will occur and how long will it last? How will the status of the heart, the brain, the liver, and the kidneys be after bathing in a solution of anger-driven stress chemicals? Will our cells be able to repair themselves properly, or will we be more vulnerable to disease while circulating the bad-feeling soup? As you can see, the cost may literally be *exorbitant*. If people thought this way, they would never dare spend themselves into such poverty. Too often, we suffer the illusion that we are rich and can squander our resources recklessly. Corrie ten Boom advises, "Forgiveness is the key that unlocks the door of resentment and the handcuffs of hatred. It is a power that breaks the chains of bitterness and the shackles of selfishness." When we forgive, newfound resources for healing may surprise us.

Practice loving the enemy

I have a patient who though only in her 60s, had a brain injury severe enough that she requires full-time care and often is not sure exactly where she is or who she is with. A kindly woman brings her to her appointments. This friend tends my patient like a mother hen would tend an injured chick. They laugh, joke, and go for lunch afterwards.

One day I commented on their friendship. I was stunned when they laughingly explained that the friend had been the "other woman" that my patient's spouse had left her for years before. Over the years of trading kids back and forth and eventually burying the husband, they had forged this caring bond. My patient had forgiven this woman and become her friend. Now, though my patient generally couldn't remember what happened five minutes prior, and wouldn't even know to thank her, the "other woman" was attending her many needs every week with great dedication and tenderness.

I was so moved to learn of such a twist of events I had tears in my eyes. Their gift to each other had rippled outward in its effect and was now a gift to me. After retelling this story to a friend, she cynically observed, "Well, that helper woman probably just feels guilty about stealing the husband in the first place and that's why she helps." I would disagree there. No guilt could sustain the tending this woman was doing, and their shared affection was unmistakable. Countless women I know would literally curse the "other woman" in their own lives. Never would most of these women even consider civil conversation with "the other woman." In light of how our emotions impact our physiology, at what unknown cost? Is there someone in your life you could practice loving, even if it is hard, it hurts, or they don't deserve it?

Swami Satchidananda said, "One day I was working in the field, and I hurt my finger. I could have ignored it, but I cleaned it and bandaged it. If I had ignored it and the finger got infected, my entire body would have suffered. The same way, if we feel that we are parts of the cosmic body, the entire universe, how can we stop from loving the other parts?" Oneness is a reality, not a concept. Just as "that helper woman" and my patient did, we must love and care for the whole in *all* of its parts.

Give the gift of love

Just a few months after I began practicing acupuncture, an elderly woman came to me for treatment. Her issues were simple and straightforward, and she responded well to treatment. Still, she was one of the most difficult patients I have ever had. This well-meaning woman talked like a freight train, sometimes for hours, and was almost impossible to interrupt. She'd sit down in the treatment room and the next thing I'd know she'd be giving me detailed reports of every meal she had eaten that week, every store she had shopped in, where there were deals going on, and what things she needed to pick up later from the grocery store. She volunteered at a nursing home so she'd tell me at excruciating length about every conversation she'd had, every card game played, and every bird glimpsed out the window. I felt like I might go mad.

After a few weeks of attempting to redirect her, cut her short, schedule her with deadlines, and every other strategy I could think of, I finally made a radical choice. I was new in practice so I had the time; I made the decision to simply love her and listen to her. I scheduled her in my book in 2.5 hour slots rather than a typical one hour slot. Everyone who knew about it thought I was nuts.

I surrendered to her stories, and began to look forward to them. I checked out some of the discount stores she mentioned and they were great. One of the restaurants she talked about every week became one of my favorites. I tried some of the recipes she described in such great detail and they were delicious.

One day she was talking at length about her weekly social visit to the nursing home. As she described in what I would have once thought of as agonizing detail about the conversations had and the card games played, she happened to mention the name of her "favorite" person she visited with each week. "I played game after game of cards and talked and joked for hours with Ellie this week" she intoned. "Ellie?" I asked, "Where do you volunteer every Friday?" Though this woman lived quite a distance from the care facility she named, I knew the facility well. *Ellie was my grandmother.*

Piglet: How do you spell "love"?
Pooh: You don't spell it...You feel it.[191]
A.A. Milne
Winnie-the-Pooh

Tolerate Change: Adjust Your Mirrors Like a Race Car Driver

Your beliefs become your thoughts.
Your thoughts become your words.
Your words become your actions.
Your actions become your habits.
Your habits become your values.
Your values become your destiny.
Mahatma Gandhi

The only person who likes change is a wet baby.
Roy Blitzer

Miracles happen more frequently than most people think. Yet they are usually not preceded by luck, but rather they are preceded by inner change. To understand how much of a challenge it is to make deep and lasting change, think for a moment how difficult it is for a coffee or soda drinker to give up their caffeine. The response from the body can include cravings, headaches, weakness, irritability, lethargy, constipation, flu-like feelings and more. There are screaming receptor sites in the brain waiting for their caffeine fix.

We also have receptor sites in our brain that grow acclimated to cortisol, adrenaline, and other biochemicals that fire off from tension, stress, and drama. If we stop those behaviors, there will be a period of withdrawal. We have to be smarter than our cravings, and outlast any reflexive gravitation toward those stimulated states. We have to feed our receptor sites a new juice. Get your brain and body addicted to Open Heart Consciousness so that you have both cravings and signs of withdrawal when you forget to live in that state.

The Heart of Healing path asks of us to radically transform our thoughts, feelings, and habits. It asks us to use every bit of the circumstances of our life, including the hardships, as opportunities to expand our ability to live playfully, freely, creatively, consciously, and lovingly. One of the challenges of change is overcoming how we are programmed to live, meaning, what we are addicted to or accustomed or habituated to. An unhealthy way of being may feel "right" even if it is "wrong." To illustrate this concept, I teach audiences how to adjust their car mirrors like a race car driver.

Remove the blind spot

What is wrong with the way most people adjust their side view car mirrors? In my talks and classes, most people practically shout out the answer to this. The way we typically adjust our mirrors leaves a huge BLIND SPOT! One thing about race car drivers is that they cannot afford a blind spot. They also cannot afford to crane their necks and glance over their shoulder every time they change lanes. For these reasons, race car drivers adjust their mirrors differently.

To adjust the mirrors without a blind spot, the mirrors must be opened much wider than most of us are used to. Instead of widening the mirrors only far enough to see a sliver of the side of the car in the reflection, they must be opened so wide that a car approaching from behind is visible first in the rear view mirror. Then, just before dropping out of sight on the rear mirror they must pop into sight in the side mirror. Then finally, just before disappearing from view of the side view mirror, they must appear in our peripheral vision directly out the side of the car window. This is exactly how a race car driver does it, and it is easy to test that they are positioned properly by checking these above-mentioned conditions while driving on a slow-moving road that has two lanes going in the same direction. (I am heartened to recently learn that drivers education is now teaching young drivers to position their mirrors much more widely, and AARP is helping older drivers convert to a wider mirror positioning through its Driver Safety course.)

As a challenge to test "change adversity," I recommend my students and patients try this "Race Car Driver Challenge." Invariably, after adjusting their mirrors in this widened way, people tell me they can barely stand the change. The reason is, instead of seeing what is expected in the reflection, suddenly they are confronted with a wonky, disconcerting image that doesn't make sense or meet expectations. It takes a month for people to grow accustomed enough to the new view to not feel totally freaked out every time they take a glance. That is if they even last a month. Many people report back to me that even though they know the new positioning is far safer, eliminating the dreaded blind spot, they revert back to the familiar after only a couple of days. As George Santayana once observed, "Habit is stronger than reason."

Make a quantum leap forward

The ways we are programmed to live may feel "right" even if they are "wrong." A new habit may be far safer, far wiser, and all around better, but if it *feels* wrong, it is going to take some effort to change. However, just as the awkwardness you first felt when you learned to drive that car soon gave way to an unconscious ease, so, too, with newly positioned mirrors and new life-affirming habits, practice fosters familiarity and ease. We just have to recognize why the new way feels "wrong" and stick with it, until it doesn't. When it comes to making a *quantum* change, we leap from where we are to a whole new experience of thinking, feeling, and acting. We leap into the space that arises from the crafting of a whole new set of biochemicals and neurotransmitters in the brain that fire from the feelings we cultivate in our heart, irrespective of circumstances. When we leap like this, our "stick with it" muscles are going to get a workout.

How change averse are you? How averse are you to feeling ongoing states of joy, bliss, and ecstatic communion with the sacred divine? How averse are you to taking charge of your health by intentionally creating your thoughts, feelings, moods, expectations, and beliefs? Living in ways that are different from what we are used to can feel unsettling and unfamiliar. Will the unfamiliarity cause you to snap back to predictable ways of thinking, feeling, and being? What will it take to make a quantum leap forward?

The old habits are MUCH HARDER than the new

People sometimes ask me why I think I had so very many symptoms and illnesses throughout my life, and whether I think I was just very unlucky or even brought it on myself. In *Man's Eternal Quest*, Paramahansa Yogananda said, "You cannot make steel until you have made the iron white-hot in fire. It is not meant for harm. Trouble and disease have a lesson for us. Our painful experiences are not meant to destroy us, but to burn out our dross, to hurry us back Home. No one is more anxious for our release than God." [192] I couldn't agree more. I never would have powerfully cultivated an inner Open Heart Consciousness had my symptoms not constantly reminded me that making Inner Molecules of Medicine was no luxury, but rather, a necessity. For me, the words of Carolyn Myss rang true, "When an illness is part of your spiritual journey, no medical intervention can heal you until your spirit has begun to make the changes that the illness was designed to inspire." [193]

Too, the following prayer by an unknown Confederate soldier comes to mind, "I asked for strength that I might achieve; I was made weak that I might learn to humbly obey. I asked for health that I might do greater things; I was given infirmity that I might do better things. I asked for riches that I might be happy; I was given poverty that I might be wise. I asked for power that I might have the praise of men; I was given weakness that I might feel the need of God. I asked for all things that I might enjoy life; I was given life that I might enjoy all things. I got nothing that I had asked for, but everything that I had hoped for. Almost despite myself, my unspoken prayers were answered; I am, among all men, most richly blessed." I feel quite the same.

The Non-Eating Saint Giri Bala purportedly told Paramahansa Yogananda in *Autobiography of a Yogi*, in response to his request that she teach her methods of living without food to the starving poor, "It appears that misery, starvation, and disease are whips of our karma that ultimately drive us to seek the true meaning of life." [194] The persistent symptoms of illness certainly whipped my attention toward Open Heart Consciousness again and again; without those symptoms causing me suffering that begged relief, I surely would have busied myself with much more mundane concerns and interests. I would know little of my rich life blessings without my path whipping me exactly and as exactingly as it did.

In the beginning of my journey of healing, I had no idea whether any of the lifestyle and habit changes I was committing to would "work." I spent money I didn't have on high quality foods and lots of supplements, and I made changes to my diet that I often quipped, "only a monk would like." I spent many hours training my attention through meditation, with no assurance that I had settled on the "right" type of meditation. I changed my attitudes, developed new habits of feeling, and focused on becoming more spontaneous, more playful, more intuitive, and more trusting in a Divine organizing intelligence. To my relief, the dividends paid back huge.

Later, I would find that the same habits that rescued me from sickness into reasonable health could be committed to with further excitement, to move toward peak performance and radical health. Again, I set out blind as to whether any of the changes I made would work or be "worth it." When I felt doubtful I would read, read, read for information and inspiration. Often, when the party line was "it can't be done," I had to seek out someone "doing it" as my sole inspiration. The unfolding results turned out again to be well worth it. People often comment that my habits and how I live are "too hard," but I look at how lethargic, uninspired, devitalized and prone to illness and ailments many such commenters are, and can assure all who are curious, living like they do as I once did is MUCH HARDER. For me, developing and nourishing my heart, mind and body are enjoyable and rewarding endeavors that I will carry on for a lifetime.

When we bloom, our fragrance uplifts all who pass by

Change can be challenging, but it is worth it. The blessing of living for a time with a weakened immune system served as my best, most unrelenting advisor. I mentioned early in this book that all that I learned would one day literally save my life. That was no exaggeration. Years ago, before I learned the many small things that I now do that add up to the big miracle of having an excellently functioning immune system, I was so ill I told my doctor, "Whatever is in me is trying to kill me." My doctor, shocked by my unusual lab results, agreed. My blood work bore so many indicators of a severe, but unidentifiable, pathological infection process that he soon had me on three different antibiotics, an anti-fungal, and a steroid pack in attempts to stem the process. That many of our ancestors died of infectious illness was no longer a foreign notion to me. The medicines did not work. For a time, I was more on the other side than this side.

For days I lay sick in bed in a semi-conscious state, feverish and filled with a sense of deep dread. I became so certain that I would soon die that I began to pray fervently for help. Mustering up a final clarity of mind, I beseeched of the heavens, *Help me, what should I do????* Not expecting a reply, I practically jumped out of my skin when a loud voice boomed back in my head, "*YOU KNOW WHAT TO DO!!!!!!!!!!*" Though many a scientist will argue that there is no such thing as a God experience and even design things like "God Helmets" that stimulate certain parts of the brain to show that simple electrical firings in the brain are what give us our holy experiences, I was and am certain that what I had was a real bona fide Divine visitation.

Buoyed by the blessing, and charged with the directive, I began to *do what I knew to do but had deemed not powerful enough to bother with.* I began to practice a Feeling Mantra and Open Heart Consciousness, even as my body was wracked with pain and so weak I could barely lift my head to sip water. Suddenly, an experience of golden light streaming into every pore of my body seemed to go on and on. Waves of euphoria bubbled in my heart. In that miraculous state of grace, it seemed that my body was almost an afterthought. Something much bigger, much more profound, and powerful unlike anything I normally associate with as "reality" was available, and awash in and over me. I was powerfully communing with an unseen force, and once again, illness slipped away. Just as the Hawaiian Kahuna had advised Keith Varnum it could: the change in my heart had activated the chemistry of immortality that came out of the blue with the power of a jackhammer, freeing my body's chemistry and instantly healing disease.

It almost mattered not whether it was the illness that slipped away, or whether I did, for what mattered only was this great huge limitless blissfully joyful love that seemed to pervade my every molecule. To know it once is to carry a flickering flame of wonderment and deep love in the heart ever after. That knowledge makes it increasingly harder to move away from the light into petty upsets, concerns, and shutdowns. Every little dislike or resistance now feels like a tourniquet squelching the ability of the Divine to get in, and demands a quick loosening.

In *The World As I See It*, Albert Einstein stated, "The most beautiful experience we can have is the mysterious. It is the fundamental emotion which stands at the cradle of true art and true science." [195] I couldn't agree more resoundingly, and we must create the conditions that invite such experiences. After absorbing the awarenesses gained through feverish Divine trance deeply over several hours, I simply got out of bed and went about living. One moment I had been ill enough to feel the proximity of death, and several hours later my consciousness had been transformed and illuminated, and I was physically, mentally, and spiritually well.

Open Heart Consciousness is available to any of us, at any time, and the transformational effects can be remarkable. I convey the stories in this book to my patients every day, but many persist for months, years, or decades in their old habits, old feelings, and old ways of being. Only a few deeply embrace the path of personal transformation. As the ancient Chinese proverb goes, "If five million people do a foolish thing, it is still a foolish thing." Shed foolishness and undertake a journey loaded with mystery, joy, awe, wonderment, and bliss. However challenging it is to adopt new habits, I promise you it is infinitely easier than living without the juice of Open Heart Consciousness coursing through your being. Please, find a way to fill your heart with a sense of ecstatic love, irrespective of circumstances. *When we bloom, our fragrance uplifts all who pass by.*

It's all bearable only through love

People inevitably demand to know, "Whatever happened with your neighbor who was angry over the parking? What did you *do?*" I knew a solution much bigger than the conciliatory pan of brownies some people professed to hope I provided was in order. Forgive and forget is fine, but I sought to *change me.* I sought to make a quantum leap forward in my progress toward that Rumi-inspired place of genuinely exhaling love through my eyes as effortlessly as my body yields its scent. I knew that my personal efforts at self-transformation would benefit much more than just the neighbor and me. I took inspiration from Brother Yun who didn't reprimand the violent prison guards, who didn't seek to forcibly right a wrong, and who did not throw the guards out of his heart. He simply gazed at each tormentor's highest self while being moved by the Holy Spirit. For months I pondered how exactly this translated to my situation and it gnawed at my creativity until a new vision of possibility bloomed in my consciousness.

The new template that arose could be used *any time* the human drama threatens to hijack higher virtues. What I realized is this: Had I been in the type of moved state where my fragrance was uplifting to all who passed by, exhaling love effortlessly from my eyes, had I been so deeply and completely living in my heart of love in that confrontative moment that what pained me most was to watch somebody forfeit such a possibility for themselves, had I been living large and able to tap into how to "Bring It!," I would have seen it then, and known what to do. I would have thrown my arms wide and shouted, "The joyous great glorious bliss of the Divine is available here, now, all around us! Breathe it in! Take it in! Worries over that which divides us only hardens our hearts and clenches our physiology too tight to receive the Divine love! Don't harm yourself that way! Be love, and in love, now! To hell with cars, spots, fights, hatred and all the parts of the human drama that would distract us otherwise! Be a vessel to receive and fill with great love and vast gloriousness!"

Though neither she nor the Jerry Springer-loving onlookers may have grasped or related to such a sentiment in that exact moment, a seed would have been planted. A seed of feeling tone and neighborhood mood that could nourish and unlock the heart of healing for a whole community, and ripple forth further and further like the butterfly flapping its weather-changing wings. To choose to respond to "fight" with "no fight" is one way. But to respond to "fight" with forgiveness, hope, and a call to love is entirely another. Johann Wolfgang von Goethe pointed out that, "If you treat an individual as he is, he will remain how he is. But if you treat him as if he were what he ought to be and could be, he will become what he ought to be and could be." And Carl Sagan said, "For small creatures such as we the vastness is bearable only through love."

A friend reading a draft of this book said, "I don't really think your resolution of the neighbor situation is very powerful; I don't get it." It is true, from a rational, linear, analytical frame of reference my solution seems "airy-fairy." From the space of alchemy, where the numinous experience trumps everything, where it becomes acutely obvious how nonsensical the human drama seems in contrast, and where it is laughable the ways we distract ourselves from the inner cultivation that liberates Open Heart Consciousness, she *would* get it. To know Oneness as an experience, and not just as an altruistic concept, prompts us to hunger for a resolution much greater than quiet tolerance. Open Heart Consciousness impels us to seek a satisfying solution that blooms from deep inside, rather than just the superficial tidying up of what could seem a commonplace and humdrum neighborly interaction. This is why I recommend that everyone hustle to overcome Divine Deficit Disorder and open themselves to embodied numinous experiences as quickly as possible. William Janes said, "Mystical consciousness is a state of insight into the depths of truth unplumbed by the discussive intellect." It changes everything.

Be the change

While a circumstance of an ill relationship in the midst of a tense neighborhood can hardly be likened to the experience of a concentration camp or filthy prison, wisdom and inspiration is available for our challenges big and small from the people who have survived severe conditions with their hearts intact. While held captive and treated brutally, Brother Yun, as he described, would "drink daily of the living waters of the holy spirit" in the presence of his tormentors.[196] Many captors, while beating and torturing this person who simply beamed up at them with complete compassion, love and forgiveness, had to quit the jobs their hearts no longer allowed them to perform. Yun saw those men as they could be, and they couldn't help but change. Not only what we *do*, but how we *be*, holds the power of healing.

There is a Sufi story about a man bereft over the suffering of humanity. Calling out to God, he asked why a loving creator would allow misery and suffering and yet do nothing about it. God replied, "I did do something about it. I made you."

Drink of the living waters that fill your heart with a feeling of the Divine, and allow what you *do* and how you *be* to spontaneously heal you, your family, your community, and the global community. Beloveds, we can afford no less.

Final Words

The writing of this book started out with the subtitle "100 Keys to Unlock Radical Health and Reverse Illness." As the length grew to over 600 single spaced 8.5x11 pages, it was groomed down multiple times to the final length you find here. There are many rich topics and beautiful stories for the next book. If you would like to see a particular topic addressed, visit me on the web at www.unlockingtheheartofhealing.com, or Follow me on Facebook under Bridget Hargadon Hughes and let me know. If you have put to use anything you learned here, and have experienced an unusual healing or unexpected outcome, I would love to hear your story. And I would be greatly blessed for your Amazon review if you have been moved or helped by this book. As a self-publishing author without a publicity budget, your word of mouth is a cherished gift.

In love,
Bridget Hughes

About the Author

Bridget Hughes M.Ac., L.Ac., NBCCH is a licensed acupuncturist with a Master's degree from the Maryland University of Integrative Health. She is co-founder of Healing Point LLC in Severna Park, Maryland, and of Healing Point Acupuncture and Healing Arts in the Cancer Resource Center at the Medical Pavilion of Howard County General Hospital/Johns Hopkins Medicine in Columbia, Maryland. She was named a 2010 and 2011 Favorite Doc in Chesapeake Family Magazine representing Anne Arundel County and the Chesapeake Bay Region. She is a past participant of the Howard County General Hospital Integrative Care Advisory Committee.

Once a child patient with Cerebral Palsy at the Kennedy Krieger Institute herself, Bridget healed beyond what was considered possible and went on to present Grand Rounds at Kennedy Krieger in 2002. Bridget is a past participant of the Kennedy Krieger Institute Complementary and Alternative Medicine Advisory Committee. She is a past member of the Kennedy Krieger Institute Ethics Committee.

Bridget holds National Board Certification as a Clinical Hypnotist and is a certified Qigong instructor. She has been interested for over 20 years in the intersection of health, wellness, brain science, energy arts, quantum physics, psychology, and peak performance. Her passion is to help clients, students, and patients to unlock peak health, peak performance, and a peak state of heart. With her husband Brandon, Bridget developed a hospital-based Recovery Movement Arts program in 2010 and is committed to bringing restorative movement therapies such as Yoga and Qigong to cancer and chronically ill patients. Their program emphasizes using self-healing practices to unlock HeartMindBody resources for healing and using meditation to access Inner Molecules of Medicine. Bridget is available for speaking and presenting workshops on a wide range of wellness topics. You can visit her on the web at www.unlockingtheheartofhealing.com.

¹ Wahls, T. L., & Adamson, E. (2014). *The Wahls Protocol: How I Beat Progressive MS Using Paleo Principles and Functional Medicine*. New York: Avery p.64

² Wiley, T. S., & Formby, B. (2000). *Lights Out: Sleep, Sugar, and Survival*. New York: Pocket Books.

³ Yuen, Jeffrey, *Cancer Care and Chinese Medicine*. Talk delivered April 3-4, 2004 Maryland. Disc 1, track 15 of the recorded version.

⁴ Varnum, K. (2012). *How to Be a Miracle Maker: Find Joy, Love, and Abundance*. eBookIt.com.

⁵ *http://www.thedream.com/index.php?option=com_content&view=article&id=153*

⁶ Glasser, R. J. (1976). *The Body is the Hero*. New York: Random House.

⁷ Marley, Z. (2007). *Love is My Religion*. Tuff Gong Worldwide.

⁸ Barasch, M. (2005). *Field Notes on the Compassionate Life: A Search for the Soul of Kindness*. Emmaus, Pa: Rodale. p.330

⁹ Waldman, M. (2010, March 27th). [Video File] retrieved from http://markrobertwaldman.com/

¹⁰ Emerson, R. (2006). *The Complete Works of Ralph Waldo Emerson: Essays*. Michigan: University of Michigan Library. p. 160

¹¹ Katz, R. (1984). *Boiling Energy: Community Healing Among the Kalahari Kung*. Harvard University Press.

¹² Feuerstein, G. (2008). *The Yoga Tradition: Its History, Literature, Philosphy, and Practice*. Arizona: Hohm Press. p.xvi

¹³ Johansson, F. (2006). *The Medici Effect: What Elephants and Epidemics Can Teach Us About Innovation*. Harvard Business Review Press.

¹⁴ Johansson, F. (2012). *The Click Moment: Seizing Opportunity in an Unpredictable World*. Portfolio Hardcover.

¹⁵ Frankl, Dr. V. (2006). *Man's Search for Meaning*. Beacon Press

¹⁶ *Nature*. "Reach and Grasp by people with tetraplegia using a neurally controlled robotic arm". 485, 372-375 (17 May 2012).

¹⁷ Barnett, K. (2013). *The Spark: A Mother's Story of Nurturing Genius*. Random House.

¹⁸ *Temple Grandin*, dir. Mick Jackson, perf. Claire Danes, DVD, HBO Films, 2010.

[19] Toussaint, C. (2013). *Battle for Grace: A Memoir of Pain, Redemption and Impossible Love.* CreateSpace Independent Publishing Platform.

[20] Jalāl, R., & Barks, C. (2003). *Rumi: The Book of Love: Poems of Ecstasy and Longing.* New York, NY: HarperOne, HaperCollins.

[21] Barasch, M. (2005). *Field Notes on the Compassionate Life: A Search for the Soul of Kindness.* Emmaus, Pa: Rodale.

[22] Starr, M., & Saint Teresa. (2013). *Saint Teresa of Avila: Passionate mystic.* Sounds True. p.2

[23] King, G. R. (1982). *Unveiled Mysteries (original).* Schaumburg, Ill: Saint Germain Press.

[24] Douillard, J. (1994). *Body, Mind, and Sport: The Mind-Body Guide to Lifelong Fitness, and Your Personal Best.* New York: Harmony Books.

[25] Fredrickson, B. (2013) *Love 2.0: Finding Happiness and Health in Moments of Connection.* Plume.

[26] Rein, Atkinson, and McCraty. *Journal of Advancement in Medicine Volume 8, Number 2, Summer 1995.* "The Physiological and Psychological Effects of Compassion and Anger"

[27] Ali, M. (2005). *Dr Ali's Weight Loss Plan.* London: Vermilion.

[28] Maltz, M. (1960). *Psycho-Cybernetics: A New Way to Get More Living Out of Life.* Englewood Cliffs, N.J: Prentice-Hall.

[29] Bernhardt, R., & Martin, D. (1977). *Self-Mastery Through Self-Hypnosis.* Indianapolis: Bobbs-Merrill.

[30] Bandler, R., & Fitzpatrick, O. (2009). *Conversations with Richard Bandler: Two NLP Masters Reveal the Secrets to Successful Living.* Deerfield Beach: Health Communications, Inc.

[31] Douillard, J. (1994). *Body, Mind, and Sport: The Mind-Body Guide to Lifelong Fitness, and Your Personal Best.* New York: Harmony Books.

[32] Turner, K. A. (2014). *Radical Remission: Surviving Cancer Against All Odds.* p.228

[33] Trungpa, C. (2002) Shambhala Classics. *Cutting Through Spiritual Materialism.*

[34] Brown, B. (2012). *Daring Greatly: How the Courage to be Vulnerable Transforms the Way We Live, Love, Parent, and Lead.* New York, NY: Gotham Books.

[35] Chopra, D. (1993). *Ageless Body, Timeless Mind: The Quantum Alternative to Growing Old.* New York: Harmony Books.

36 Church, D. (2008). *The Genie in Your Genes: Epigenetic Medicine and the New Biology of Intention*. Santa Rosa, California: Energy Psychology Press. p. 170

37 Leonard, G., & Murphy, M. (1995). *The Life We are Given*. New York: Putnam.

38 Leonard, G., & Murphy, M. (1995). *The Life We are Given*. New York: Putnam. p.100

39 Connelly, D. M. (2009). *Medicine Words: Language of Love for the Treatment Room of Life*. Laurel, Md: Tai Sophia Press.

40 http://www.eurekalert.org/pub_releases/2006-04/aps-jte033006.php

41 Chopra, D. (1987). *Creating Health: Beyond Prevention, Toward Perfection*. Boston: Houghton Mifflin.

42 Church, D. (2008). *The Genie in Your Genes: Epigenetic Medicine and the New Biology of Intention*. Santa Rosa, California: Energy Psychology Press. p. 17

43 Murakami, K. (2006). *The Divine Code of Life: Awaken Your Genes & Discover Hidden Talents*. Hillsboro, Ore: Beyond Words Pub.

44 Chopra, D. (1987). *Creating Health: Beyond Prevention, Toward Perfection*. Boston: Houghton Mifflin.

45 Bandler, R., & Fitzpatrick, O. (2009). *Conversations with Richard Bandler: Two NLP Masters Reveal the Secrets to Successful Living*. Deerfield Beach: Health Communications, Inc. p.207

46 Childre, D. L., Martin, H., Beech, D., & Institute of HeartMath. (1999). *The HeartMath Solution*. San Francisco, CA: Harper San Francisco.

47 Rohr, R. (2003). *Simplicity: The Freedom of Letting Go*. New York: Crossroad Pub.

48 Adiswarananda. (2003). *Meditation & its Practices: A Definitive Guide to Techniques and Traditions of Meditation in Yoga and Vedanta*. Woodstock, Vt: SkyLight Paths Pub.

49 Krishnamurti, J. (1975). *Think on These Things*. San Francisco: Harper Collins.

50 Ladinsky, D. (2002) *Love Poems From God: Twelve Sacred Voices From the East and West*. Penguin. p.10

51 Ware, B. (2012). *The Top Five Regrets of the Dying: A Life Transformed by the Dearly Departing*. Carlsbad, Calif: Hay House.

52 Yogananda. (1998 reprint). *Autobiography of a Yogi*. Self-Realization Fellowship.

53 Bandler, R., & Fitzpatrick, O. (2009). *Conversations with Richard Bandler: Two NLP Masters Reveal the Secrets to Successful Living*. Deerfield Beach: Health Communications, Inc.

54 Matthieu, R. (2001). *The Quantum and the Lotus: A Journey to the Frontiers Where Science and Buddhism Meet*. New York: Crown Publishers. (p. 261)

55 Nhất, H., & Kotler, A. (1987). *Being Peace*. Berkeley, Calif: Parallax Press.

56 Sood, M.D., A. (2010). *Train Your Brain Engage Your Heart Transform Your Life: A Course in Attention & Interpretation Therapy*. CreateSpace Independent Publishing Platform.

57 Surya, D. (1999). *Awakening to the Sacred: Creating a Spiritual Life From Scratch*. New York: Broadway Books.

58 Osho. (2004). *Meditation: The First and Last Freedom*. New York: St. Martin's Griffin. p.29

59 Ramachandran, V. S. (2011). *The Tell-Tale Brain: Unlocking the Mystery of Human Nature*. London: William Heinemann.

60 Hoff, B. (1983). *The Tao of Pooh*. Penguin.

61 Hamilton, A. J. (2008). *The Scalpel and the Soul: Encounters With Surgery, the Supernatural, and the Healing Power of Hope*. New York: Jeremy P. Tarcher/*Putnam*.

62 Goethe, J. *Faust*. Various publishers and dates.

63 Ragnar, P. (2005). *The Awesome Science of Luck: Your Guide to Winning all the Time*. Asheville, NC: Roaring Lion Pub.

64 Byrne, R. (2006). *The Secret*. New York: Atria Books.

65 Feuerstein, G. (1974). *Wholeness or Transcendence? Ancient Lessons for the Emerging Global Civilization*. Larson Publications. p.19

66 Gallwey, W. T. (1974). *The Inner Game of Tennis*. New York: Random House.

67 Bandler, R., & Fitzpatrick, O. (2009). *Conversations with Richard Bandler: Two NLP Masters Reveal the Secrets to Successful Living*. Deerfield Beach: Health Communications, Inc.

68 Gallwey, W. T. (1974). *The Inner Game of Tennis*. New York: Random House.

69 Beck, M. N. (2008). *Steering by Starlight: Find Your Right Life, No Matter What!* New York: Rodale.

70 Dispenza, J. (2007). *Evolve Your Brain: The Science of Changing Your Mind*. Dearfield, FL: Health Communications.

71 Dispenza, J. (2013). *Breaking the Habit of Being Yourself: How to Lose Your Mind and Create a New One*. Hay House.

72 Dispenza, J. (2014). *You are the Placebo: Making Your Mind Matter*. Hay House.

73 Dispenza, J. (2007). *Evolve Your Brain: The Science of Changing Your Mind*. Dearfield, FL: Health Communications.

74 Walters, J. D., & Yogananda. (2004). *Conversations with Yogananda*. Nevada City, Calif: Crystal Clarity Publishers. p.20

75 Dispenza, J. (2014). *You are the Placebo: Making Your Mind Matter*. Hay House.

76 Covey, S., Merrill, A., Merrill, R. (1996). *First Things First*. Free Press. p.180

77 Mehl-Madrona M.D., L. (1998). *Coyote Medicine: Lessons From Native American Healing*. Touchstone. p.262

78 Murphy, M., White, R. A., & Murphy, M. (1995). *In the Zone: Transcendent Experience in Sports*. New York: Penguin/Arkana. p.150

79 Braden, G. (2006). *Secrets of the Lost Mode of Prayer: The Hidden Power of Beauty, Blessings, Wisdom, and Hurt*. Hay House.

80 Kriyananda. (2009). *The New Path: My Life with Paramahansa Yogananda*. Nevada City, Calif: Crystal Clarity Publishers.

81 Hall, HR., Minnes, L., Tosi, M., Olness, K. "Voluntary Modulation of Neutrophil Adhesiveness Using a Cyberphysiologic Strategy." *International Journal of Neuroscience*. 1992 Apr;63(3-4):287-97.

82 Redman, Jason, (2013). *The Trident: The Forging and Reforging of a Navy SEAL* Leader. William Morrow.

83 Chopra, D. (1994). *Journey Into Healing: Awakening the Wisdom Within You*. Harmony.

84 Hanson, R. (2013). *Hardwiring Happiness: The New Brain Science of Contentment, Calm, and Confidence*.

85 Amen, D. (1999). *Change Your Brain, Change Your Life*. Harmony.

86 Walters, J. D., & Yogananda. (2004). *Conversations with Yogananda*. Nevada City, Calif: Crystal Clarity Publishers.

87 Holmes, E. (1999). *Words That Heal Today*. Deerfield Beach, Fla: Health Communications. p.46

88 Hanson, R. (2013). *Hardwiring Happiness: The New Brain Science of Contentment, Calm, and Confidence*. Harmony.

89 Rankin, L. (2013). *Mind Over Medicine: Scientific Proof You Can Heal Yourself*. Hay House. p.134

90 Gallwey, W. Timothy. (1977). *Inner skiing*. New York: Random House.

91 Tolle, E. (2004). *The Power of Now: A Guide to Spiritual Enlightenment*. New World Library. p.64

92 *A Beautiful Mind*. Dir. Ron Howard. Perfs. Russell Crowe, Ed Harris, Jennifer Connelly, Paul Bettany. Universal Pictures, 1991.

93 Niequist, S. (2010). *Cold Tangerines: Celebrating the Extraordinary Nature of Everyday Life*. Zondervan

94 Goss, T. (1995). *The Last Word on Power: Executive Re-Invention for Leaders Who Must Make the Impossible Happen*. Crown Business.

95 Chopra, D. (1987). *Creating Health: Beyond Prevention, Toward Perfection*. Boston: Houghton Mifflin.

96 Ragnar, P. (2005). *The Awesome Science of Luck: Your Guide to Winning all the Time*. Asheville, NC: Roaring Lion Pub.

97 Boone, J. A. (1954). *Kinship With All Life*. New York: Harper. p.83

98 Boone, J. A. (1954). *Kinship With All Life*. New York: Harper. p.91

99 Lipton, B. H., & Bhaerman, S. (2009). *Spontaneous Evolution: Our Positive Future (and a Way to Get There From Here)*. Carlsbad, Calif: Hay House.

100 Gallwey, W. Timothy. (1977). *Inner Skiing*. New York: Random House.

101 Cleary, T. (1991). *The Secret of the Golden Flower: The Classic Chinese Book of Life*. New York: HarperCollins. p.2

102 Jwing-Ming, Y. (2003). *Qigong Meditation: Embryonic Breathing*. Boston: YMAA Publication Center. p.21

103 Gallwey, W. T. (1974). *The Inner Game of Tennis*. New York: Random House. p.38

104 Gallwey, W. T. (1974). *The Inner Game of Tennis*. New York: Random House. p.81

105 Tolle, E. (2004). *The Power of Now: A Guide to Spiritual Enlightenment*. New World Library.

106 Church, D. (2008). *The Genie in Your Genes: Epigenetic Medicine and the New Biology of Intention*. Santa Rosa, California: Energy Psychology Press. p.198

107 Gallwey, W. Timothy. (1977). *Inner skiing*. New York: Random House.

108 Spielman, E. (1979). *The Mighty Atom: The Life and Times of Joseph L. Greenstein*. New York: Viking Press.

109 Douillard, J. (2004). *Perfect Health for Kids: Ten Ayurvedic Health Secrets Every Parent Must Know*. Berkeley, Calif: North Atlantic Books. p.305

110 Ibid.

111 Lee, A., & Campbell, D. (2009). *Perfect Breathing: Transform Your Life, One Breath at a Time*. New York: Sterling.

112 Pelton, Ph.D., R. (1989). *Mind Food & Smart Pills: A Sourcebook for the Vitamins, Herbs, and Drugs That Can Increase Intelligence, Improve Memory, and Prevent Brain Aging*. New York: Doubleday. p.247

113 Wahls, T. (2011, November 30th). [Video File] retrieved from http://terrywahls.com/minding-your-mitochondria-dr-terry-wahls-at-tedxiowacity/

114 Ratey, MD, John J. & Manning, Richard. (2014). *Go Wild: Free Your Body and Mind From the Afflictions of Civilization*. New York: Little Brown & Co. p.23

115 Osho. (2004). *Meditation: The First and Last Freedom*. New York: St. Martin's Griffin

116 Ratey, MD, John J. & Manning, Richard. (2014). *Go Wild: Free Your Body and Mind From the Afflictions of Civilization*. New York: Little Brown & Co. p.256

117 Hayflick, L. (1994). *How and Why we Age*. New York: Ballantine Books. p.281

118 Philpott, W. H., & Kalita, D. K. (2000). *Brain Allergies: The Psychonutrient and Magnetic Connections*. Los Angeles: Keats Pub.

119 Pelton, Ph.D., R. (1989). *Mind Food & Smart Pills: A Sourcebook for the Vitamins, Herbs, and Drugs That Can Increase Intelligence, Improve Memory, and Prevent Brain Aging*. New York: Doubleday. p.275

120 Hoffer M.D., A. (1999). *Vitamin B-3 & Schizophrenia: Discovery, Recovery, Controversy*. Quarry Press. p.68

121 Somers, S. (2006). *Ageless: The Naked Truth About Bioidentical Hormones*. New York: Crown Publishers.

122 Walsh, W. (2012). *Nutrient Power: Heal Your Biochemistry and Heal Your Brain*. New York, NY: Skyhorse Pub.

123 Kalita, D. K., & Williams, R. J. (1977). *A Physician's Handbook on Orthomolecular Medicine*. New York: Pergamon Press.

124 Rochlitz, S. (1991). *Allergies and Candida: With the Physicist's Rapid Solution*. New York: Human Ecology Balancing Sciences.

125 Rapp, D. J. (1991). *Is This Your Child?: Discovering and Treating Unrecognized Allergies*. New York: W. Morrow.

[126] Philpott, W. H., & Kalita, D. K. (2000). *Brain Allergies: The Psychonutrient and Magnetic Connections*. Los Angeles: Keats Pub.

[127] Buhner, S. H. (1999). *Herbal Antibiotics: Natural Alternatives for Treating Drug-Resistant Bacteria*. Pownal, Vt: Storey Books.

[128] Ibid.

[129] Webster, JP., Lamberton, PH., Donnelly, CA., Torrey, EF. *Proceedings of the Royal Society of Biological Sciences* 2006 Apr 22;273(1589):1023-30. *"Parasites as causative agents of human affective disorders? The impact of anti-psychotic, mood-stabilizer and anti-parasite medication on Toxoplasma gondii's ability to alter host behaviour."*

[130] Singh, K. D., & Stauth, C. (2001). *Meditation as Medicine: Activate the Power of Your Natural Healing Force*. New York: Pocket Books.

[131] Buhner, S. H. (2013). *Herbal Antivirals: Natural Remedies for Emerging Resistant and Epidemic Viral Infections*. Pownal, Vt: Storey Books.

[132] Pauling, L. (1986). *How to Live Longer and Feel Better*. New York: W.H. Freeman. p.122

[133] Buhner, S. H. (2013). *Herbal Antivirals: Natural Remedies for Emerging Resistant and Epidemic Viral Infections*. Pownal, Vt: Storey Books.

[134] Buhner, S. H. (1999). *Herbal Antibiotics: Natural Alternatives for Treating Drug-Resistant Bacteria*. Pownal, Vt: Storey Books.

[135] Bowden, J. (2008). *The Most Effective Natural Cures on Earth: The Surprising, Unbiased Truth About What Treatments Work and Why*. Beverly, Mass: Fair Winds Press.

[136] Murray, M. T. (1995). *The Healing Power of Herbs: The Enlightened Person's Guide to the Wonders of Medicinal Plants*. Rocklin, CA: Prima Pub.

[137] Yance, D. R. (2013). *Adaptogens in Medical Herbalism: Elite Herbs and Natural Compounds for Mastering Stress, Aging, and Chronic Disease*. Healing Arts Press.

[138] Grandin, T. (1995). *Thinking in Pictures: And Other Reports from my Life with Autism*. New York: Doubleday. p.198

[139] Swimme, B. (1995). *Canticle to the Cosmos*. Sounds True.

[140] Peace Pilgrim. (1996). *Peace Pilgrim: Her Life and Work in Her Own Words*. Salem, Or: Oregon State Library.

[141] Yogananda. (2005). *Spiritual Diary: An Inspirational Thought for Each Day of the Year*. Self-Realization Fellowship.

[142] Blake, W. (1908). *The Poetical Works*. "Jerusalem (The Holiness of Minute Particulars)." London, New York: Oxford University Press.

[143] May, R. (2009). *Man's Search for Himself*. W. W. Norton & Co.

[144] Lewis, C.S. (2009). *The Problem of Pain*. HarperOne.

[145] Ratey, MD, John J. & Manning, Richard. (2014). *Go Wild: Free Your Body and Mind From the Afflictions of Civilization*. New York: Little Brown & Co. p.131

[146] Wiley, T. S., & Formby, B. (2000). *Lights Out: Sleep, Sugar, and Survival*. New York: Pocket Books. p.164

[147] Engel, C. (2003). *Wild Health: Lessons in Natural Wellness from the Animal Kingdom*. Mariner Books

[148] Steiger, B. (1973). *Revelation, the Divine Fire*. Englewood Cliffs, N.J: Prentice-Hall.

[149] Pullig Schatz, M.D., M. (1992). *Back Care Basics: A Doctor's Gentle Yoga Program for Back and Neck Pain Relief. Rodmell Press*. p.14

[150] Colbin, A. (1998). *Food and Our Bones: The Natural Way to Prevent Osteoporosis*. New York: Penguin Group.

[151] Soerjomataram MD, I., et. al. "Global burden of cancer in 2008: a systematic analysis of disability-adjusted life-years in 12 world regions." *The Lancet*. Volume 380, Issue 9856, Pages 1840-1850, 24 November 2012.

[152] O'Regan, B., Hirshberg, C. (1993) *Spontaneous Remission An Annotated Bibliography*. Institute of Noetic Sciences

[153] Seligman, M. E. (2011). *Flourish: A Visionary New Understanding of Happiness and Well-Being*. New York: Free Press.

[154] Wiley, T. S., & Formby, B. (2000). *Lights Out: Sleep, Sugar, and Survival*. New York: Pocket Books.

[155] Iyengar, B.K.S. (2005). *Lights on Life: The Yoga Journey to Wholeness, Inner Peace, and Ultimate Freedom*. Rodale. p.22

[156] Ibid. p.15

[157] Buhner, S. H. (1999). *Herbal Antibiotics: Natural Alternatives for Treating Drug-Resistant Bacteria*. Pownal, Vt: Storey Books.

[158] Robinson, J. (2014). *Eating on the Wild Side: The Missing Link to Optimum Health*. Little, Brown & Company. p.50

[159] Bassler, B. (February, 2009). *How bacteria "talk"* [Video file]. Retrieved from: http://www.ted.com/talks/bonnie_bassler_on_how_bacteria_communicate?language=en

[160] Reid, D. (1994). *The Complete Book of Chinese Health and Healing: Guarding the Three Treasures*. Boston: Shambhala. p.148

[161] Fuhrman, J. (2011). *Eat to Live: The Amazing Nutrient-Rich Program for Fast and Sustained Weight Loss*. New York: Little, Brown and Co.

[162] Hartmann, T. (2003). *The Edison Gene: ADHD and the Gift of the Hunter Child*. Rochester, Vt: Park Street Press.

[163] Wiley, T. S., & Formby, B. (2000). *Lights Out: Sleep, Sugar, and Survival*. New York: Pocket Books. p.38

[164] Gallwey, W. Timothy. (1977). *Inner skiing*. New York: Random House.

[165] Gatto, J. T. (2009). *Weapons of Mass Instruction: A Schoolteacher's Journey Through the Dark World of Compulsory Schooling*. Gabriola Island, B.C: New Society Publishers. p.126-7

[166] Ibid. (p.xiv)

[167] Angelo, L., Kuzrock, R. "Turmeric and Green Tea: A Recipe for the Treatment of B-Chronic Lymphocytic Leukemia." *Clinical Cancer Research* February 15, 2009; 15(4): 1123-1125.

[168] *Become an Epigenetic Engineer*. Jeanne Wallace, Ph.D., CNC. Healing Journeys, 2012.

[169] Holmes, E. (1952). *This Thing Called You*. Dodd Mead Co.

[170] Augustine., Thomas., Pusey, E. B., & Benham, W. (1909). *The Confessions of St. Augustine*. New York: P.F. Collier & Son.

[171] Morowitz, H. J. (1979). *The Wine of Life, and Other Essays on Societies, Energy & Living Things*. New York: St. Martin's Press.

[172] Vujicic, Nick. (2010). *Life Without Limits: Inspiration for a Ridiculously Good Life*. New York: Doubleday.

[173] Jalāl, R., & Barks, C. (2003). *Rumi: The Book of Love: Poems of Ecstasy and Longing*. New York, NY: HarperOne, HaperCollins.

[174] Chopra M.D., D. (1990). *Quantum Healing: Exploring the Frontiers on Mind/Body Medicine*. Bantam. p.237

[175] Mogel, W. (2008). *The Blessing of a Skinned Knee: Using Jewish Teachings to Raise Self Reliant Children*. New York: Scribner.

[176] Ibid.

[177] Turner, K. A. (2014). *Radical Remission: Surviving Cancer Against All Odds*. p.65

[178] Walters, J. D. (2002). *The Art and Science of Raja Yoga: Fourteen Steps to Higher Awareness*: Based on the Teachings of Paramahansa Yogananda. Nevada City, Calif: Crystal Clarity Publishers. p.102

[179] ten Boom, C., Sherrill, J., Sherrill, E. (1984.) *The Hiding Place*. Bantam.

[180] ten Boom, C., Sherrill, J., Sherrill, E. (1984.) *The Hiding Place*. Bantam.

[181] Barasch, M. (2005). *Field Notes on the Compassionate Life: A Search for the Soul of Kindness*. Emmaus, Pa: Rodale. p. 340

[182] Grant, A., Hofmann, D. *Psychological Science* 2011 Dec;22(12):1494-9 "It's not all about me: motivating hand hygiene among health care professionals by focusing on patients."

[183] Siegel, M.D., B. (1988) *Love, Medicine & Miracles*. HarperCollins.

[184] Le, G. U. (1971). *The Lathe of Heaven*. New York: Scribner.

[185] Ram, D., & Das, R. (2010). *Be Love Now: The path of the Heart*. New York: HarperOne.

[186] Grabhorn, L. (2000). *Excuse Me, Your Life is Waiting: The Astonishing Power of Feelings*. Charlottesville, Va: Hampton Roads Pub. Co.

[187] Gandhi., & Desai, M. H. (1993). *An Autobiography: The story of My Experiments with Truth*. Boston: Beacon Press.

[188] Barasch, M. (2005). *Field Notes on the Compassionate Life: A Search for the Soul of Kindness*. Emmaus, Pa: Rodale.

[189] Shadyac, T. (Director). (2010). *I Am* [Motion picture].

[190] *Predicability: Does the Flap of a Butterfly's wings in Brazil set off a tornado in Texas?* Edward N. Lorenz Sc.D. Presented before the American Association for the Advancement of Science, December 29, 1972.

[191] Milne, A.A. (1992). *Winnie-the-Pooh*. Puffin.

[192] Yogananda. (1975). *Man's Eternal Quest*. Los Angeles: Self-Realization Fellowship.

[193] Myss, C. (1998). *Why People Don't Heal and How They Can*. Harmony.

[194] Yogananda. (1998 reprint). *Autobiography of a Yogi*. Self-Realization Fellowship. p.516

[195] Einstein, A., & Rouben Mamoulian Collection (Library of Congress). (1949). *The World as I See It*. New York: Philosophical Library.

[196] Brother Yun, Hattaway, P. (2002) *The Heavenly Man: The Remarkable True Story of Chinese Christian Brother Yun*. Kregel Publications.